CHECKERBOARD PRESS
Geography
Encyclopedia

CHECKERBOARD PRESS
New York

Contents

THE EARTH WE LIVE ON
The Earth in Space	8
The Planet Earth	10
The Earth's Atmosphere	12
The Face of the Earth	14
Climates	16
Soil and Vegetation	18
Weather and Forecasting	20
Polar Lands	22
Deserts	24
Jungles and Forests	26
Grasslands	28
Mountains	30
Animals of the World	32
Oceans	34
Waves, Tides, and Currents	36

SHAPING THE EARTH
Volcanoes	38
Earthquakes	40
Wind and Weather	42
Rivers and Ice	44
The Underground World	46

THE HUMAN WORLD
How People Live	48
Race and Language	50
Developed and Developing Countries	52
Food and Farming	54
Wealth from the Sea	56
Wealth from the Earth	58
The Continents	60

EUROPE 62
Northern Europe	64
British Isles	66
Low Countries	68

EDITORIAL
Frances M. Clapham
Jennifer L. Justice
Cover: Denise Gardner

Germany	70	ASIA	100
France	72	China	102
Mountain Countries	74	Japan and Korea	104
Mediterranean Lands	75	Southeast Asia	106
Eastern Europe	78	India and its Neighbors	110
Union of Soviet Socialist Republics	80	Southwest Asia	114
		AFRICA	118
NORTH AMERICA	82	Northern Africa	120
Canada	84	West Africa	124
United States of America	86	Central Africa	126
Central America and the West Indies	90	East Africa	128
		Southern Africa	130
SOUTH AMERICA	92	OCEANIA	132
Northern South America	94	Australia	134
Brazil, Peru, and Bolivia	96	New Zealand and the Pacific Islands	136
Southern Lands	98	Index	138

The Earth in Space

Our planet, the Earth, is one of nine planets that rotate around the Sun. This group of heavenly bodies is called the Solar System. It also includes asteroids, comets, dust, gas, meteors, and moons. The Sun is only one of millions of stars in our galaxy, the Milky Way. This galaxy is a flattened disk of dust, gas, and stars. Beyond our galaxy are millions of others.

The Earth is only a tiny speck in space. Space is so huge that scientists measure distances in *light-years*. A light-year is the distance traveled by light in one year. Light travels at a speed of 186,282 miles a second. So one light-year is equal to nearly 6 trillion miles.

Scientists have several ideas about how the Earth was formed. Today most think that the Solar System formed from a vast cloud of whirling gas and dust. Some of this condensed, or was drawn together, to form the Sun. The rest condensed to form the planets and other heavenly bodies, which were bound to the Sun by the force of gravity.

Above: The setting Sun. As the Earth rotates on its axis, the Sun appears to rise, move across the sky, and set. But it is actually the Earth that is moving. Astronomers used to believe that the Sun, Moon, and planets all circled the Earth, and that Earth was the center of the universe.

Below: Our seasons occur because the Earth is tilted on its axis. When the North Pole is tilted toward the Sun, the Northern Hemisphere gets most sunlight and has its summer. When it tilts away from the Sun, the Northern Hemisphere gets less sunlight and has its winter. The Southern Hemisphere's seasons occur in reverse.

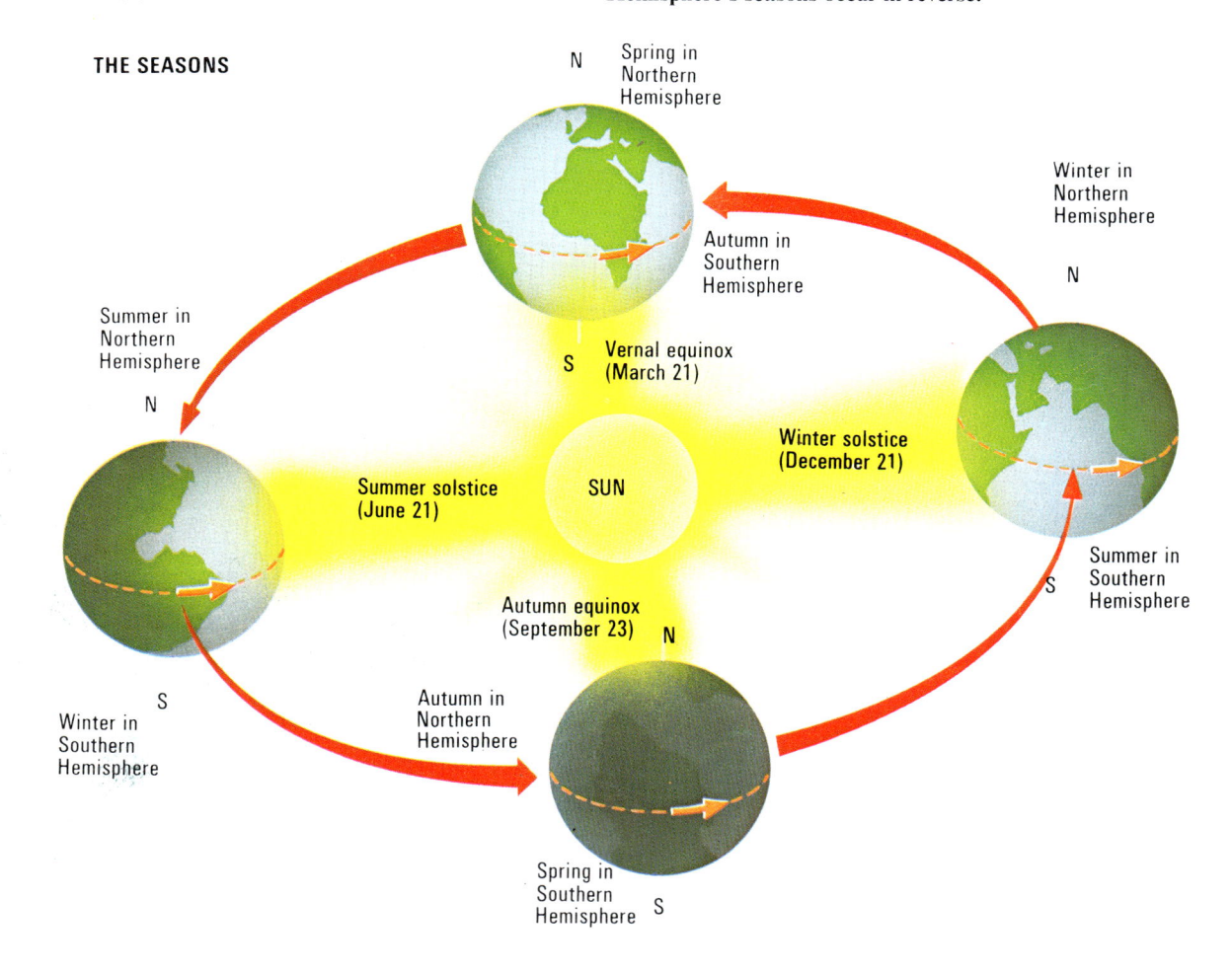

THE SEASONS

Right: The Earth is part of the Solar System. It is the third planet from the Sun. Like Mercury, Venus, Mars, and Pluto, the Earth is a *terrestrial* planet – that is, a dense, rocky body. The Earth is the largest of the terrestrial planets. Jupiter, Saturn, Uranus, and Neptune are *giant* planets – low-density balls of gas.

1 Mercury
2 Venus
3 Earth
4 Mars
5 Jupiter
6 Saturn
7 Uranus
8 Neptune
9 Pluto

Below right: The Earth photographed from the Apollo 11 spacecraft in July 1969. Night has fallen on eastern Asia, but the Sun is still shining on Southwest Asia, Europe, and Africa. Cloud covers parts of the land and much of the sea. Such views of the Earth from space help weather experts to work out the paths of hurricanes and so to warn ships of dangerous storms.

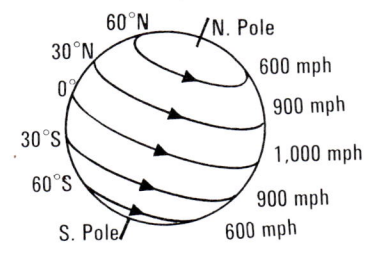

Above: The Earth moves in three main ways: It moves around its axis, an imaginary line drawn through the poles. The speed at which the Earth rotates is greatest at the Equator. It slows down as it gets closer to the poles.

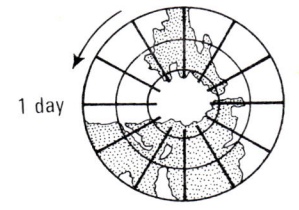

The Earth rotates once on its axis in 23 hours, 56 minutes, and 4.1 seconds.

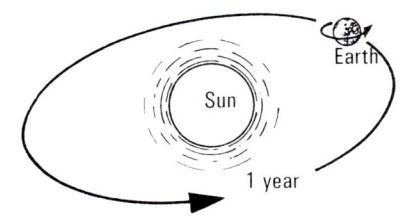

The Earth revolves around the Sun in one solar year, 365 days, 6 hours, and 9 minutes.

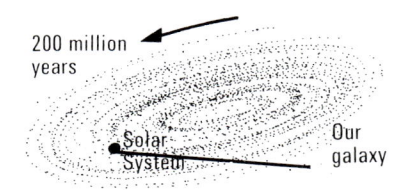

The entire Solar System rotates once around the Milky Way galaxy every 200 million years.

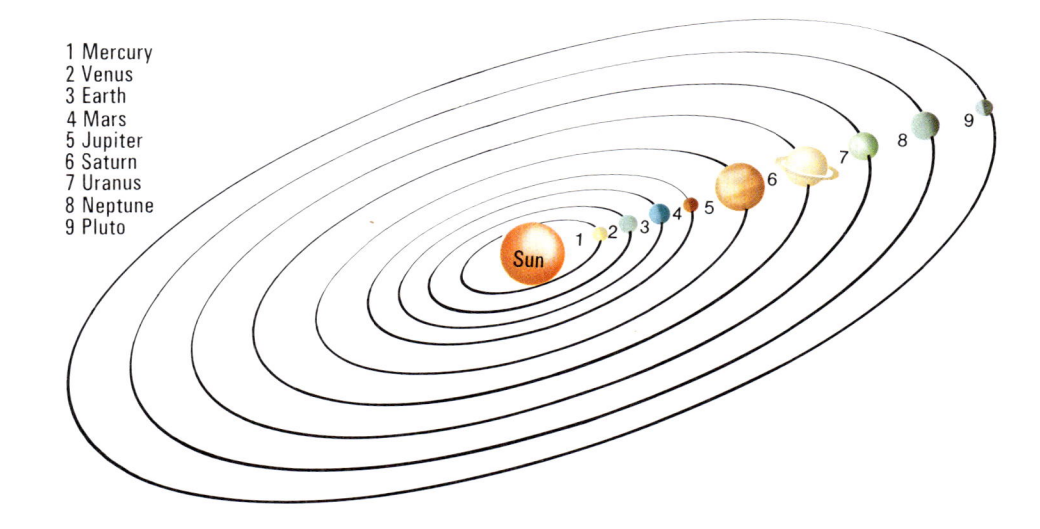

The Planet Earth

The surface of the Earth, the part we live on, was formed about 4½ billion years ago. At first, the Earth's surface, or *crust*, was probably largely covered by hot, molten rock. As the Earth cooled, the surface rock hardened. But molten rock still sometimes pushed up to the surface. It spilled out from the holes and cracks we now call *volcanoes*.

These volcanic eruptions also released gases and steam from the rocks. Above the Earth's surface, steam cooled to water vapor and fell back as rain. So began the oceans and rivers. The pull of gravity held

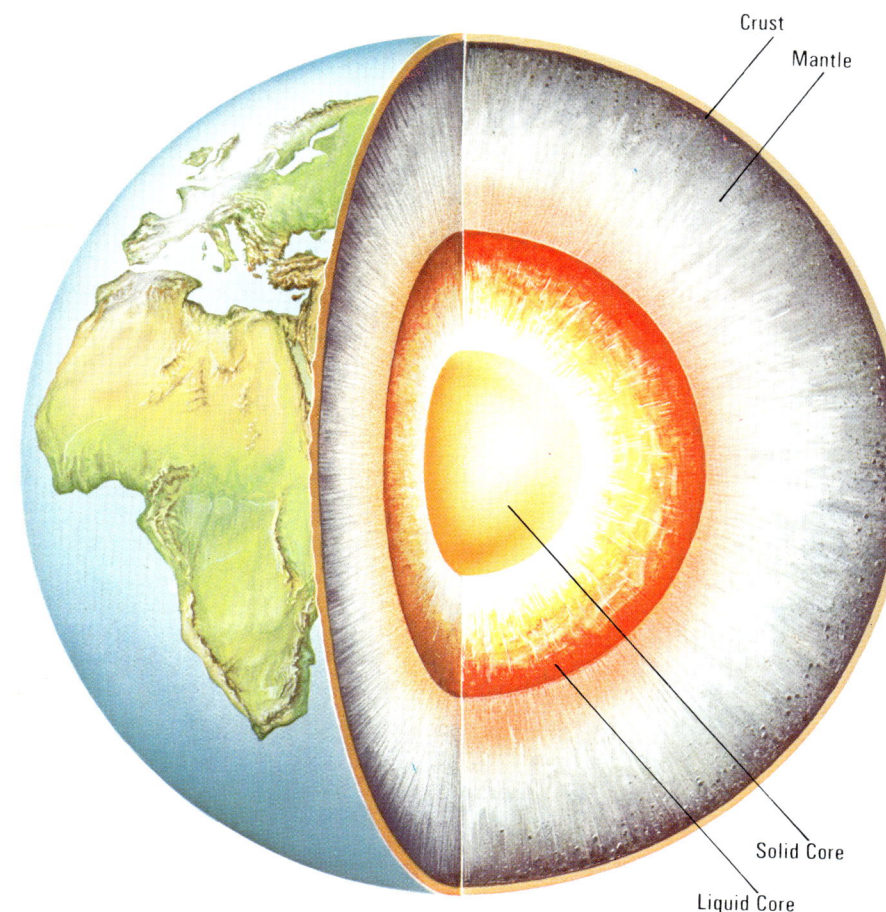

Right: The inside of the Earth is made up of three main sections: the crust, mantle, and core. The mantle contains extremely dense rocks. The core has a liquid outer part and a solid center.

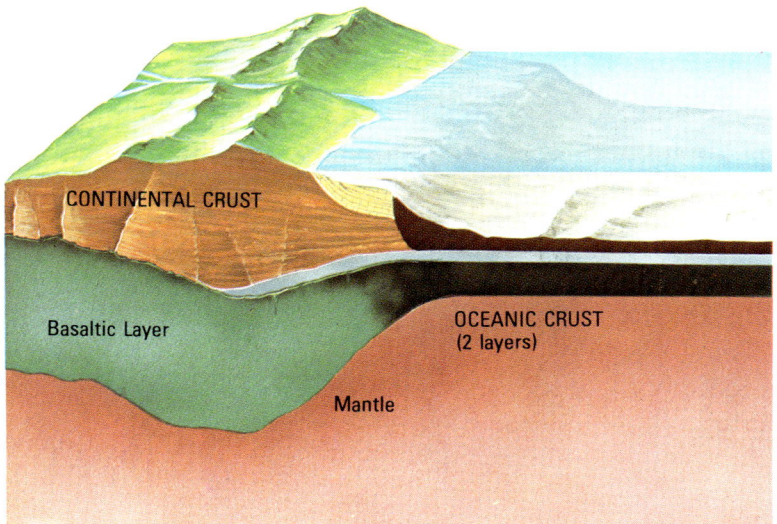

Left: A slice through the Earth's crust. Two thin layers make up the ocean floors. Beneath the continents the crust is thicker and more complicated. The *continental shelf* extends out beyond the ocean shores.

most of the other gases close to the Earth's surface. They formed the Earth's early atmosphere.

Life on Earth

Hundreds of millions of years after the Earth first formed, the warm oceans were like a rich soup of chemicals. Sunshine acting on certain chemicals may have produced the first living things – tiny particles able to use food to grow and reproduce themselves. By about 3 billion years ago, tiny plants were drifting in the oceans. But it was a long time before complicated kinds of plants and animals appeared.

Modern life began about 600 million years ago. The seas began to teem with familiar living things, such as jellyfish and seaweeds. Later came sea animals with backbones, and plants and animals that lived on land. Birds and mammals evolved only much more recently. Fossils in the rocks today tell scientists the story of how modern plants and animals got where they are today.

Facts about the Earth
Diameter at Equator: 7,926 miles
Circumference around poles: 24,860 miles
Density: 5.52 (density of water is 1)
Mass: 6.6 sextillion short tons
Area: 197,000,000 square miles
Surface: 71 percent water, 29 percent land
Temperature: Lowest known, −126.9°F; highest 136°F
Highest peak: Mount Everest, 29,028 feet
Deepest ocean trench: 36,198 feet
Escape velocity: 32,736 feet per second
Turns on axis in: 23 hours, 56 minutes, 4.1 seconds
Distance from Sun: 92.9 million miles
Orbits Sun in: 365 days, 6 hours, 9 minutes
Orbital velocity: 18.5 miles per second
Moons: One

THE DEVELOPMENT OF LIFE

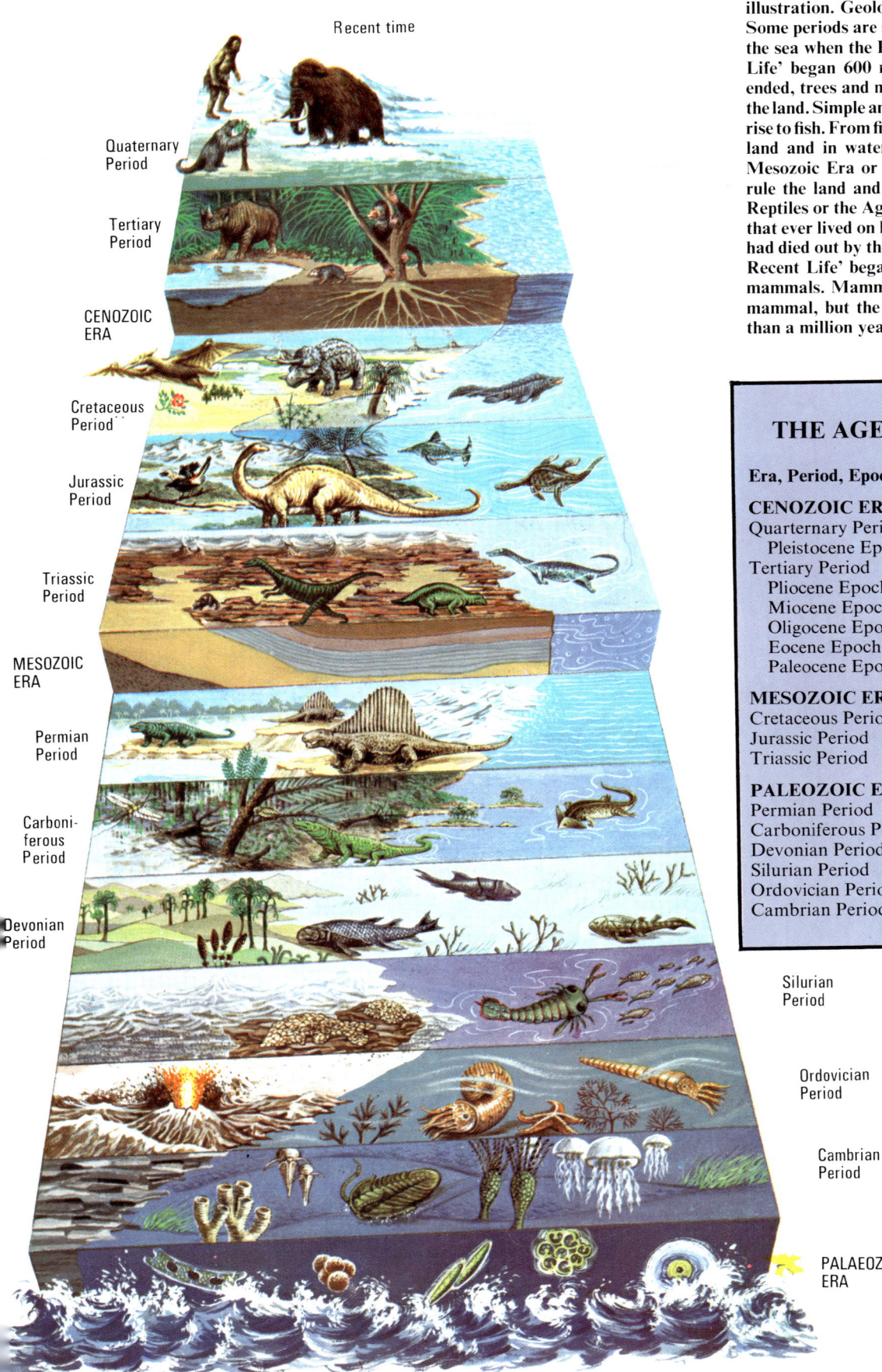

Recent time

Quaternary Period
Tertiary Period

CENOZOIC ERA

Cretaceous Period
Jurassic Period
Triassic Period

MESOZOIC ERA

Permian Period
Carboniferous Period
Devonian Period
Silurian Period
Ordovician Period
Cambrian Period

PALAEOZOIC ERA

PRE-CAMBRIAN TIME

Life on Earth has evolved in three great ages of Earth history, called eras. Each era makes up one step in the illustration. Geologists divide each era into periods. Some periods are split into epochs. Life flourished in the sea when the Palaeozoic Era or 'Age of Ancient Life' began 600 million years ago. By the time it ended, trees and many other plants were growing on the land. Simple animals without backbones had given rise to fish. From fish came amphibians, which lived on land and in water. From them came reptiles. The Mesozoic Era or 'Age of Middle Life' saw reptiles rule the land and seas. It is also called the Age of Reptiles or the Age of Dinosaurs. The biggest beasts that ever lived on land flourished in this era. But they had died out by the time the Cenozoic Era or 'Age of Recent Life' began. Reptiles gave rise to birds and mammals. Mammals ruled the land. Man, too, is a mammal, but the first men like ourselves lived less than a million years ago.

THE AGES OF THE EARTH

Era, Period, Epoch	Millions of Years Ago
CENOZOIC ERA	
Quaternary Period	
Pleistocene Epoch	10,000 years – 2 million
Tertiary Period	
Pliocene Epoch	2–5
Miocene Epoch	5–25
Oligocene Epoch	25–40
Eocene Epoch	40–55
Paleocene Epoch	55–65
MESOZOIC ERA	
Cretaceous Period	65–135
Jurassic Period	135–200
Triassic Period	200–225
PALEOZOIC ERA	
Permian Period	225–280
Carboniferous Period	280–345
Devonian Period	345–395
Silurian Period	395–440
Ordovician Period	440–500
Cambrian Period	500–600

The Earth's Atmosphere

The EXOSPHERE is the outer part of the atmosphere, which gradually merges into space. It is above the ionosphere, which ends about 300 miles above the Earth.

The IONOSPHERE extends between 50 and 300 miles above the Earth. Disturbances in the ionosphere are caused by streams of particles from the Sun. They take the form of glowing lights called *aurorae*. The ionosphere gets its name because most of the gas molecules in this layer are ionized, or electrically charged, by cosmic or solar rays. Many artificial satellites orbit the Earth in the ionosphere.

The STRATOSPHERE lies between the tropopause and about 50 miles above the Earth. The layer of ozone gas in the stratosphere filters out some of the ultraviolet radiation from the Sun. This radiation would be fatal to life on Earth if it reached the surface. Jet aircraft often fly in the lower stratosphere.

The TROPOSPHERE contains most of the mass of the atmosphere, including the winds and clouds that give us our weather. It extends to about 10 miles over the Equator, 6–7 miles over middle latitudes, and 5 miles over the poles. The troposphere ends at the TROPOPAUSE, where the temperature is about −131°F.

Look up at a clear night sky. Nothing seems to lie between you and the stars. But in fact you are gazing up through air – the layer of invisible gases making up the Earth's atmosphere. Air is chiefly made of nitrogen and oxygen, but there are other gases, too. Air also holds tiny particles of dust and water. Balloons carrying instruments have shown scientists that the Earth's atmosphere has four main layers.

Air for Life and Weather

The lowest layer of the atmosphere is called the *troposphere*. This layer is between 5 and 10 miles thick. Most of the air is concentrated in this layer. Only the troposphere holds enough air for people and other living things to breathe.

Here, too, is the world's weather factory, where the winds and rain begin. The Sun warms up the air more over some parts of the Earth's surface than over other parts. Warmed air rises, and heavier, cooler air flows in to take its place. This causes winds. Warming and cooling also produce water vapor, clouds, rain, sleet, and snow. The kind of weather a region gets over many years is called its *climate*. The kind of climate a region has influences the kind of plants that grow in it.

Where Air Grows Thin

Above the cold upper level of the troposphere lies the atmospheric layer called the *stratosphere*. The stratosphere rises to about 40 miles above the Earth's surface. It holds a layer of ozone – a form of oxygen that shields the Earth's living things from harmful radiation caused by ultraviolet rays sent out by the Sun. Above the stratosphere lies a level sometimes called the *mesosphere*, the coldest level of all.

Above: The air we breathe clings to the Earth's surface like a thin, invisible skin. Its main ingredients are nitrogen and oxygen. The atmosphere is held around the Earth by the force of gravity. It provides the gases needed for human, animal, and plant life.

COMPOSITION OF AIR

The three main gases in air, making up 99.97 percent of the total, are nitrogen (78.09 percent), oxygen (20.95 percent), and argon (0.93 percent). The remaining 0.03 percent is made up of minute amounts of carbon dioxide, helium, hydrogen, krypton, methane, neon, ozone, and xenon. Carbon dioxide is important because plants use it for photosynthesis. Air also contains water vapor and specks of dust and salt (from sea spray).

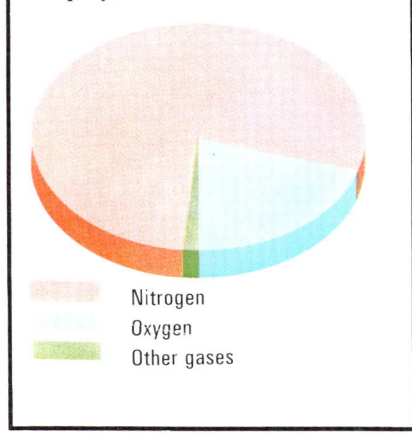

- Nitrogen
- Oxygen
- Other gases

Right: The huge Saturn V rocket, which thrust manned satellites out of Earth's gravity and into orbit in space. The spacecraft carried by these rockets are designed to protect astronauts from the dangers of leaving and reentering the Earth's atmosphere. Just 6 miles up, the air is too thin to breathe. At 12 miles deadly bubbles form in the blood. Seven miles higher still the temperature is −131°F. At 24 miles the effect of ultraviolet rays is dangerous. On the return journey, fierce heat is caused by air friction as the space capsule hurtles back into the atmosphere. The capsule would burn up if it were not protected against these high temperatures.

Above the mesosphere come the even sparser gases of the *ionosphere*. Here, the Sun's fierce radiation *ionizes* the gas atoms; that is, it knocks off electrons, and makes the atoms electrically charged.

The *exosphere* – the outer layer of the atmosphere – is made up of the lightest gases: helium and hydrogen. Many hundreds of miles out, the atmosphere thins to nothing.

The Weight on Our Shoulders

The atmosphere is held around the Earth by the force of gravity. It is estimated that the total weight of the atmosphere is about $5\frac{1}{2}$ quadrillion short tons. This means that a column of air weighing about one short ton is constantly pressing down on our shoulders. We do not feel this pressure, because we are supported on all sides by an equal pressure, just as fish survive the great pressures in the ocean depths.

The Face of the Earth

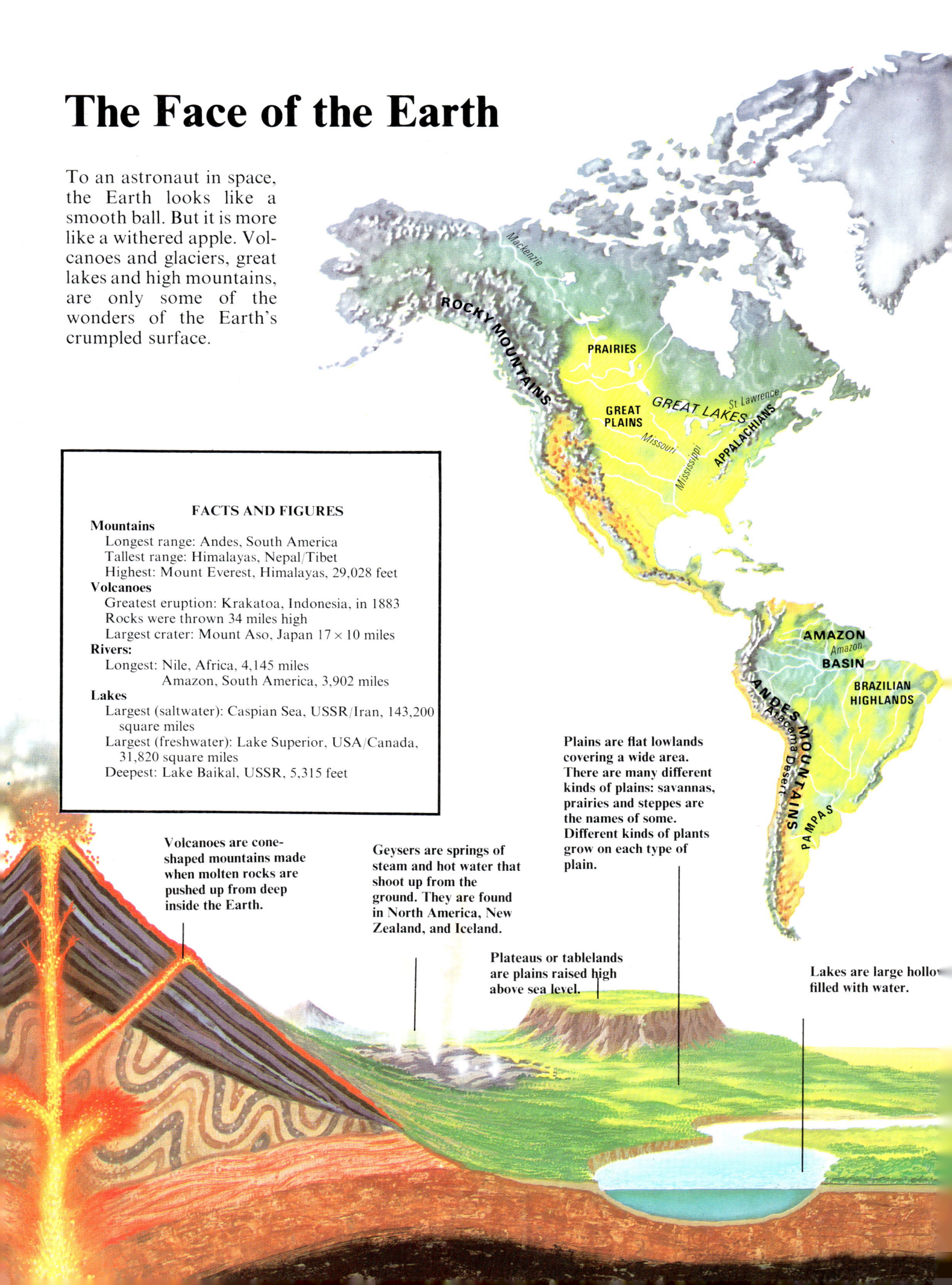

To an astronaut in space, the Earth looks like a smooth ball. But it is more like a withered apple. Volcanoes and glaciers, great lakes and high mountains, are only some of the wonders of the Earth's crumpled surface.

FACTS AND FIGURES

Mountains
 Longest range: Andes, South America
 Tallest range: Himalayas, Nepal/Tibet
 Highest: Mount Everest, Himalayas, 29,028 feet

Volcanoes
 Greatest eruption: Krakatoa, Indonesia, in 1883
 Rocks were thrown 34 miles high
 Largest crater: Mount Aso, Japan 17 × 10 miles

Rivers:
 Longest: Nile, Africa, 4,145 miles
  Amazon, South America, 3,902 miles

Lakes
 Largest (saltwater): Caspian Sea, USSR/Iran, 143,200 square miles
 Largest (freshwater): Lake Superior, USA/Canada, 31,820 square miles
 Deepest: Lake Baikal, USSR, 5,315 feet

Volcanoes are cone-shaped mountains made when molten rocks are pushed up from deep inside the Earth.

Geysers are springs of steam and hot water that shoot up from the ground. They are found in North America, New Zealand, and Iceland.

Plains are flat lowlands covering a wide area. There are many different kinds of plains: savannas, prairies and steppes are the names of some. Different kinds of plants grow on each type of plain.

Plateaus or tablelands are plains raised high above sea level.

Lakes are large hollows filled with water.

Map Labels

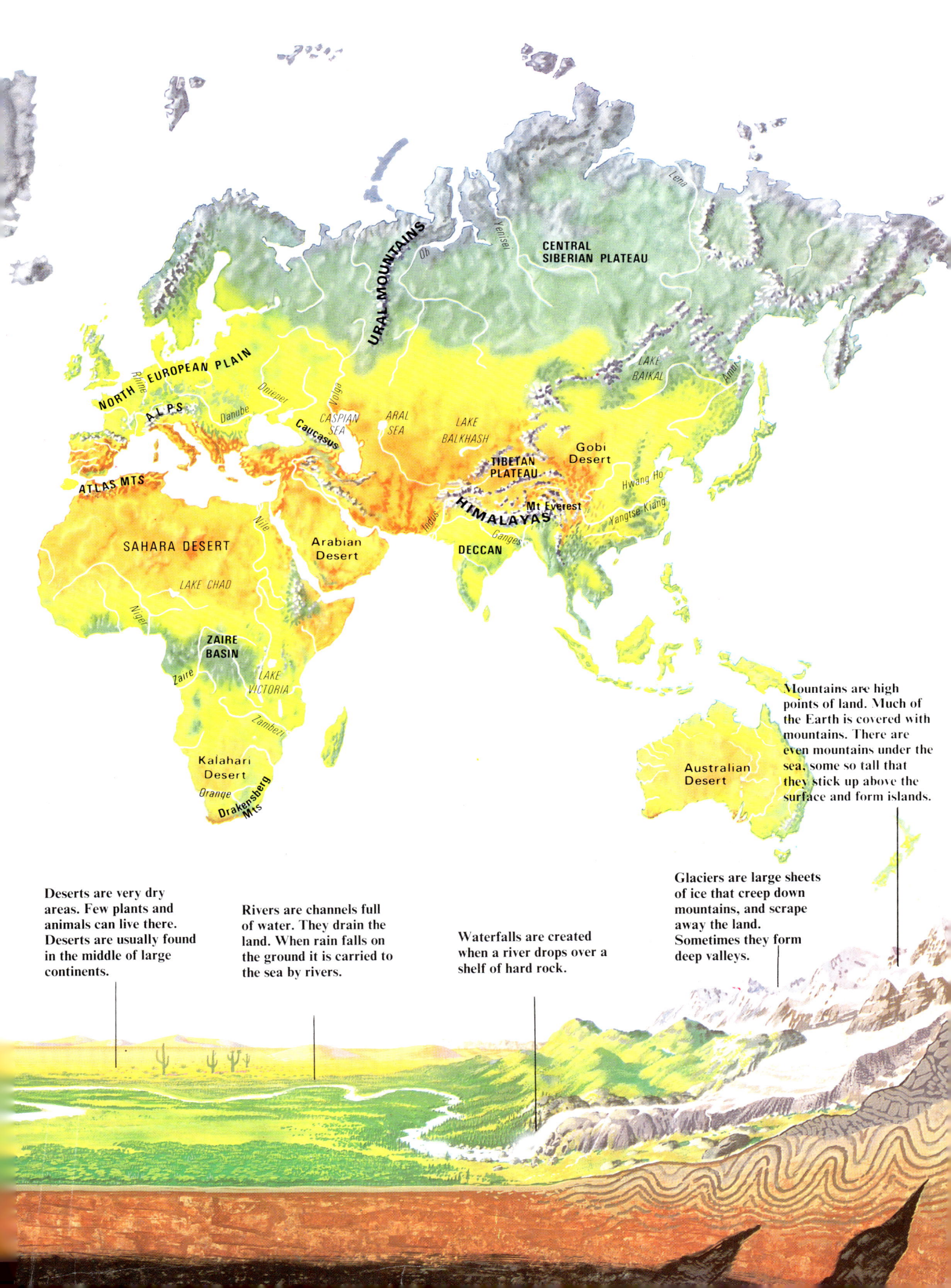

- CENTRAL SIBERIAN PLATEAU
- URAL MOUNTAINS
- Lena
- Yenisei
- Ob
- NORTH EUROPEAN PLAIN
- Rhine
- ALPS
- Dnieper
- Danube
- Volga
- CASPIAN SEA
- ARAL SEA
- LAKE BALKHASH
- LAKE BAIKAL
- Amur
- Caucasus
- Gobi Desert
- TIBETAN PLATEAU
- HIMALAYAS
- Mt Everest
- Hwang Ho
- Yangtse Kiang
- ATLAS MTS
- SAHARA DESERT
- Nile
- Arabian Desert
- Indus
- Ganges
- DECCAN
- LAKE CHAD
- Niger
- ZAIRE BASIN
- Zaire
- LAKE VICTORIA
- Zambezi
- Kalahari Desert
- Orange
- Drakensberg Mts
- Australian Desert

Captions

Deserts are very dry areas. Few plants and animals can live there. Deserts are usually found in the middle of large continents.

Rivers are channels full of water. They drain the land. When rain falls on the ground it is carried to the sea by rivers.

Waterfalls are created when a river drops over a shelf of hard rock.

Glaciers are large sheets of ice that creep down mountains, and scrape away the land. Sometimes they form deep valleys.

Mountains are high points of land. Much of the Earth is covered with mountains. There are even mountains under the sea, some so tall that they stick up above the surface and form islands.

Climates

The word "climate" comes from the Greek word *klima* (slope) because the ancient Greeks thought that the Earth "sloped" southward to the hot Equator and northward to the icy poles. Today we know that the climate of a particular place on Earth is decided by three things. The first is its *latitude* – that is, how far north or south of the Equator it lies. The second is how near or far the place is from the sea. And the third is its surface features – whether it has mountains or plains, and whether it lies at sea level or on a high plateau.

Latitude affects climate because the Sun's rays are stronger at the Equator than at the poles, so lands nearer the Equator are usually hotter. But even in a hot place, the temperatures at the top of a mountain or on a high plateau are cold.

The sea warms and cools the land near it, and so coastal areas usually have fewer extremes of temperature than the centers of continents. Cold and warm ocean currents also affect the climate on land.

Right: The average temperatures in different parts of the world in January and July. Lands nearest the Equator have the highest temperatures. In polar regions, temperatures in January can fall to as low as –90°F.

Below left: The wind shapes wave-like sand dunes in many deserts. Dry climates have an average of less than 10 inches of rainfall per year. What little rain does fall evaporates quickly. Dry climates include deserts and steppelands.

Below: The Swedish port of Luleå on the Baltic Sea is important for shipping iron ore from inland mines. But in winter, the Baltic Sea freezes over and blocks the port. Icebreakers (bottom) now keep the port open, but until recently all the ore was shipped through the Norwegian port of Narvik. Narvik lies far to the north of the Arctic Circle, but it is ice-free in winter. The map shows the reason why. A warm ocean current called the North Atlantic Drift flows along the Norwegian coast. The warmth of the current keeps the coastal waters of Norway ice-free. It also brings a fairly mild climate to the coast itself.

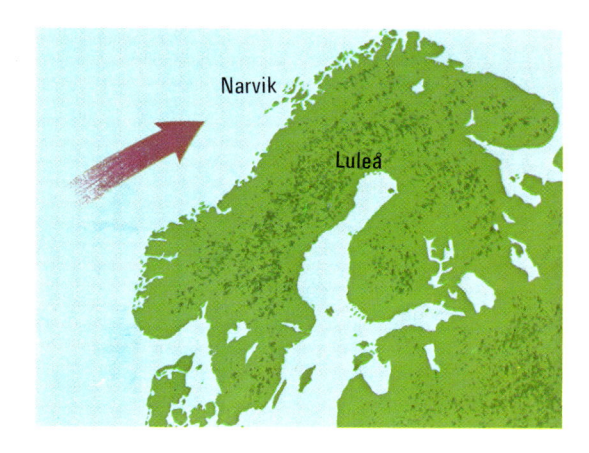

F°	
	Over 85
	65–85
	50–65
	32–50
	15–32 **JULY TEMPERATURES**

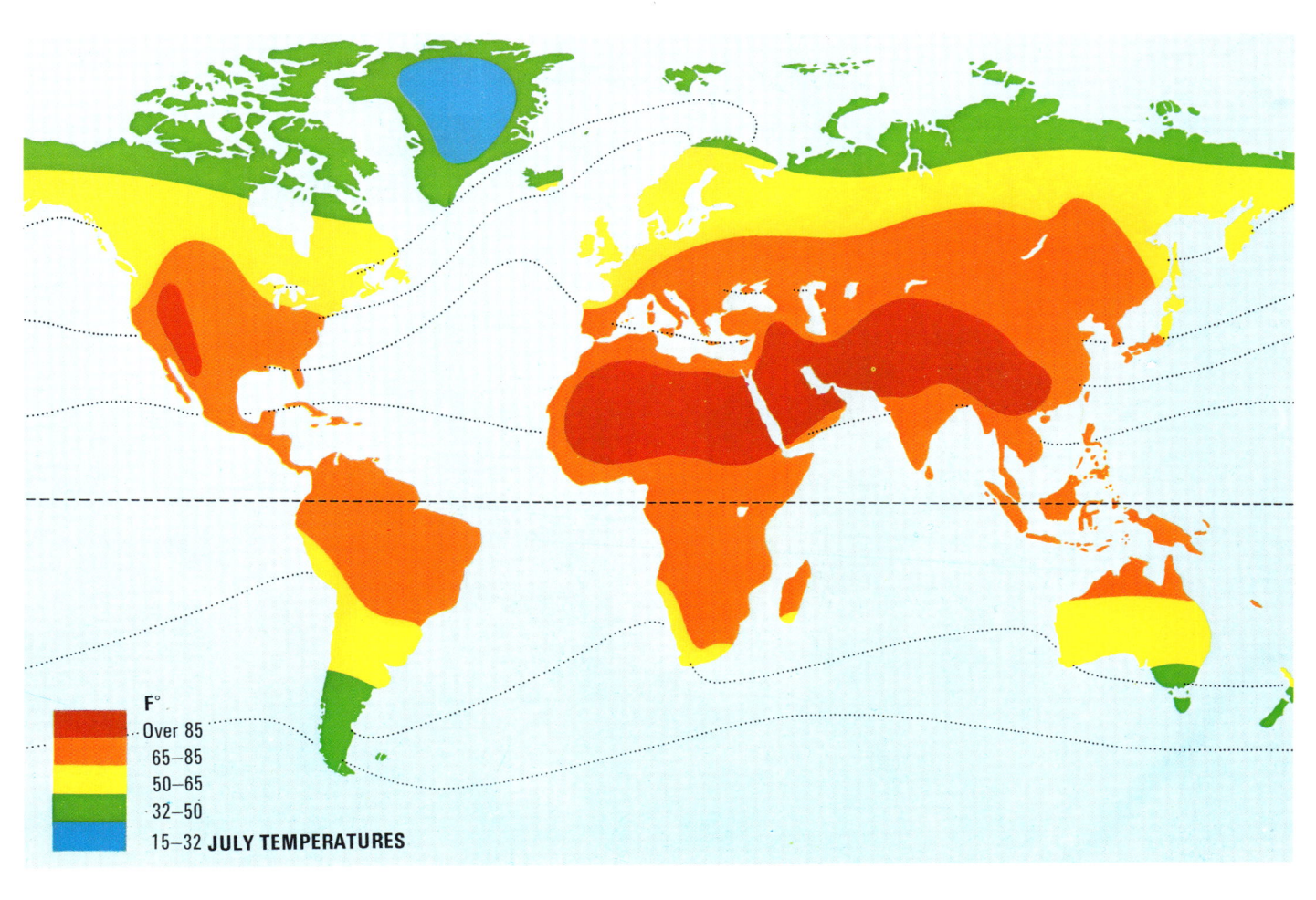

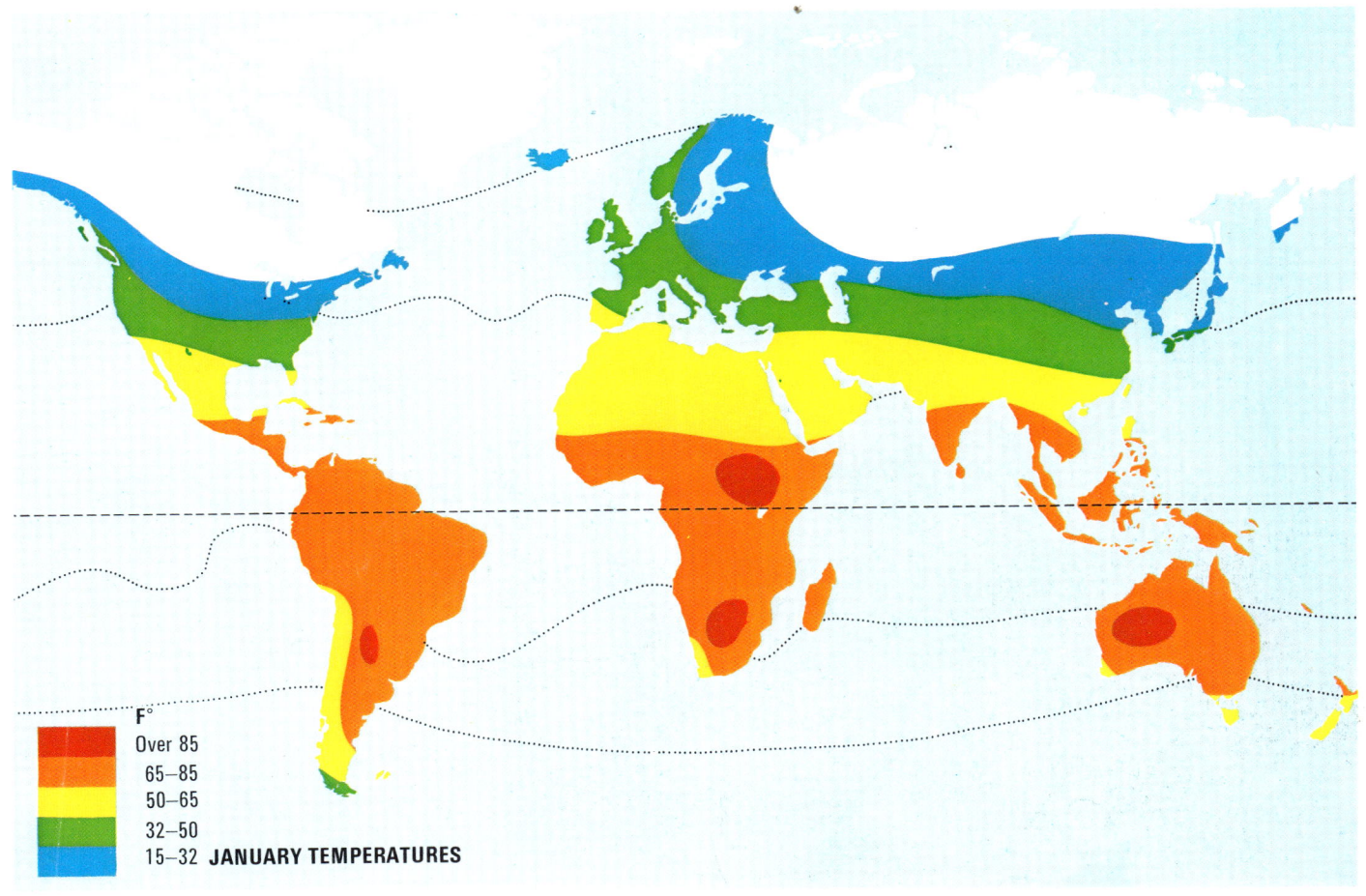

F°	
	Over 85
	65–85
	50–65
	32–50
	15–32 **JANUARY TEMPERATURES**

Soil and Vegetation

Without soil, there would be few plants on Earth. Soil stores heat, food, and water for plants. It also supports their roots.

Soil is mostly made up of tiny rock fragments. Most soils also contain *humus* – the decayed remains of dead plants, animals, and animal excretions. Soils with plenty of humus are usually dark in color.

Climate plays a large part in determining the kind of soil in a region. In tropical rainy climates, the soil may be red and heavily *leached* – that is, the rain dissolves many chemicals out of the topsoil. These soils are rich in bauxite but poor for farming. The plants that grow in tropical climates are those of the dense, tall, evergreen rain forest.

Dry deserts often contain red, sandy soils and salt. These soils support scrubby plants or plants like cacti that store water. Grasslands usually have what are called *chestnut-brown soils*. These soils are unleached and are brown because they contain a great deal of humus.

Above: Conifers, or cone-bearing trees, are the main trees that grow in cold forests. Many have sloping sides and leaves like soft green needles. Snow can slip off such trees without damaging their branches. Forests of conifers ring the world's cool lands near to the tundra.

Below: Three kinds of grassland soils. Even grassland soils differ according to the dryness, or aridity, of the climate. Soils have three layers. The top, or A, layer contains grains of rock and humus. The B layer often contains material leached (dissolved) from the A layer. The C layer contains soil and rocks from the bedrock below.

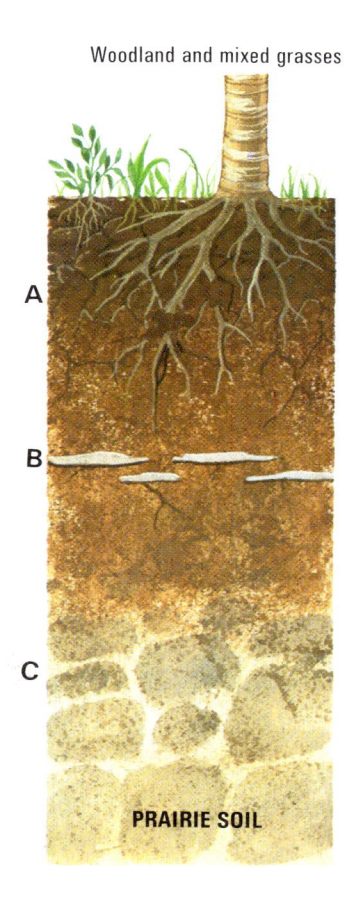

Increasing aridity

Woodland and mixed grasses | Tall bunch grass | Short grass and xerophytic shrubs

PRAIRIE SOIL | CHERNOZEM SOIL | CHESTNUT BROWN SOIL

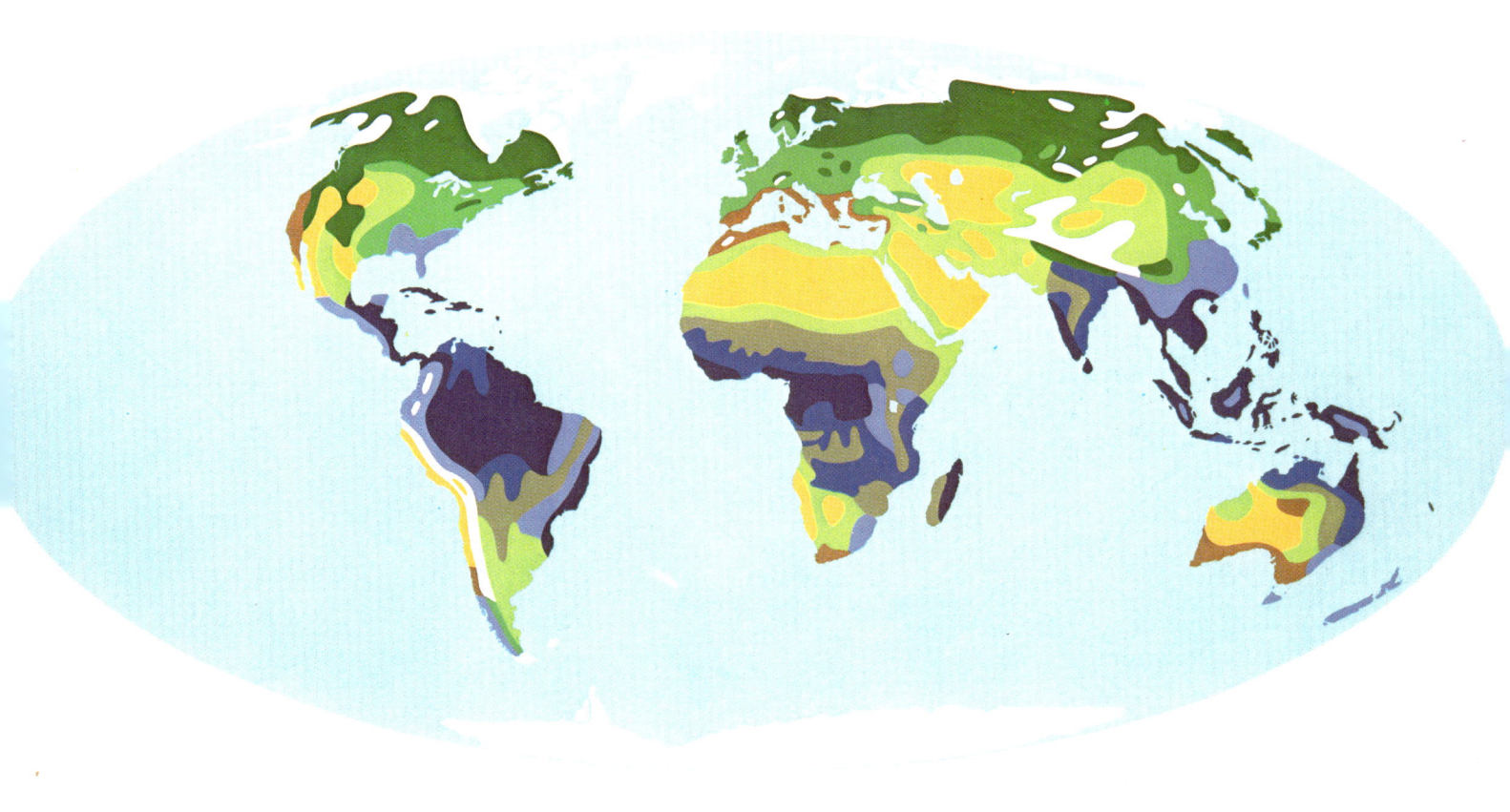

The main vegetation zones of the world. Vegetation is determined by climate, soils, altitude, and the effects of people and animals.

Polar climates are too cold for plants except for low-growing, shallow-rooted plants such as lichens, mosses, grasses, shrubs, and tiny trees.

Similar plants tend to do well in similar climates, even if an ocean separates them. Some such plants are closely related. They evolved together before the sea opened up between them. But many plants just happen to look alike. They developed to suit the same climate.

- Polar tundra and alpine tundra
- Needleleaf forest (cool coniferous)
- Sclerophyll forest (Mediterranean woodland) and maquis (chaparral)
- Deciduous temperate forest
- Evergreen temperate forest
- Steppe and grassland
- Desert and semi-desert
- Savanna
- Tropical deciduous seasonal forest
- Evergreen tropical forest

Rivers and streams also affect soil and vegetation. Where sluggish rivers meet the sea, they drop their loads of silt and mud. These soils are often rich and good for farming.

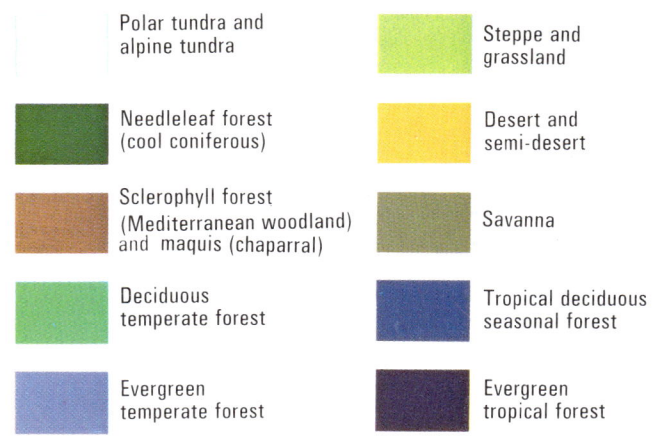

The narras melon of South Africa is a plant designed for life in hot deserts. Its long roots reach down to suck moisture from the soil. Little water can escape from its spiky leaves.

Weather and Forecasting

Below: The meteorologist's tools. Psychrometers measure humidity. Barographs record changing air pressures on a rotating drum.

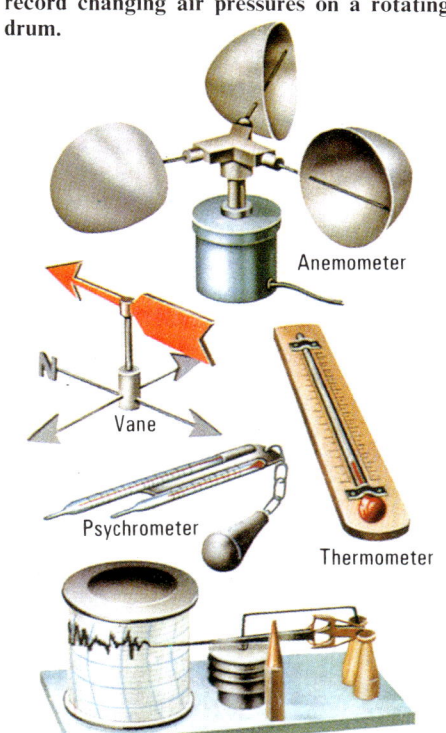

Weather is the condition of the air from day to day and even from hour to hour. Weather is different from climate, which is a description of the typical or average weather of a region.

Depressions and Anticyclones
Our weather is decided by the movements of huge air systems. Low-pressure air systems, or depressions, usually bring rainy and windy weather. They are between 95 and 1,800 miles across, and winds rotate around them in a counterclockwise direction in the Northern Hemisphere and in a clockwise direction in the Southern, Anticyclones are high-pressure air systems. They bring fairly stable weather, including warm sunny weather in summer and cold weather in winter. The winds in an anticyclone rotate in the opposite direction to those in a depression.

At a Weather Station
At weather stations on land and at sea, weather experts, or *meteorologists*, make regular measurements of the air conditions that make up our weather. These include the air temperature, measured by thermometers; the movement of air (winds), measured by anemometers; and the changing air pressure, measured by barometers. Weather balloons (radiosondes) carrying instruments and artificial satellites help meteorologists to study and forecast the weather.

Left: In the eastward-moving depression, a wedge of warm air is enclosed between areas of cold air. Beyond the edge of the warm air, called the *warm front*, warm air rises over the cold air, and clouds form.

Right: One way in which rain is formed. The Sun heats the surface of the Earth and hot air, containing invisible water vapor, rises rapidly. As it rises, the air cools and the vapor condenses to form water droplets. These develop into rain clouds and the droplets fuse into raindrops, which fall to the ground.

Below: A whirling tornado sweeps over a town in Texas. Tornadoes are violent windstorms with wind speeds of up to 400 miles an hour. They form when a long, funnel-like column of air sinks down from a rain cloud as warm air rises and rotates around it. Tornadoes can explode buildings, uproot trees, and lift people into the air.

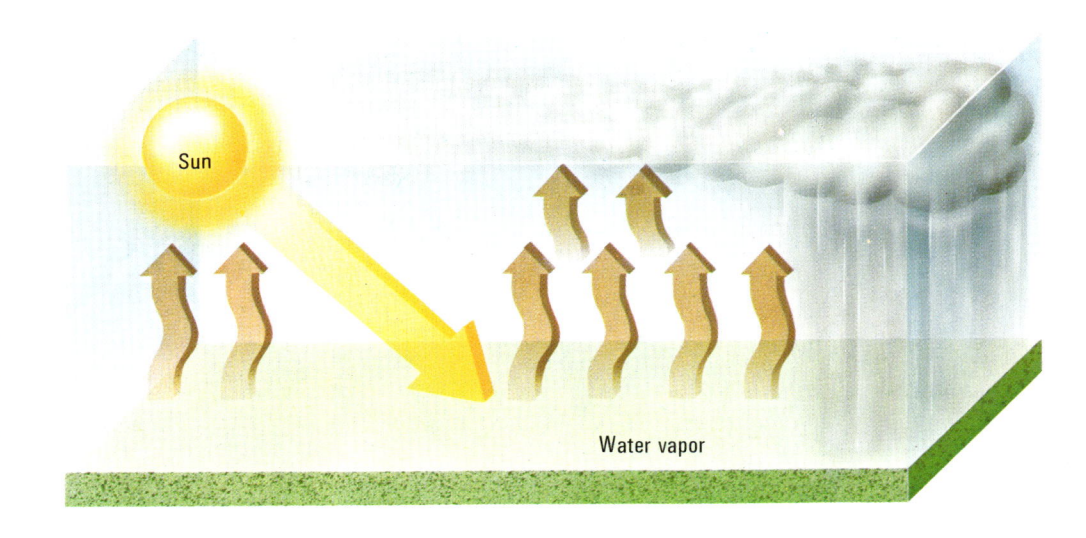

THE BEAUFORT SCALE
The Beaufort scale, used to classify wind strength, is numbered from 0 to 12. Winds with Beaufort number 0 blow at up to 1 mph. Conditions are calm. Beaufort number 1 indicates a wind speed of 1–3 mph, number 2, 4–7 mph, and number 3, a gentle breeze, 8–12 mph. Beaufort number 4 is a wind of 13–18 mph, number 5, 19–24 mph, and number 6, a fresh breeze, 25–31 mph. Number 7 is a wind of 32–38 mph, number 8, 39–46 mph, number 9, 47–54 mph, and number 10, a gale, 55–63 mph. Number 11, 64–73 mph, is a storm wind. Number 12, over 74 mph, is a hurricane-force wind.

Right: A weather map gives a summary of the weather at a particular time. So much information is needed for forecasting that symbols are used to show warm and cold fronts, wind speed, amount of cloud, and whether there is mist, fog, rain, snow, hail, or thunderstorms.

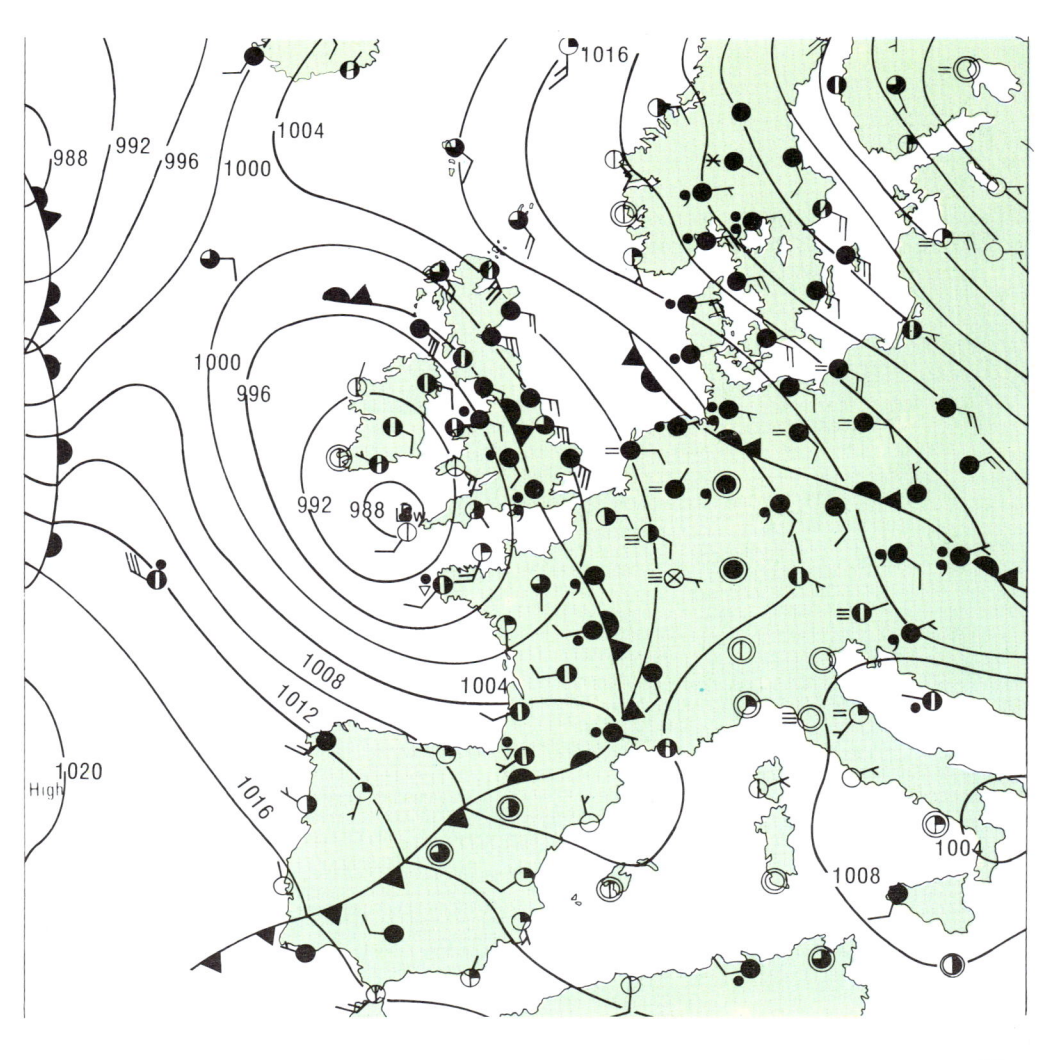

Polar Lands

North Pole

South Pole

Snowy owl

Polar bear

Arctic Circle

ASIA

Arctic Ocean

Lemming

Arctic fox

NORTH AMERICA

North Pole

Ptarmigan

Arctic hare

Long-tailed duck

EUROPE

GREENLAND

Walrus

ICELAND

Reindeer

Ringed seal

The Arctic

The area around the North Pole is called the Arctic. Most of it consists of the Arctic Ocean, which is frozen for much of the year. Winters are long and bitterly cold, and for months the Sun never rises. But in the short, mild summer, the Sun never sets and the warm south winds blow. As the ice melts, bright flowers, moss, and small bushes grow. Eskimos and Lapps live in the Arctic. On the left, you can see Eskimos fishing through a hole in the ice. Their igloo home, made from blocks of frozen snow, and some huskies can be seen in the background.

The Antarctic

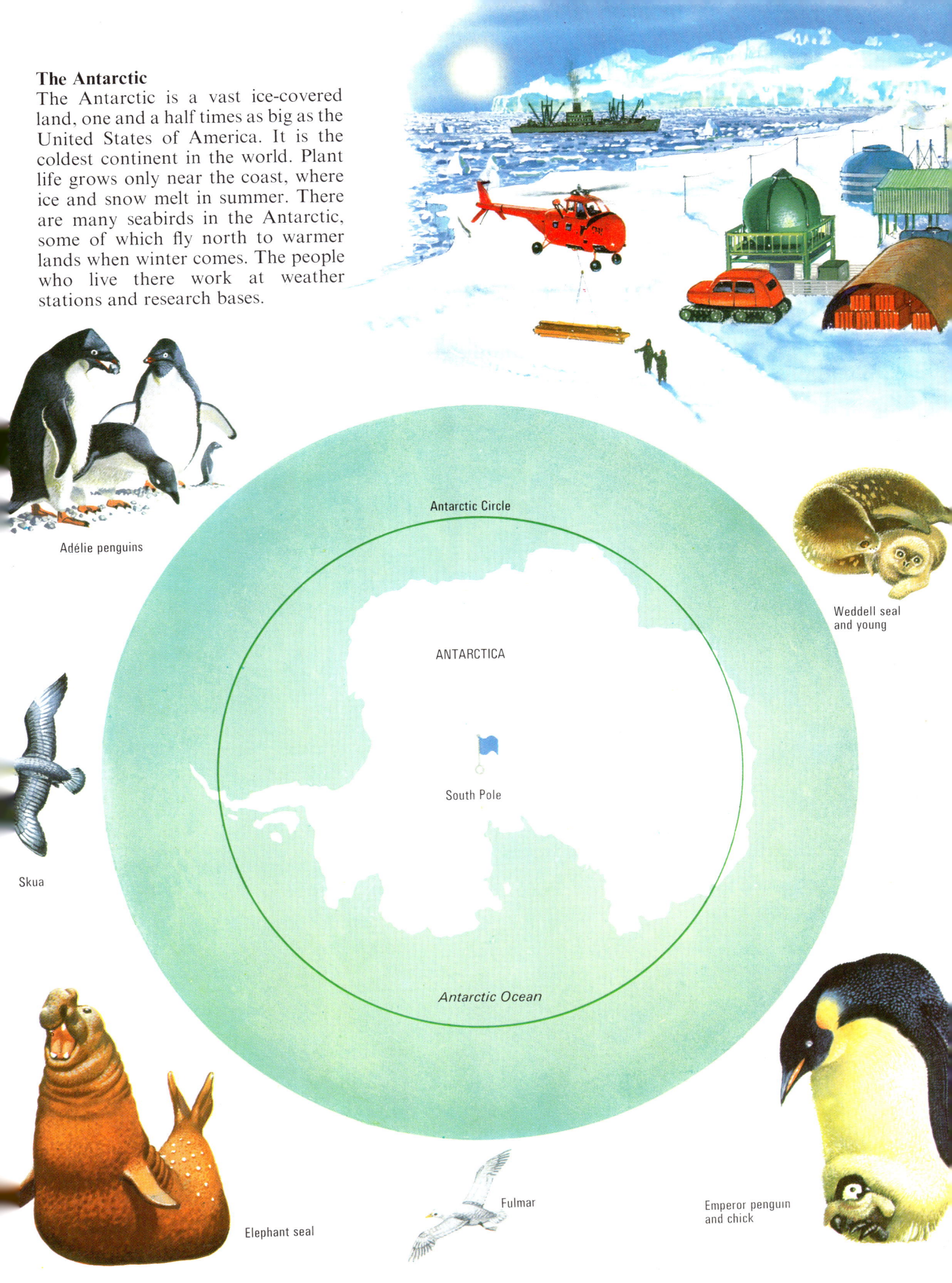

The Antarctic is a vast ice-covered land, one and a half times as big as the United States of America. It is the coldest continent in the world. Plant life grows only near the coast, where ice and snow melt in summer. There are many seabirds in the Antarctic, some of which fly north to warmer lands when winter comes. The people who live there work at weather stations and research bases.

Adélie penguins

Weddell seal and young

Skua

Antarctic Circle

ANTARCTICA

South Pole

Antarctic Ocean

Elephant seal

Fulmar

Emperor penguin and chick

Stationary dune Direction of wind Migrating dune

Deserts

Every continent except for Antarctica and Europe has large, dry deserts. People often think of deserts as vast seas of sand, but sand only covers one-fifth of the deserts. There are three main kinds of desert scenery. Their names come from Arabic words first used by the desert peoples of North Africa. Sand desert is called *erg*. Bare, rocky desert, without sand, is called *hammada*, and stony desert, covered by loose gravel or pebbles, is called *reg*.

Deserts are too dry for most kinds of plants. And because there are few plants to hold the soil in place, the wind can make many changes in the desert scenery. Sandstorms are one unpleasant kind of desert storm. During sandstorms, grains of sand are lifted up, blown forward, and bounced along the surface. The sand acts like a natural sandblaster. It strips paint off cars and frosts the glass on windscreens. It can even cut through wooden telegraph poles unless they are protected by metal or by a pile of stones around the base.

Windblown sand also polishes rocks and cuts caves in cliffs. It can create beautiful formations in the rock. But it is a hazard to people and animals. Sand dunes blown by the wind move slowly forward, burying everything in their paths.

Above: Winds can move desert sand dunes forward. The slope facing the wind is usually gentle. Sand grains are blown up this slope and tumble over the crest down the steep slope that lies away from the wind. This constant movement of sand causes the dunes to move forward, burying all in their paths. The only way to stop them is to plant grasses and trees, whose roots anchor the sand.

Man-made Deserts

Some deserts are created by people. In several parts of the world, dry, grassy plains have been plowed and converted to farmland. But too much farming and grazing makes the soil less fertile, so that crops will not grow. Without plants to hold the soil, it is exposed to erosion (wearing away) by the wind. The loose, powdery soil is then blown away by the wind. This occurred in the 1930s in the central plains of the United States, which became known as the Dust Bowl.

Left: In the hot deserts, only a few nomads can survive in the harsh conditions.

Right: Hot deserts support little plant or animal life. But they can be beautiful. Bare rocks are carved by windblown sand into strange shapes, and the sands are rippled by the wind.

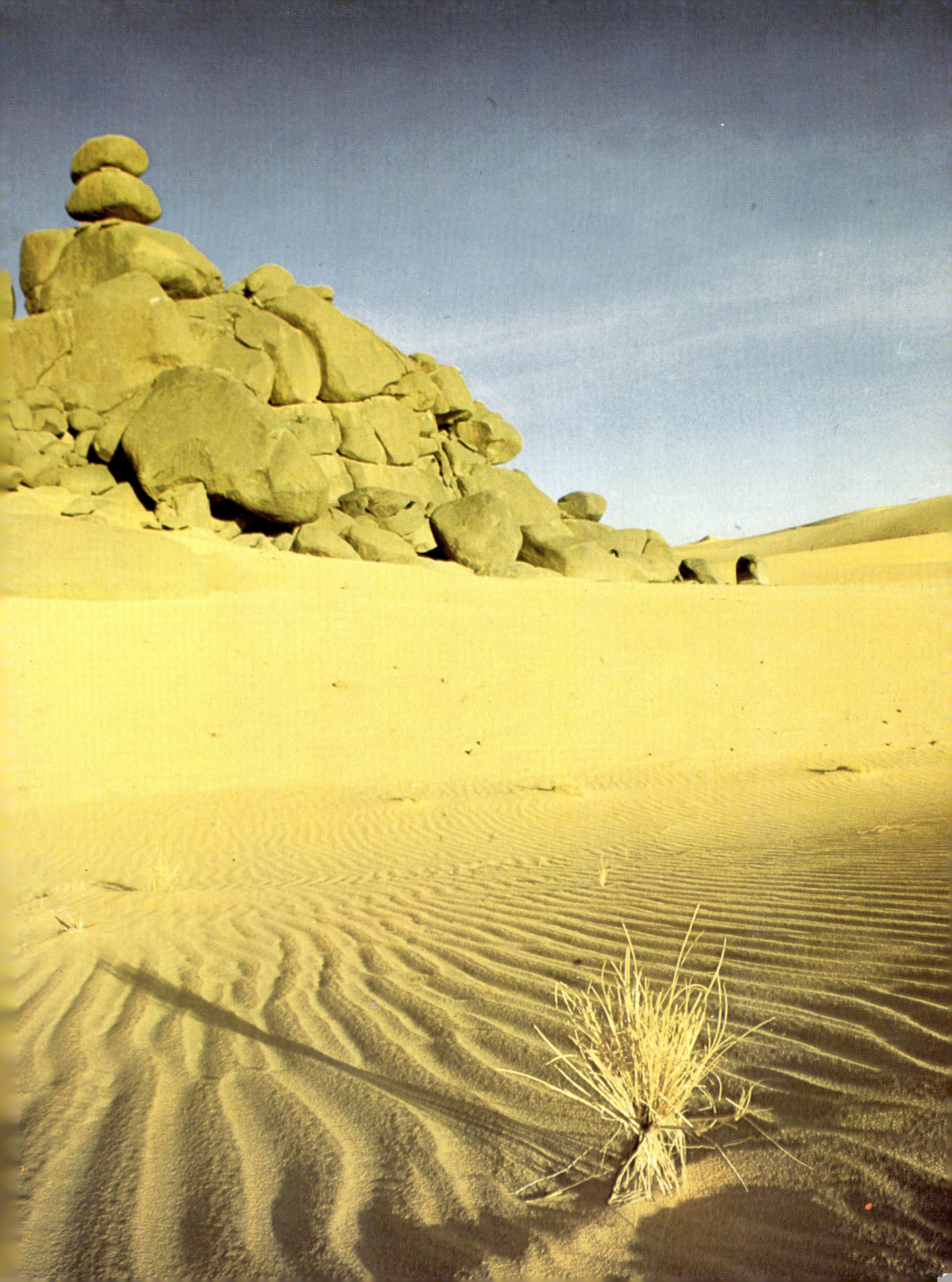

Jungles and Forests

Forests are where trees grow thickly together to cover the land. Great forests of evergreen, cone-bearing trees (conifers) grow in the cool lands of the world. Broad-leaved trees grow in lands with temperate climates, warm in summer and cold in winter. They are called *deciduous* trees because they shed their leaves in autumn. Deciduous trees include oaks, birches, elms, and beeches.

Parts of the tropics are very hot and very wet. Some of the world's greatest jungles, or rain

Above left: Inside an oak forest. Its trees shed their leaves for winter. Such deciduous forests grow in many temperate lands near the coniferous forests. But most of the world's deciduous forests have been cut down by man. Above center: Tropical vegetation is usually dense forests of high trees. People in these regions clear plots of land for cultivation. Above right: Part of a great forest of evergreen, cone-bearing trees. Coniferous forests ring the world's cool lands near the tundra.

Below: This map shows the location of softwood and hardwood forests in the world, together with mixed and tropical forests.

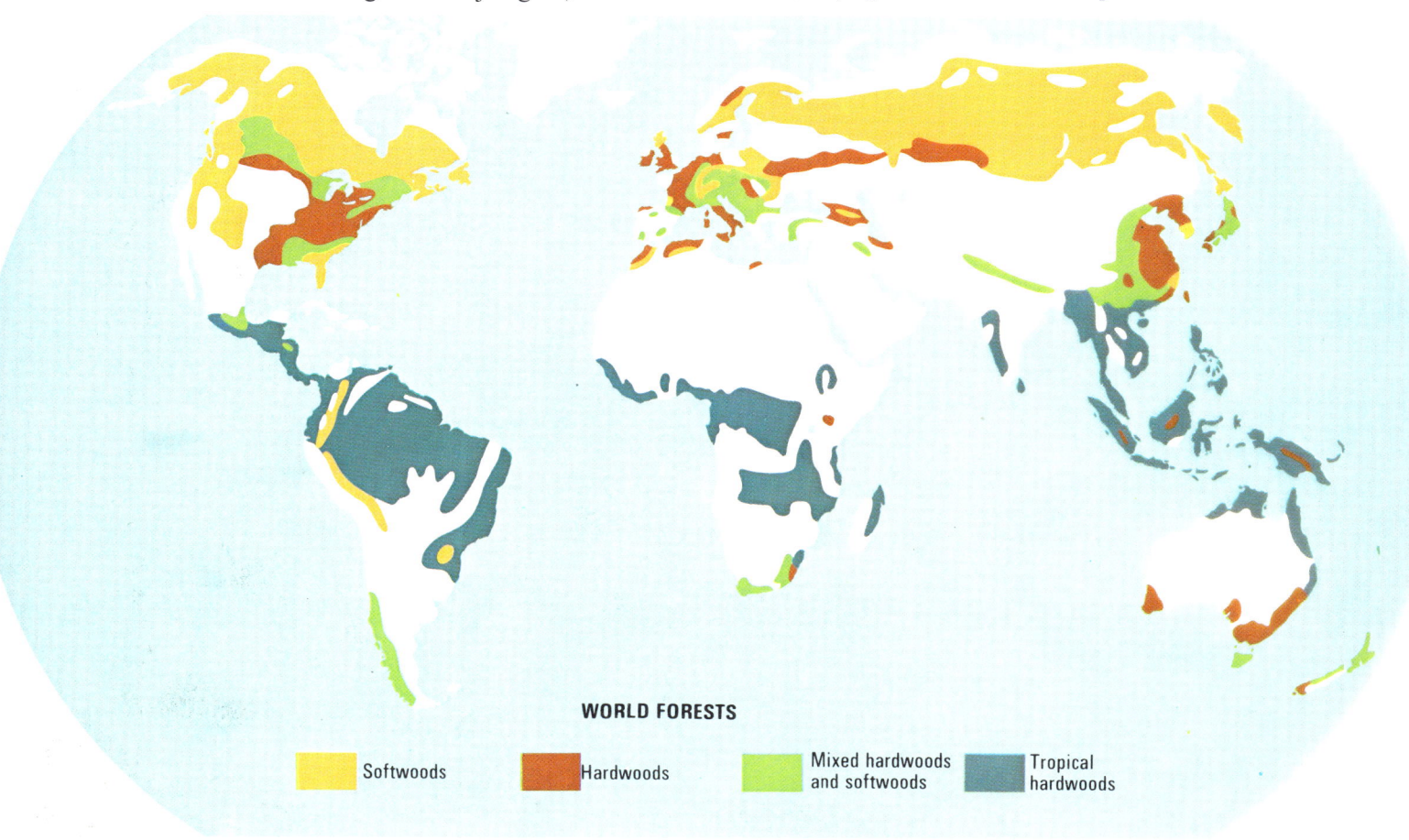

WORLD FORESTS

- Softwoods
- Hardwoods
- Mixed hardwoods and softwoods
- Tropical hardwoods

forests, grow here. Their trees are tall, broad-leaved, and evergreen. Some rain forests are so dense that very little sunlight filters down to the forest floor. But these jungles are home for a great variety of animals, from large and beautiful butterflies, colorful birds and amphibians, to large, powerful mammals such as jaguars, gorillas, and elephants.

Forests and Man

Wood is an extremely useful material – for building, furniture, and many other products, including paper. The northern forests produce many softwoods, including pines, cedars, and spruces. Tropical forests contain valuable hardwoods, including mahogany, used to make fine furniture; rosewood, used in musical instruments; and teak, also valued by furniture makers.

Below: A family of rhesus monkeys at home among Sri Lanka's forest trees. The warm wet tropics are rich in wildlife. Most jungle mammals live in the trees. They include monkeys, gorillas, and chimpanzees in Africa, and orangutans and gibbons in Asia.

Grasslands

Grasslands occur naturally in many parts of the world where rainfall is not sufficient to allow most trees to grow but where conditions are not dry enough to produce deserts. There are also many "artificial" grasslands, produced by the grazing of domestic animals in areas that would otherwise be woodland.

Kinds of Grassland

Natural grasslands are of two main types – tropical and temperate. Tropical grasslands are never cold, but there is usually a wet season and a dry season. Temperate grasslands have cold winters and warm summers, but rain can fall at

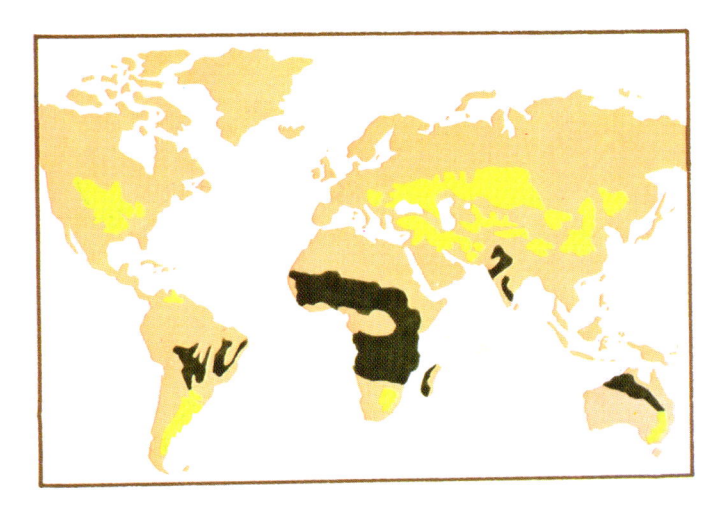

Above: A map showing the grasslands of the world. The light green areas are temperate grasslands, the dark green tropical. Below: A prairie dog "town" on the North American prairie. Much of the prairie is now farmland.

Sheep have helped to form the grasslands of Western Europe. The need for pasture has led to many woodlands being cut down, and the animals' nibbling prevents young trees from growing.

Giraffes graze on the open grasslands of the African savanna. The strange umbrella shape of the acacia trees behind is caused by giraffes eating their lower branches.

any time. The grass is usually taller in the tropical grasslands, and there may be scattered trees.

Tropical grasslands occur in Africa (the savanna) and in parts of southeastern Asia, northern Australia, India, and South America. The main temperate grasslands are the North American prairies, the Eurasian steppes, the South African veld, the Australian and New Zealand downs, and the South American pampas.

Most tropical grasslands lie between forests and semideserts. The yearly rainfall and the rate at which water evaporates are usually high. Savanna grasslands are dotted with such trees as acacia and baobab. In moist areas, elephant grass may reach 16 feet high, but toward the desert it becomes increasingly shorter. The trees are never able to develop into forests, however – partly because the hordes of grazing animals nibble off the seedlings, and partly because fires often sweep over the grassland during the dry season. The grasses survive the fires and quickly send up new shoots from their underground roots or buried seeds.

Today there are few temperate grasslands that have been left in their natural state. Most have been turned into farmland or grazing land. Even dry grasslands are pastures for the flocks of wandering nomads. Here, long droughts sometimes occur, causing the deaths of many animals and starvation among the nomads.

American bison (sometimes wrongly called *buffalo*) used to graze on North American grasslands. They are now rare outside reservations, where they are protected. Between July and September (the mating season), males often fight one another.

Mountains

If you were circling the Earth in a spacecraft, you would notice that much of the land looked like a wrinkled rug. The humps would be mountains, and the dips between them valleys.

Some areas are more mountainous than others. From the spacecraft you might be able to pick out two very long rows of mountains. One runs east from northwest Africa and southern Europe through Asia. This line includes the European Alps and the Himalayas, separating India from China. Some of the highest mountains in the world are in the Himalayas.

A second great chain of mountains runs from

MOUNTAINS – FACTS AND FIGURES
The world's highest peak is Mount Everest. It is 29,028 feet above sea level.
The world has 109 peaks above 24,000 feet. All of them are in Asia, and 96 of them are in the Himalaya-Karakoram Range.
The greatest of all mountain systems is the Mid-Atlantic Ridge, 10,004 miles long. Most of its peaks lie beneath the ocean.
The tallest active volcano is Cotopaxi in the Andes of Ecuador. It is 19,347 feet high.

Above: The Himalayas, the world's highest fold mountains.
Below: Different kinds of fold mountains. A *nappe* is a fold pushed forward over the rocks. A fold may be tilted over to form a *recumbent fold*. Below right shows how block mountains are thrown up. The blocks of land pushed upward are called *horsts*. The steep slopes bordering horsts are called *fault scarps*.

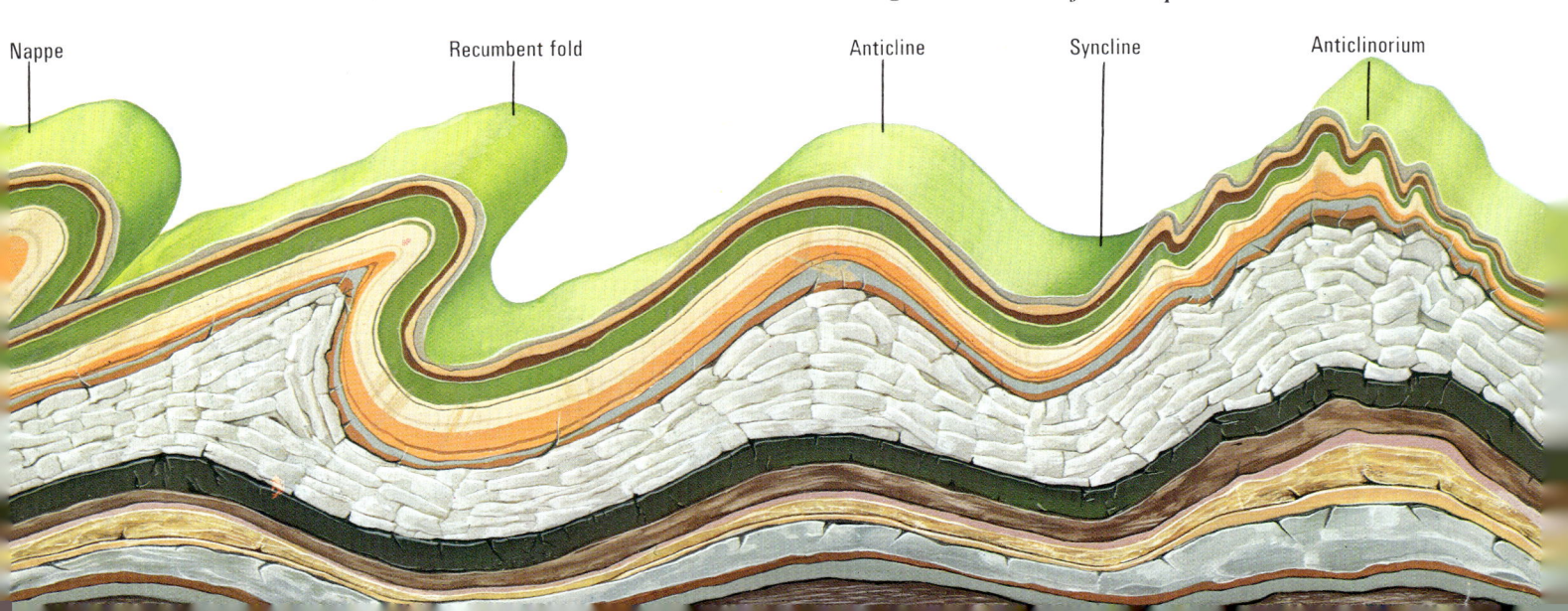

Nappe　　Recumbent fold　　Anticline　　Syncline　　Anticlinorium

north to south, close to the western coast of the Americas. This row includes the Rocky Mountains of North America, and South America's great mountain chain, the Andes.

There are other lower, shorter, groups of mountains. For example, there are mountains on the edge of the Great Rift Valley of East Africa. The Great Dividing Range runs close to Australia's eastern coast. Antarctica is also mountainous, but a thick ice blanket hides all but its highest peaks.

Fold Mountains
The Himalayas and the Rockies are examples of *fold mountains*. They were formed when two great land masses collided millions of years ago. Rocks that had been on the sea floor were pushed upward. Some rocks were folded over onto others. So, over millions of years, the mighty mountain chains were formed.

Movements of the Earth also produce *block mountains*. Great pressures inside the Earth may open up parallel cracks, or *faults*, in the land. A block of land between two such faults may be forced up by pressure from each side.

Not all mountains build up in lines. Some of the largest are built up separately as volcanoes. Indeed, the largest mountain in the world is a volcano. Mauna Loa in Hawaii rises 31,988 feet from the ocean floor.

Fossil animals in its rocks show that this mountain's limestone formed under the sea 250 million years ago. Movements of the Earth later forced it upward. What had once been seabed rocks were pushed up into high mountains.

The Dolomite Mountains are part of the folded Alpine mountain system, straddling northeastern Italy and the Austrian Tyrol. The Dolomites contain superb scenery and attract many climbers who enjoy the challenge of their rugged cliffs and jagged peaks.

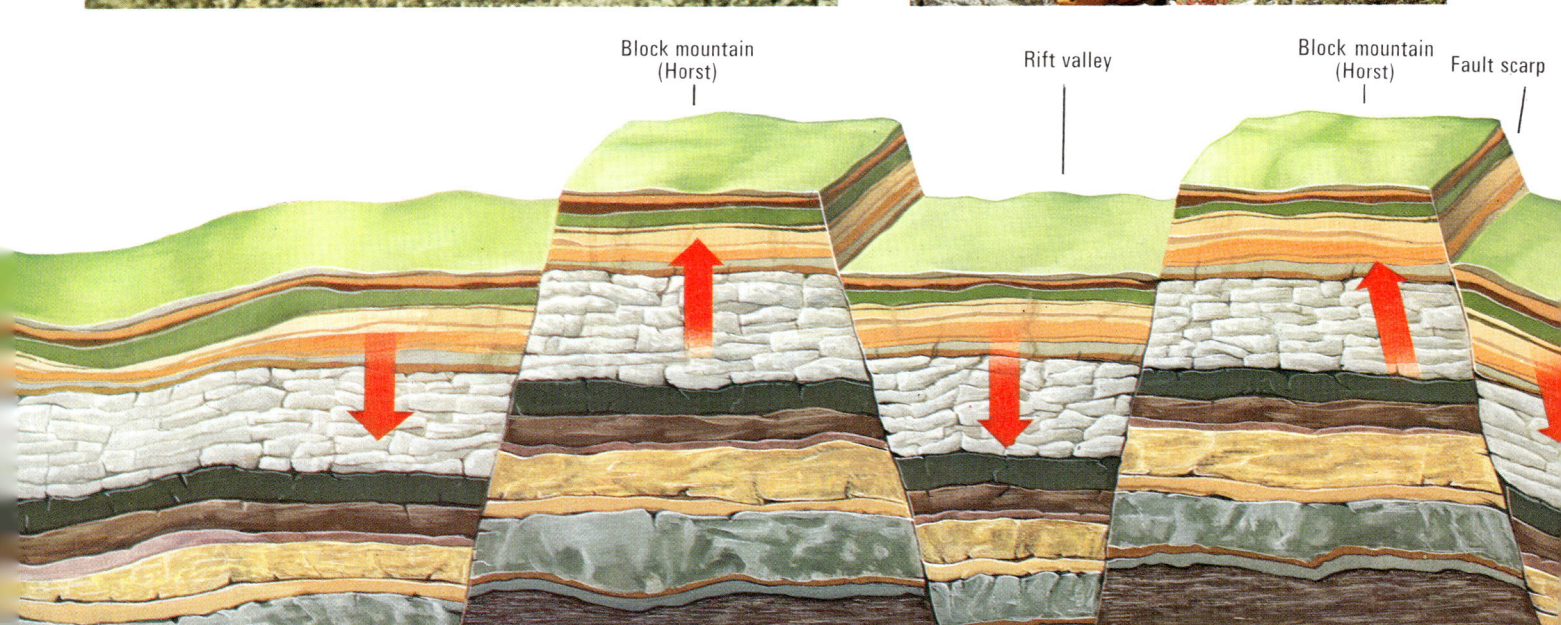

Block mountain (Horst) — Rift valley — Block mountain (Horst) — Fault scarp

Animals of the World

Like plants, many groups of animals are better suited to the climate of one region than to that of others. Some have stayed in one region because they evolved only after the sea or rising mountain ranges had cut off their region from the rest of the world.

Above left: Zebras drinking at a water hole in Africa. Zebras, antelopes, lions, gorillas, and ostriches are among the animals that live in parts of the Ethiopian Realm.
Above: The wild cat is a predator of the European forests. It looks rather like a domestic tabby, but is larger, with pointed ears and ringed, bushy tail.

The Animal Realms
Zoologists have divided the world into six main animal regions, or realms, shown in the map below. Many zoologists now lump the Nearctic and Palaearctic Realms into one realm. They call this the Holarctic realm. More beasts are special to the Nearctic than to the Palaearctic area. Nearctic animals include the North American antelope (the pronghorn), two lizard families, and the bowfin, an ancient type of freshwater fish.

The Neotropical Realm of Central and South America has an even richer store of animals peculiar to one realm. New World monkeys, sloths, anteaters, and many rodents are among its special mammals.

There are many animals special to the Ethiopian Realm. Its unique mammals include giraffes, hippopotamuses, the aardvark, and some lemurs.

The strangest animals of all inhabit Australasia. This region is the home of most marsupial mammals, whose mothers raise their babies in a pouch – the kangaroo and koala are examples. Here, too, live the platypus and the echidna, the only mammals that lay eggs.

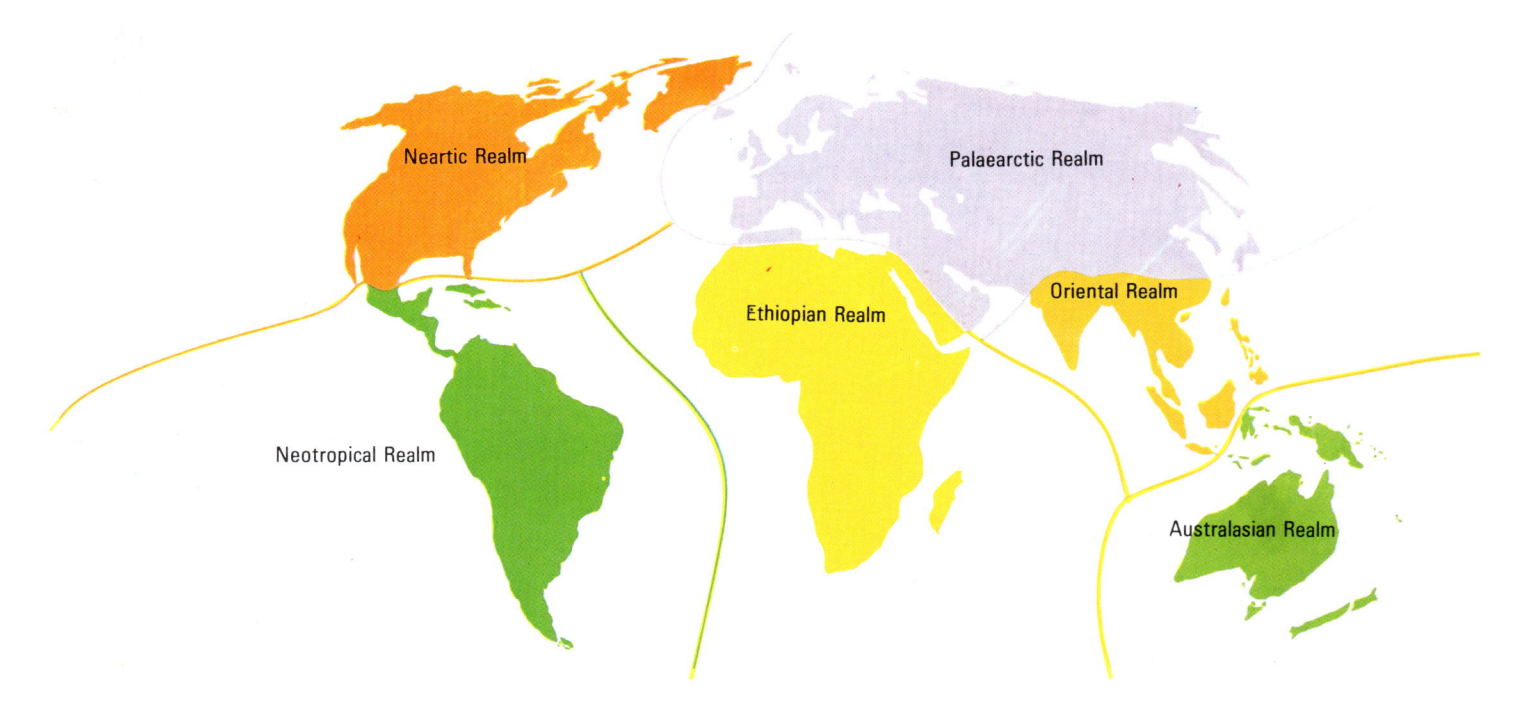

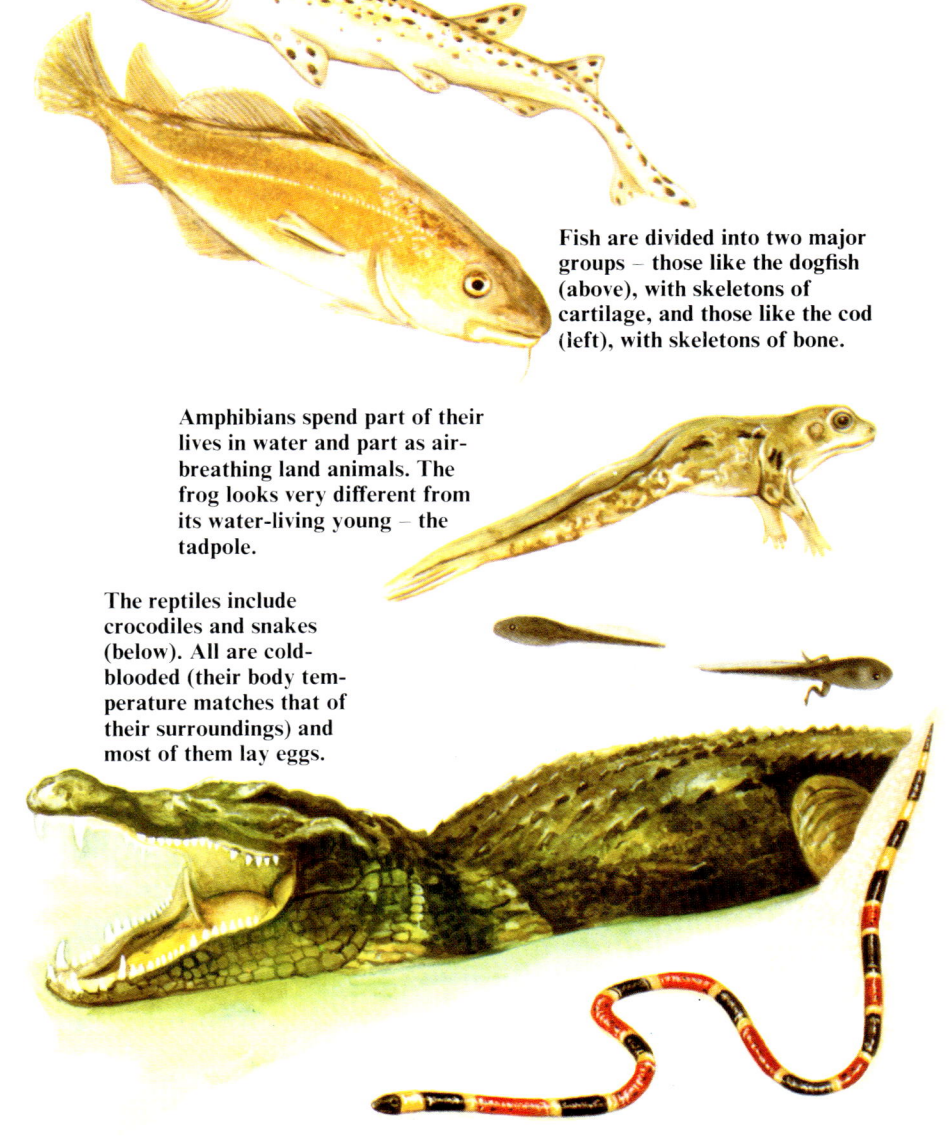

Fish are divided into two major groups – those like the dogfish (above), with skeletons of cartilage, and those like the cod (left), with skeletons of bone.

Amphibians spend part of their lives in water and part as air-breathing land animals. The frog looks very different from its water-living young – the tadpole.

The reptiles include crocodiles and snakes (below). All are cold-blooded (their body temperature matches that of their surroundings) and most of them lay eggs.

Top left: Gibbons live in the Oriental Realm, in South and Southeast Asia. The Oriental Realm – the smallest – has many strange beasts, such as tree shrews, flying lemurs, and the spiny dormouse.

Above: The common hedgehog is a mammal that belongs to Europe and northern Asia, part of the Palaearctic Realm. This realm covers Europe and most of Asia.

Below left: Mammals, such as this pony suckling its foal, are found throughout the world. They are warm-blooded animals that feed their young on milk from the mother's body. All mammals have hair – but some, like humans, do not have very much! Mammals are the most advanced of the animals.

Below: A platypus swims underwater. One of the world's strangest animals, it is one of only two mammals that lay eggs. Both live in the Australasian Realm.

33

Oceans

The oceans cover nearly three-quarters of the Earth's surface. Largest of all is the Pacific. You could fit all the world's lands into the Pacific Ocean, which is also the world's deepest ocean. The Pacific lies between Asia and Australasia in the west and North and South America in the east.

The Atlantic Ocean is the second-largest ocean. It separates the Americas from Europe and Africa. The Indian Ocean, the third-largest ocean, is bordered by Africa, Asia, and Australia. The Arctic Ocean is smaller, shallower, and colder than the other three. Much of it lies under ice.

Ocean water is salty. This is because rivers dissolve salts from the land and wash them into the sea. When seawater evaporates (turns into water vapor) the salts stay in the sea. As a result over millions of years the oceans have become too salty to drink.

OCEANS – FACTS AND FIGURES
Extent of oceans: 71 percent of Earth's surface
Average depth: 11,660 feet
Greatest depth: 36,198 feet
Volume: 308,431,601 cubic miles
Weight: 0.022% of the Earth
Largest ocean: Pacific Ocean
Smallest ocean: Arctic Ocean

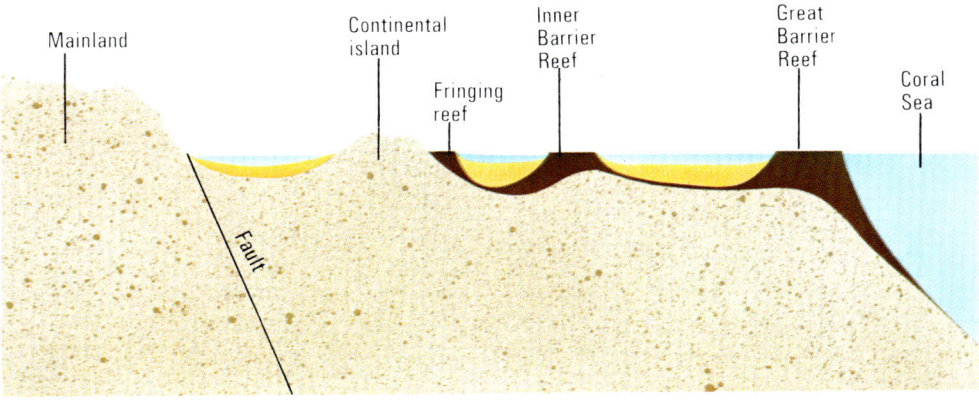

Above left: The islands of Fiji in the South Pacific are called *oceanic islands* because they rise steeply from the sea floor. Continental islands, such as the British Isles, are parts of the continental land masses and rise from the continental shelf.

Left: The Great Barrier Reef off the coast of Australia may have been formed when a section of the coast sank downward along a fault. As the land sank, coral gradually built up islands and reefs.

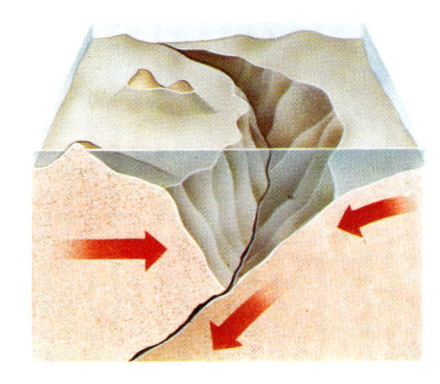

Above: The deepest parts of the oceans are the oceanic trenches. They lie along the edges of plates (sections of the Earth's crust) where one plate is pushed down beneath another.

Below: Echo-sounders are used to map the ocean floor. A pulse of sound is sent down to the sea bottom from a ship's transmitter. The pulse bounces off the ocean floor and back to a receiver. From the time it takes to receive this echo, scientists can work out the depth at that point.

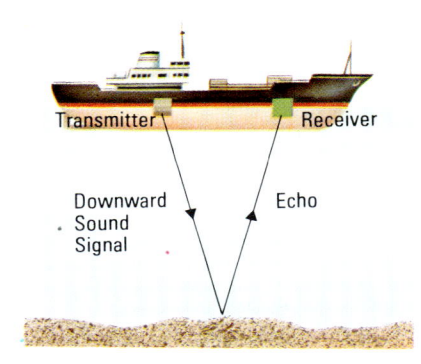

Above right: The diagram shows the chief features of the oceans. Sunlight penetrates to a depth of only 650 to 980 feet, so that plants can grow only in this zone. While the average depth of the oceans is about 11,000 feet, the ocean trenches plummet to more than 36,000 feet.

Below: A cutaway view of the floor and currents of the North Atlantic Ocean. The great underwater Mid-Atlantic Ridge runs down the middle. Here and there its tips peep from the sea as islands. Near the land, the floor rises in a steep slope, up to the shallow continental shelf around North America and Europe. The arrows show ocean currents. The Gulf Stream sends warm water from America to Europe. The Labrador Current (blue arrows) brings cold water from the Arctic to chill the northeastern shores of North America.

Below right: Views of the Earth from space help us to realize that oceans cover nearly three-quarters of the Earth's surface.

Top: Waves are mostly caused by winds. They break on the shores of land masses.

Spilling breaker

Plunging breaker

Above: Spilling breakers occur on gentlysloping beaches. As the waves move up the beach, their crests spill over. Plunging breakers occur on steeper slopes.

Right: Spring tides are the highest tides. They occur when the Sun's gravitational pull is combined with the Moon's. Neap tides are the lowest tides. They occur when the pull of the Moon is at right angles to that of the Sun.

Waves, Tides and Currents

Sometimes the ocean surface is calm. At other times the wind whips up waves. The waves move through the water. But the water stays where it is as each wave passes by. This movement makes boats bob up and down.

Strong, steady winds keep parts of the ocean surface moving as currents. Some carry warm water to cold parts of the world. Others bring cold water to warm areas.

Because the Earth spins from west to east, ocean currents bend to the

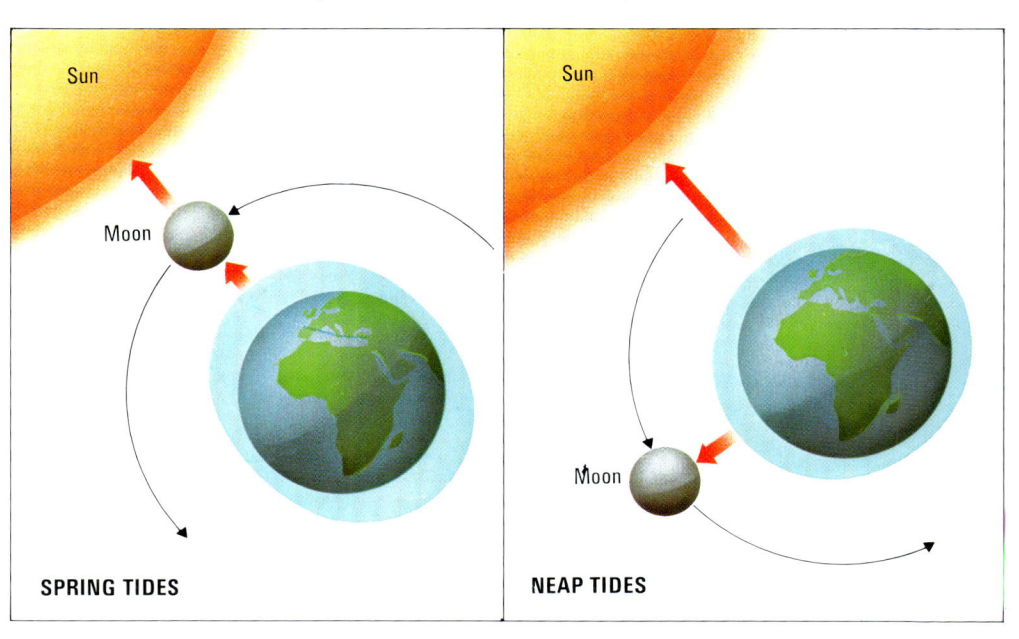

SPRING TIDES

NEAP TIDES

right north of the Equator. South of the Equator currents bend to the *left*. Some currents flow in huge circles. Cold currents flow deep down, often in different directions from those on the surface.

The Restless Tides

Rises and falls of the sea are called *tides*. They occur twice every 24 hours 50 minutes – one complete orbit of the Moon around the Earth. Tides are caused mainly by the gravitational pull of the Moon and, to a lesser extent, of the Sun. On the side of the Earth facing the Moon, the Moon's pull draws ocean water up toward it. The solid Earth is also moved but not so strongly. This pull draws it away from the water on the far side of the world. The result is high tides on opposite sides of the world.

Wave action excavates caves on both sides of a headland.

The caves meet in a natural arch, with a blowhole in the surface.

When the natural arch collapses, the tip of the former headland remains as a rocky islet, or stack.

Above: These cliffs show where sea attacks the land, forming rocky stacks from the tips of former headlands.

Below: A map showing the world's ocean currents.

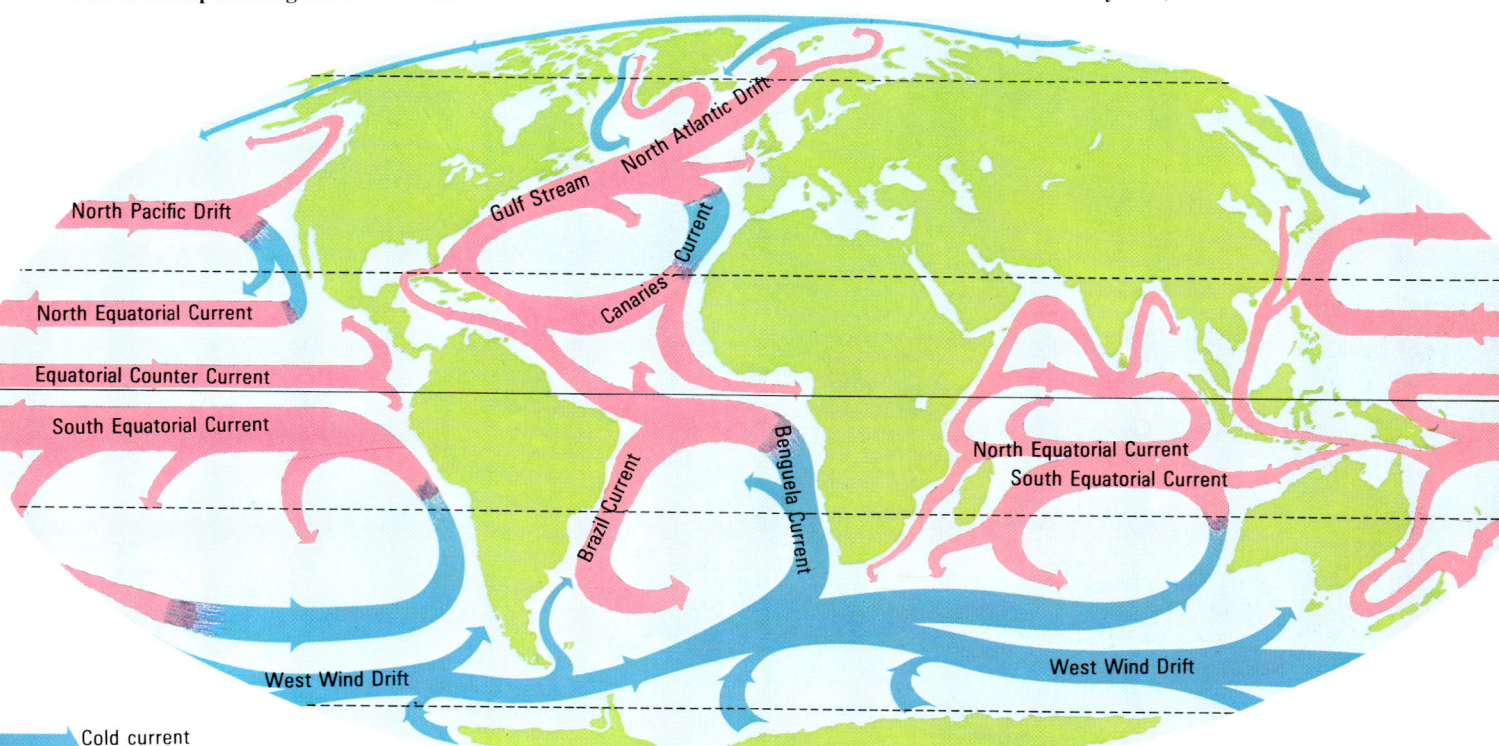

North Pacific Drift
North Atlantic Drift
Gulf Stream
Canaries Current
North Equatorial Current
Equatorial Counter Current
South Equatorial Current
Brazil Current
Benguela Current
North Equatorial Current
South Equatorial Current
West Wind Drift
West Wind Drift

Cold current
Warm current

37

Volcanoes

Volcanoes are holes in the ground through which hot, liquid rock and gases escape from below the surface. Much of the Earth's crust and many of its mountains originally came from volcanoes.

Volcanoes are fiery clues to the great heat and pressures deep down in the Earth. They occur where the Earth's crust is weakest, especially where two plates (sections of the Earth's crust) meet or separate. Here, pressure may force melted rock and other substances up from the mantle and onto the surface of the Earth.

There are three main types of volcano. Sudden, violent eruptions occur if the molten rock has many hot gases trapped in it that expand explosively in eruption. Others are much quieter, spilling molten rock, or lava, to make a gently sloping volcano. The third type of volcano often explodes violently, but it also pours out flows of lava.

FAMOUS VOLCANOES

Greatest explosion: In about 1470 BC, a volcano exploded on the island of Thera (Santorini) in the Aegean Sea. Scientists have estimated that this was the most powerful volcanic explosion – about 130 times as powerful as the greatest H-bomb explosion. About 15 cubic miles of rock was removed by the explosion. The Santorini explosion generated a massive *tsunami* – a huge tidal wave – that battered the island of Crete, probably destroying its Minoan civilization. Some people believe that the destruction of Santorini gave rise to the legend of the lost island of Atlantis.

Greatest recent explosion: In 1883, Krakatoa, a volcanic island in the Sunda Strait between Java and Sumatra, was largely destroyed by a volcanic explosion, and a tsunami drowned 36,000 people in Java and Sumatra. The explosion had only about one-fifth of the power of Santorini.

Greatest eruption: In terms of the amount of material discharged, the eruption of a volcano on the island of Sumbawa, Indonesia, in 1815, was the world's greatest. The eruption discharged about 36 cubic miles of rock.

A cutaway view of one volcano. Pressure forces molten rock (magma) from the mantle to the surface through a weakness in the crust. The magma rises through basalt, granitic, metamorphic, and folded rocks. It escapes from a vent in the surface. In time, volcanoes stop erupting. If they stop for good, scientists describe them as *extinct*. But some volcanoes are only *dormant*. They may lie quiet for hundreds of years and then erupt with sudden violence. Krakatoa in Indonesia exploded in this way.

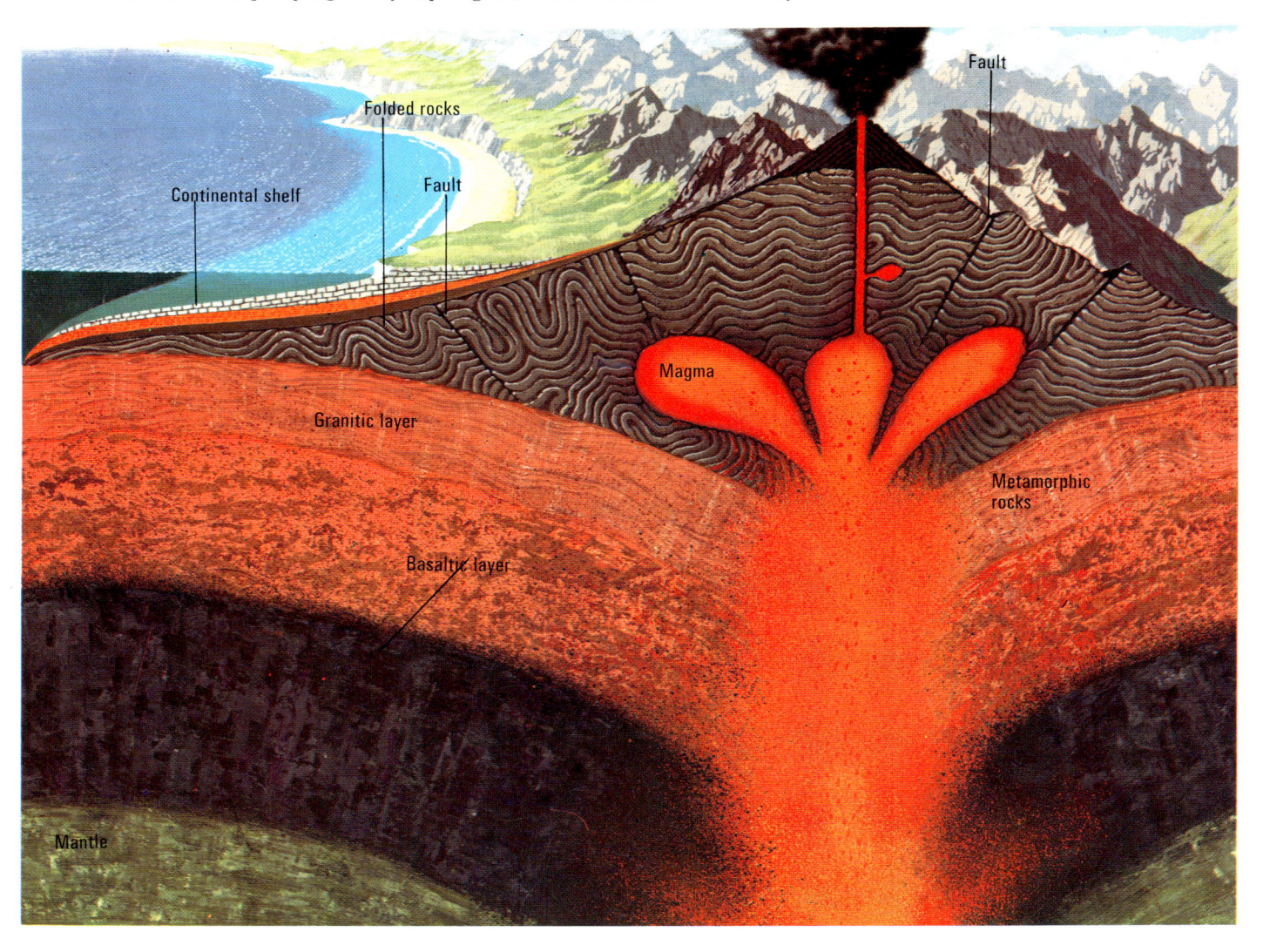

Runny lava flows far and builds a shield volcano.

Thicker lava and ash form layers that build up a cone-shaped volcano.

Very thick lava may harden and plug the volcano until pressure blasts it out.

Quiet volcanoes, such as those on Hawaii, discharge little gas, so there are no explosive eruptions.

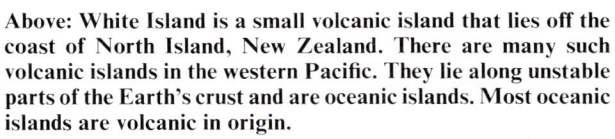

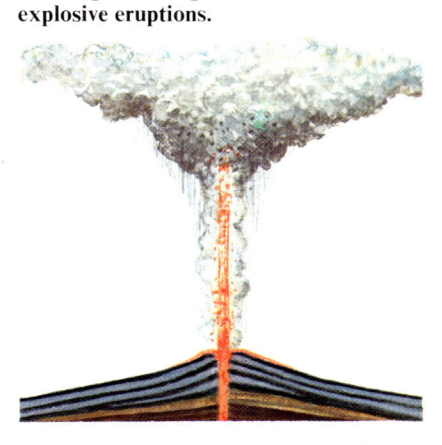

Above: White Island is a small volcanic island that lies off the coast of North Island, New Zealand. There are many such volcanic islands in the western Pacific. They lie along unstable parts of the Earth's crust and are oceanic islands. Most oceanic islands are volcanic in origin.

Below: The world's volcanoes. Most of them occur when magma (molten rock) wells up to the surface in places where crustal plates collide or separate.

Above: How different types of volcano are formed. A plug of solid lava may block a volcano so that it lies dormant for hundreds of years.

⇨ Direction plate is moving
— Collision zone
▲ Volcanoes

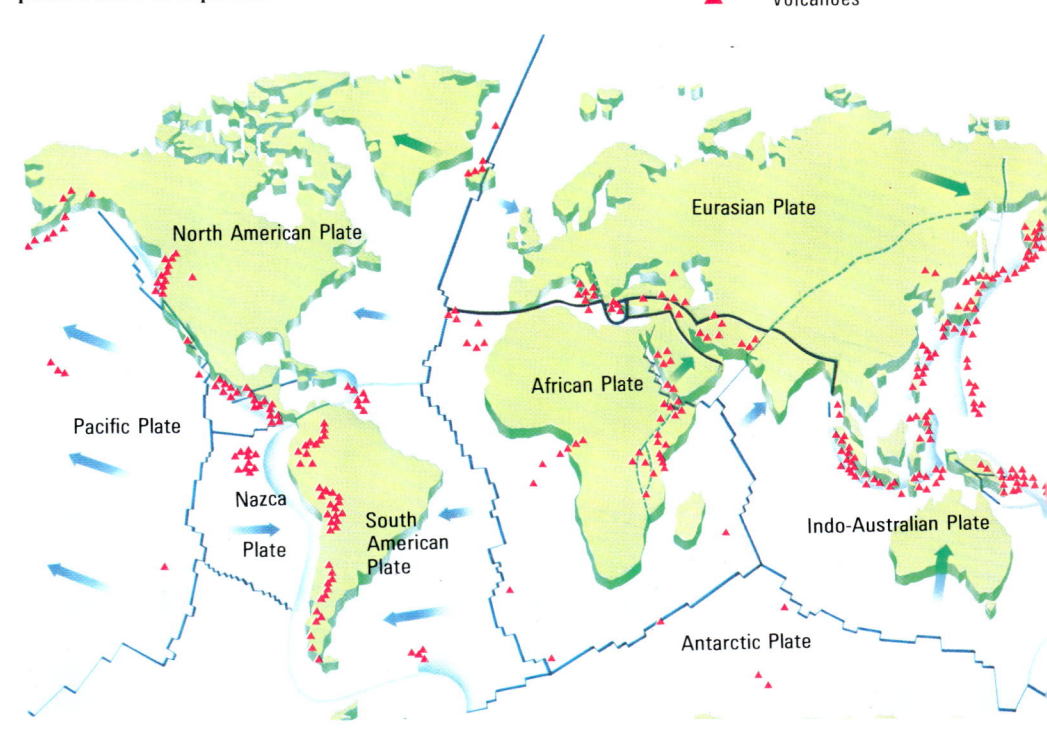

Explosive volcanoes erupt dramatically, shooting clouds of hot ash and rock into the air.

When Mount Pelée erupted in 1902, a "nuée ardente" (glowing cloud) of hot gas and dust rolled downhill.

North American Plate
Eurasian Plate
Pacific Plate
African Plate
Nazca Plate
South American Plate
Indo-Australian Plate
Antarctic Plate

39

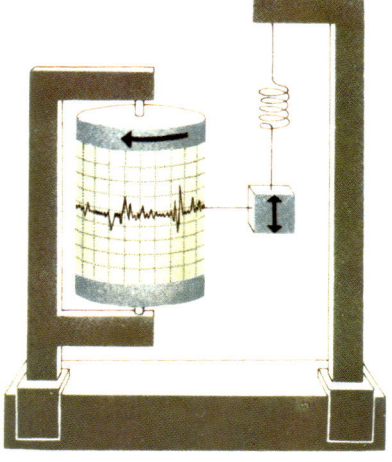

Above: A seismograph shows earth tremors as wriggles in a line traced on a turning drum.

Left: The town of Lice in Turkey was devastated by a 1975 earthquake that killed 2,312 people.

Earthquakes

When earthquakes strike, buildings sometimes tumble as the ground they stand on heaves and splits apart. In some years, earthquakes somewhere in the world destroy thousands of lives and buildings. But most earthquakes are too slight to be felt.

Like volcanoes, earthquakes tend to happen where the great plates of the Earth's crust slowly crash together. Where plate rims are dragged below the ocean trenches, great forces set up strains in the surface rocks. At times, these forces tear a gash across the land. At other times, the rock on one side of such a crack, or *fault*, moves up, down, or sideways.

Such movements produce a shock that travels through the crust and sets the surface trembling. Most earthquakes have their origin, or focus, within 12 miles of the surface. Some are even launched by a landslide or avalanche. The most damaging earthquakes come from less than 40 miles below the surface.

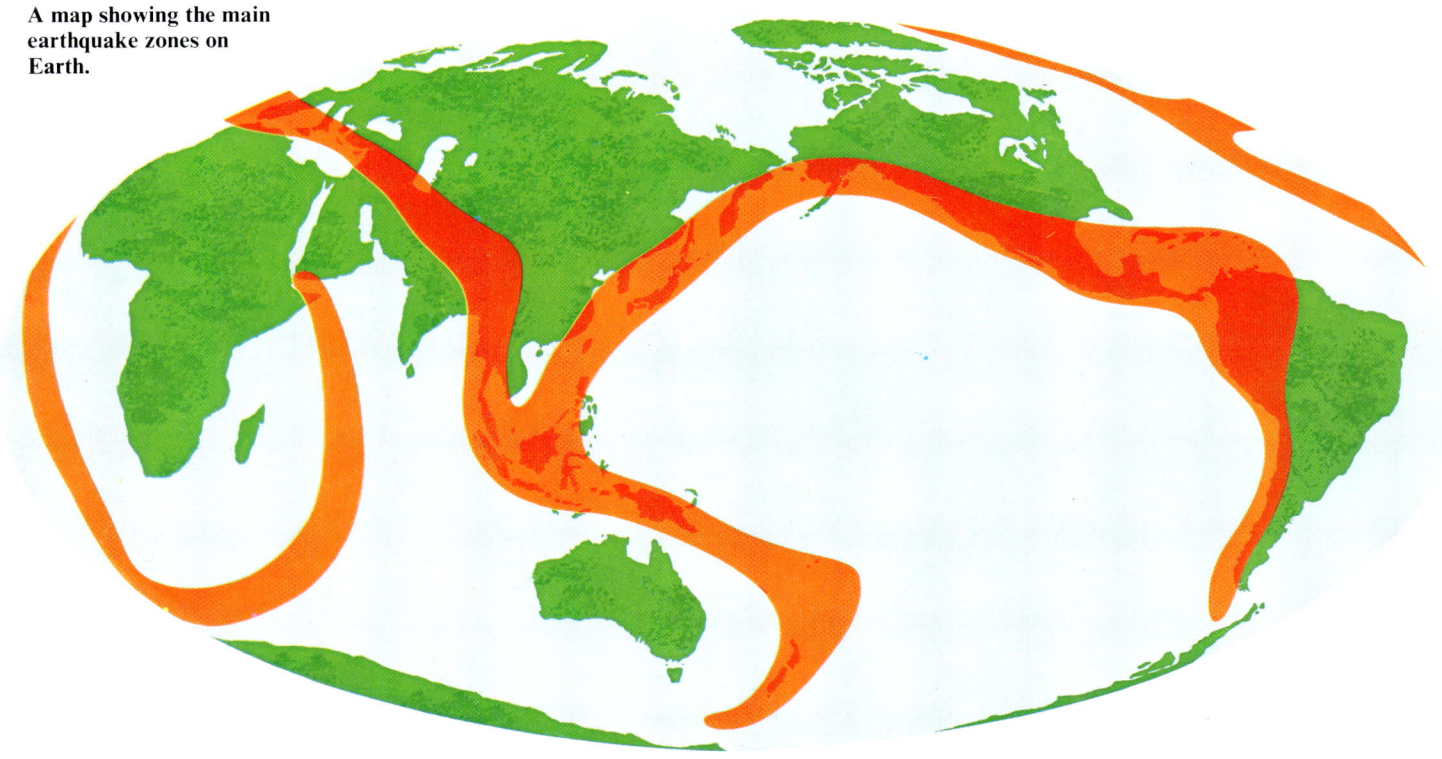

A map showing the main earthquake zones on Earth.

Below: In California, two plates meet at the San Andreas Fault. The western plate moves northwest but is forced west and then north, where it meets the Sierra Nevada. The movements of this plate against its neighbor have caused thousands of earthquakes. The small-scale map at the bottom shows the main lines of weakness responsible for California's earthquakes. Movements of land on both sides of such lines helped to produce the blocks of land shown in the diagram.

Above: Buildings shattered and tilted by the San Francisco earthquake of 1906. This earthquake killed 700 people and destroyed 497 buildings. Most of the destruction and death was caused by the fires that followed the earthquake and not by the quake itself.

EARTHQUAKES – FACTS AND FIGURES

About half a million earthquakes are recorded every year.

One in five can be felt. Only one in 500 does any damage.

The severest earthquake in modern times struck Alaska in 1964. It measured 8.9 on the Richter scale and unleashed the mightiest known ocean wave – 220 feet high.

The most earthquake deaths have occurred in China. In 1556 about 800,000 died in Shensi Province. In 1976 nearly as many may have died at Tangshan.

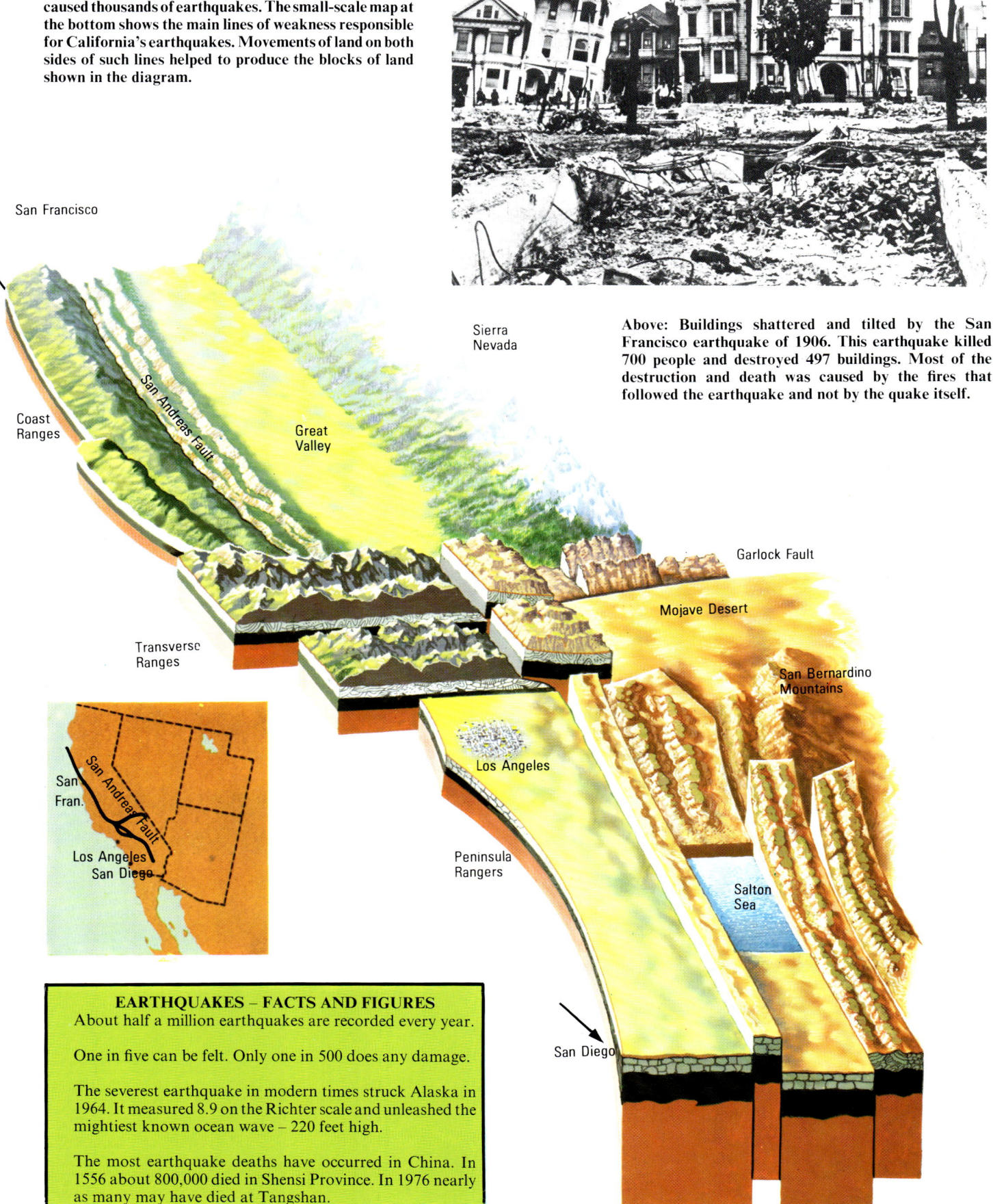

Wind and Weather

Land is built up by volcanoes and colliding continents. But as soon as land appears above the sea, it comes under attack. Sun, wind, frost, ice, chemicals, and moving water combine to wear it down. Their work is slow.

It may well take millions of years to wear a mountain down to the level of the sea. But weathering has worked on all but the newest volcanoes, and has shaped all other hills and the mountains, and every plain and valley in the world today.

Weathering at Work
Weathering is the rotting or splitting up of solid surface rock. Changing temperatures can split up rock in several ways. In hot lands, the Sun heats up the surface rock, making it expand more than the rock below. The surface rock may flake off, much like the outer layer of an onion.

Above: Wind-worn rocks in the Algerian part of the Sahara. Wind hurls loose sand grains against the bases of the rocks. In time the rocks are undercut and topple.

In cool lands, rain may fill up the cracks in the rocks. On cold days or nights the water freezes. Because ice takes up more space than liquid water, it presses outward in the cracks and makes them larger. Over the years, freezing and thawing breaks the rock surface into stones and boulders.

Rock is also broken up by chemicals contained in rainwater that dissolve or rot the rock away.

Above left: Broken fragments of rocks weathered by freezing and thawing tumble downhill, piling up in heaps of loose rock called *scree*.

Left: Temperature changes between day and night greatly affect desert scenery. Desert travelers are sometimes awakened at night by a loud sound like a pistol shot. This is really the sound of rocks breaking apart – the result of being overheated by day and rapidly cooled at night.

For instance, falling rain collects carbon dioxide gas from the air. The two form a weak acid that eats into limy rocks such as chalk and limestone. Some limestone hills have many caves gnawed out by water flowing underground.

The Work of Wind

Wind shapes the land by a process called *erosion*. In deserts, weathered particles of rocks form sand. Windblown sands strike the bottom of rocks with stinging force. They undercut boulders, and gouge caves and hollows in the ground. Winds not only erode loose rock, they carry it from one place to another.

Below right: One way to prevent soil erosion is to plow fields and plant crops following the shape, or contour, of the land. Here, a farmer is harvesting such a crop.

Bottom right: In parts of the world, forests of deciduous trees were cut down and the fertile soils were plowed. At first the land yielded good harvests, but the soil soon lost its fertility. Exposed to the weather, the soil was gradually worn away. On sloping land, the rain collected into small streams and gouged out gullies, such as those in Tunisia shown here.

Plants may also help to wear away the land. A young sapling may take root in a small crack in a boulder. As the tree grows, the roots push downward and sideways, gradually forcing the rock apart.

Above: Barchans are crescent-shaped sand dunes moved like waves by the wind.
Below: A mushroom rock carved by windblown sand.

43

Rivers and Ice

Running water and moving ice do most to change the surface of the land. Rivers have cut valleys from the uplands or dropped loads of mud and silt upon low-lying plains. Young, upland rivers carve out steepsided valleys. In time, a river carves a deep, broad valley from the land. The river winds along the valley floor in bends called *meanders*. Near its mouth, a river may reach "old age." It winds slowly toward the sea over broad, level land. This *floodplain* may end in an *estuary* or *delta*.

Much of the world's fresh water is frozen. A huge ice cap covers Antarctica. *Glaciers* (rivers of ice) form from thick layers of snow and fill many mountain valleys. As they move downhill, rocks stuck in the ice deepen and widen the valleys into a U-shape.

RIVERS – FACTS AND FIGURES
The world's rivers hold about 55,180 cubic miles of water.
The longest river is the Nile. It is 4,145 miles long.
The largest river is the Amazon. It pours 157,000 cubic yards of water per second into the sea.

Above: A cross-section of Niagara Falls between the USA and Canada. The rock at the top of the falls is hard dolomite; the lower layers are shales, limestones, and sandstones. The softer shales are gradually undercut as the water lashes against them.

Left: Waterfalls like this unleash huge quantities of energy. That energy can be used to spin wheels and generate electricity. Such hydroelectric power plants have been built at many major waterfalls.

Right: The continent of Antarctica is the coldest place on Earth. It is mostly covered by a thick blanket of ice, but some peaks, called *munataks*, rise through the ice. At the coast, the ice breaks off to form flat-topped icebergs. The largest known iceberg covered an area of about 12,000 square miles. The ice from Antarctica flows outward under the force of gravity.

Above: The shape of the delta of the river Nile looks like the shape of the Greek letter delta (Δ).

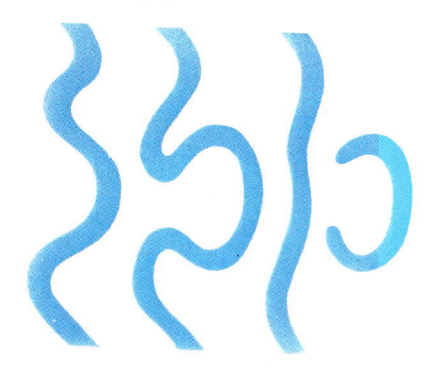

Above: Rivers slowly form bends, or meanders, by eroding one bank and depositing material on the other. Gradually the river cuts a straight channel through the neck of the bend, leaving a separate loop called an *oxbow lake*.

Above: Deposits of eroded material, called silt, slowly build up along river banks, creating natural *levees* (low embankments).

Above: Rivers often cut back at their sources and "capture" other rivers, which become tributaries.

Left: A glacier (river of ice) moves slowly down a mountain valley. As it creeps downhill, the glacier picks up stones that deepen and widen the valley. At the same time, the melting and freezing of snow and ice break up rocks at the top of the valley. This helps the glacier to eat back into the mountain peaks and steepen their slopes.
Below: During the Ice Age, ice spread over much of North America and northern Europe. The ice retreated and advanced several times during the Ice Age, which lasted from about 600,000 years ago to about 15,000 years ago. The map shows the maximum extent of the ice.

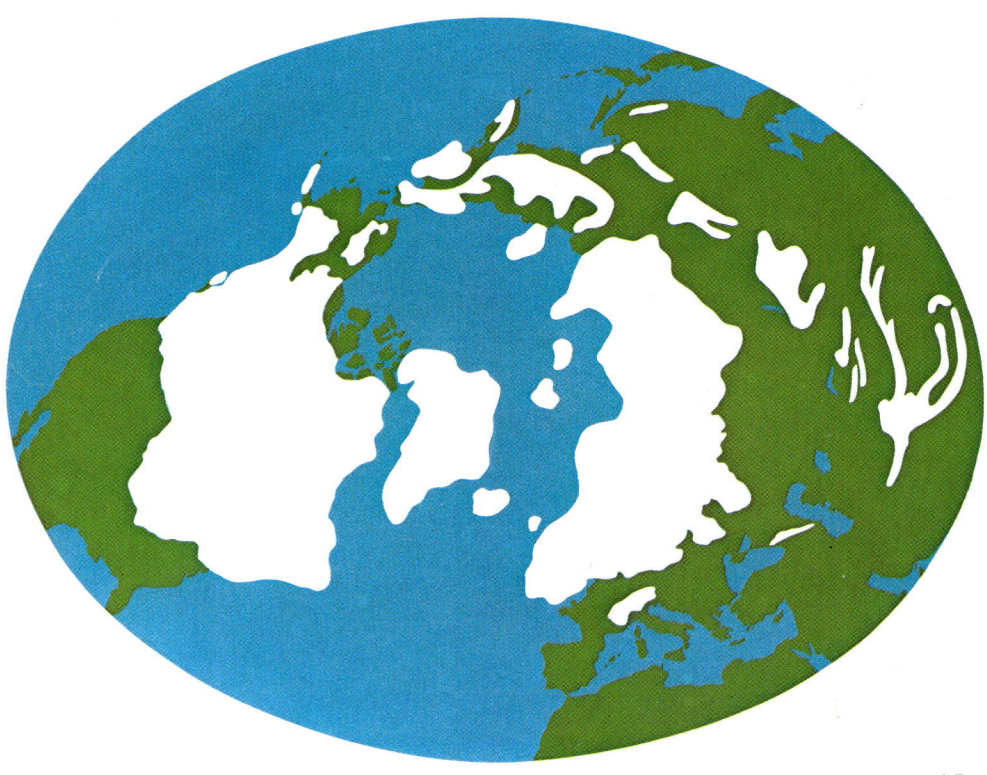

The Underground World

Caves are some of the most curious and fascinating of all the natural formations. There are several kinds of caves. These include ice caves in glaciers, lava caves in hardened lava flows, and sea caves carved into cliffs. But the largest and most spectacular caves occur in rocks such as limestone or dolomite.

Limestone caves are carved out by a chemical process. As rain falls, it absorbs carbon dioxide from the air to form a mild acid. This acid dissolves the calcium carbonate in limestone, which will not dissolve in plain water. As the acid eats away the rock, it widens cracks into passageways and finally caverns under the ground.

The world's largest cavern is the Big Room in the Carlsbad Caverns of New Mexico. The Big Room is 1,312 feet below the surface. It is about 4,000 feet long, nearly 330 feet high, and 656 feet wide.

The World Below
Many caverns are festooned with strange features. Water running through caves often contains dissolved minerals. As drops of water seep through cracks in the cave's ceiling, they hang for a while before dropping. Some of the water evaporates, leaving a thin film of mineral deposit behind. A second droplet deposits another film, and, layer by layer, the deposit grows downward, forming a long *stalactite*. Water droplets that fall to the cave floor may build up columns in the same way. These are called *stalagmites*.

Flows of water across a cave floor can build up flowstones. Water dripping from wavy cracks in the ceiling sometimes forms stone features called *fringed curtains*. And, on the roofs of some caves, there are branching formations that resemble flowers.

Few animals live in caves. Bats are guided by their radar systems. Blind newts and shrimp swim in underground pools.

The whiskered bat and the noctuid moth are two animals that have adapted to life under the ground. Both spend the winter in hibernation inside caves, protected from the cold weather outside. Droplets of dew form on the animals' hairy bodies, which keep them moist and prevent them from drying out. The animals wake up again when they feel the warmth of spring.

THE FORMATION OF A LIMESTONE CAVE

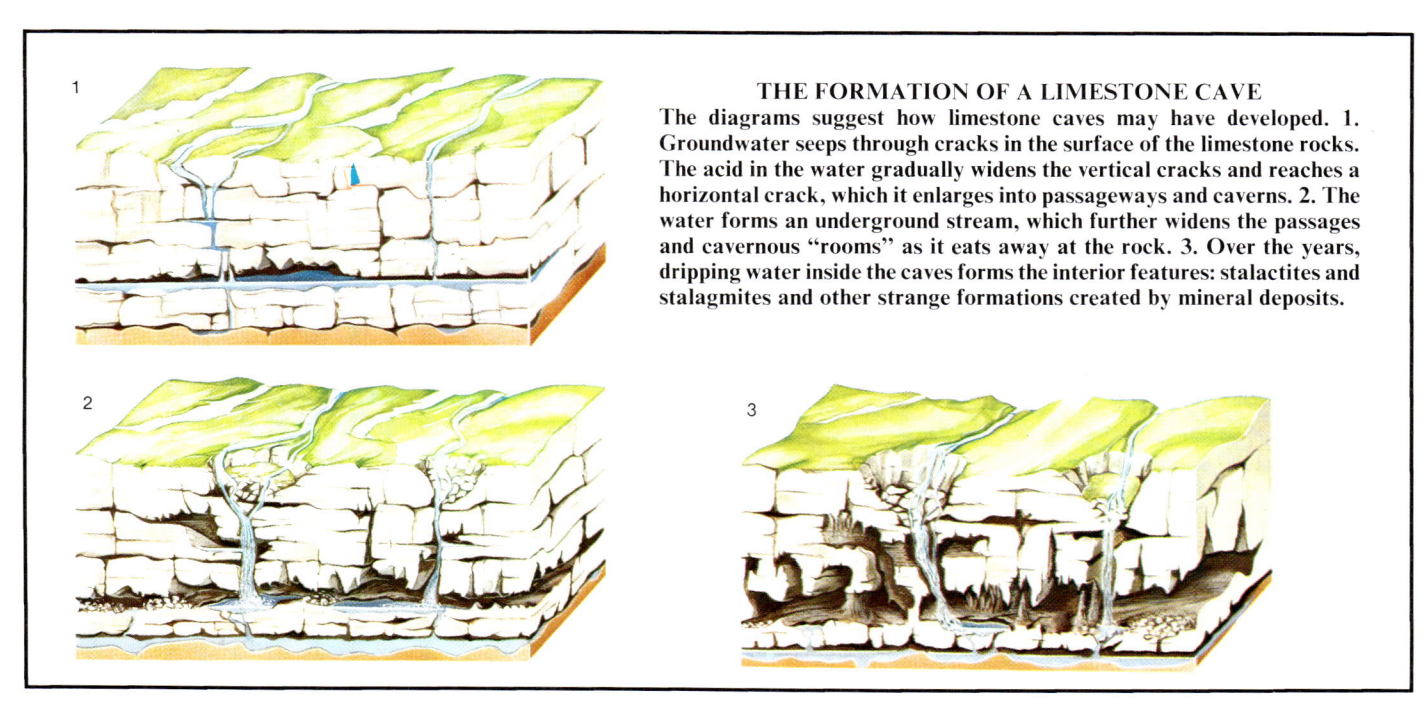

The diagrams suggest how limestone caves may have developed. 1. Groundwater seeps through cracks in the surface of the limestone rocks. The acid in the water gradually widens the vertical cracks and reaches a horizontal crack, which it enlarges into passageways and caverns. 2. The water forms an underground stream, which further widens the passages and cavernous "rooms" as it eats away at the rock. 3. Over the years, dripping water inside the caves forms the interior features: stalactites and stalagmites and other strange formations created by mineral deposits.

A cross-section of a limestone cave system. The cave explorer, or *potholer*, passes a cave called a *dry gallery* before reaching the deeper cave containing a stream. Many different stalactite and stalagmite forms decorate the underground chambers. At right, a stream plunges down a dissolved *sink* to the cave floor below. The underground stream reappears on the surface at left.

Above: The small British colony of Hong Kong is one of the world's most crowded places. Thousands of people live on boats because there is not enough space for them on the land.

Below: Harvesting pumpkins on a farm in New England. Although the United States is a leading industrial manufacturing nation, it is also one of the world's major agricultural producers.

How People Live

Farms, mines, and factories have changed the ways in which people live. Once, most people were farmers, producing food and living on the land. Now one farmer, helped by modern know-how and machines, can feed large numbers of people. There is no need for everyone to work on the land. Many people leave the land and make their homes in cities. They work in factories, offices, shops, schools, hospitals, trains, or buses. Many people now have cars, television sets, and many other goods their ancestors never dreamed of – as well as nourishing, abundant food, and modern hospitals and medicines to cure disease. Most people in industrialized countries now lead longer, more comfortable lives than people long ago enjoyed. But even today not everyone lives in such comfort, or for so long.

Some countries are poor. They cannot produce enough food to feed their people, and they have very little industry to provide wealth. Most people living there are also poor. Most die young from hunger or disease.

More and More People

The population of the world is rising fast. In fact, the number of people has been increasing for the last 10,000 years or so. The world fed perhaps a mere 5 million people in the Old Stone Age, when people relied on hunting for food. In the New Stone Age, farming helped to feed four times that many mouths.

Trade between the farmers and the first cities led to another jump in population. There were perhaps 300 million people 1,000 years ago. In the 1800s the total passed 1 billion. Now, more than 4 billion people live on Earth. If numbers go on rising at this rate the population of the world may more than double in your lifetime. We already face problems of overcrowding, pollution, and the diminishing of natural resources. These problems must be solved to make the Earth a good place to live for future generations.

Above: Bushmen in southern Africa still lead a primitive way of life. They obtain food by hunting wild animals, while the women and girls gather berries and plant roots.

Left: An open-air market in Tbilisi in European Russia. Marketplaces, an age-old institution, are still an important feature of life in many modern nations.

LARGEST COUNTRIES

THE LARGEST NATIONS

Country	Area (sq mi)
USSR	8,600,383
Canada	3,831,033
USA	3,679,201
China	3,630,747
Brazil	3,265,075
Australia	2,967,909
India	1,237,061
Argentina	1,068,301
Sudan	967,500
Algeria	919,595

THE MOST POPULATED NATIONS

Country	Population (1988 est)
China	1,062,000,000
India	800,300,000
USSR	284,000,000
USA	244,000,000
Indonesia	175,000,000
Brazil	141,500,000
Japan	123,000,000
Nigeria	109,000,000
Bangladesh	107,200,000
Pakistan	105,000,000

Race and Language

Scientists describe modern humans as *Homo sapiens*. In the past, there were other forms of humans. But about 35,000 years ago, *Homo sapiens* became dominant and other types, such as *Neanderthal Man*, probably became extinct. Though today we all belong to one species, anthropologists (scientists who study humans) divide humankind into three main subgroups or races: *Caucasoids*, *Mongoloids*, and *Negroids*.

Caucasoids include most Europeans and many Asian and North African peoples. Since the age of exploration, European Caucasoids have settled in most parts of the world.

There are twelve main kinds of Caucasoids: early Mediterranean; Mediterranean; Nordic; Alpine; East Baltic; Lapps; Irano-Afghans; the southern Indian group; the Mediterranean-type Indians; northern Africans; eastern Africans; and mixed groups. Many Caucasoids speak *Indo-European* languages, the world's chief language family (see the diagram on the opposite page).

Mongoloids, the second-largest group, have yellowish skin and straight black hair. The eyes of many Mongoloids have a slanted appearance, because of an internal skinfold in the upper eyelid. Most Mongoloids speak a language either in the Sino-Tibetan group or the Japanese and Korean group.

Negroid peoples have very dark skins, curly or tightly coiled hair, thick lips, and broad noses. Most African Negroids speak languages of the *Niger-Congo* and *Sudanic* families or one of the *Bantu* languages. Other Negroid peoples include the Papuans of New Guinea and the Negritos of Australasia.

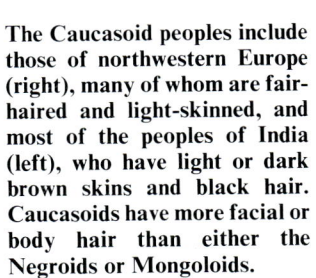

Above: The black African belongs to the Negroid group, which also includes the bushmen of southern Africa and the pygmies of Central Africa.

Above: Australian Aborigines belong to the Caucasoid group. They are of mixed origin, but their features are mainly Caucasoid.

The Caucasoid peoples include those of northwestern Europe (right), many of whom are fair-haired and light-skinned, and most of the peoples of India (left), who have light or dark brown skins and black hair. Caucasoids have more facial or body hair than either the Negroids or Mongoloids.

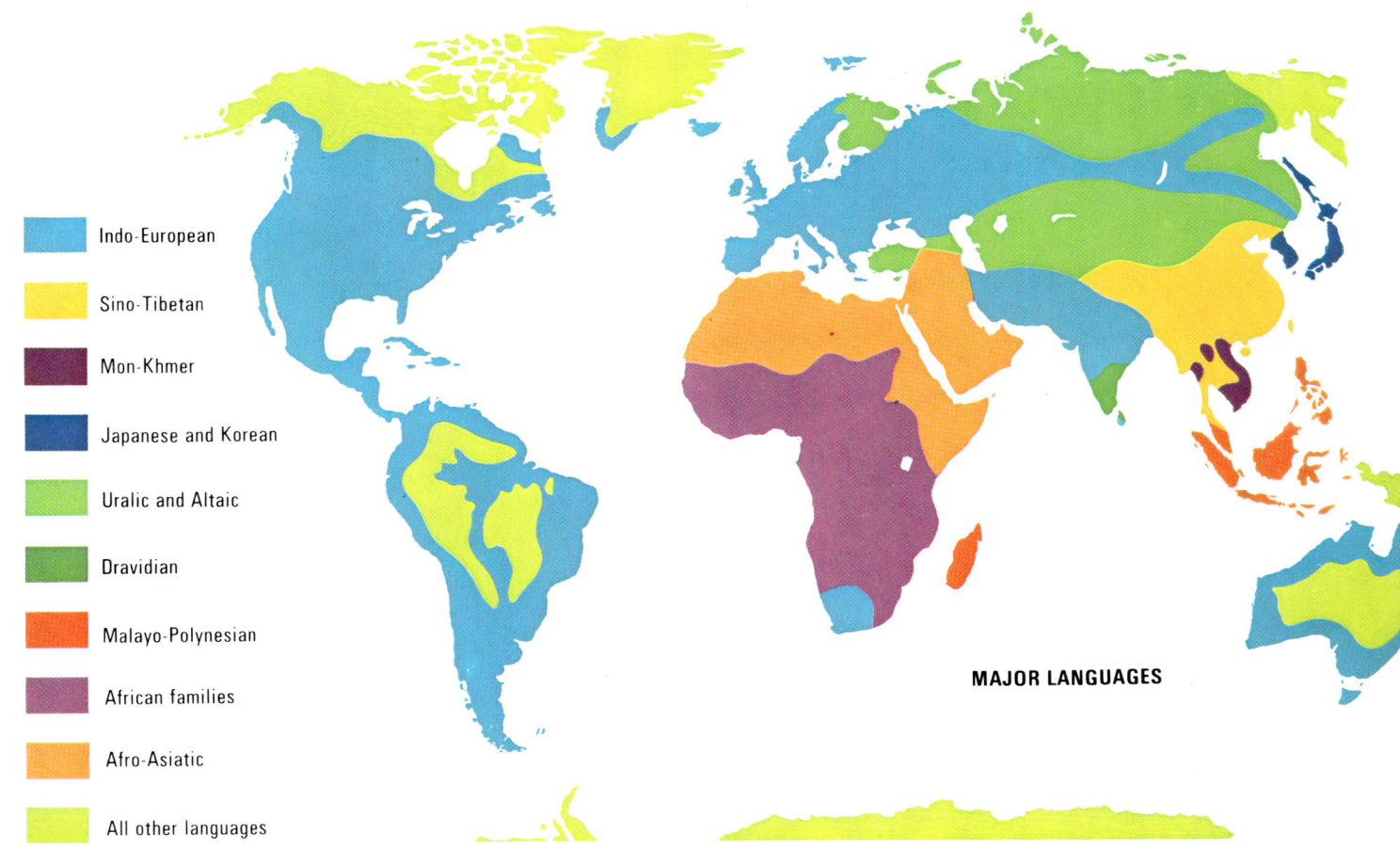

- Indo-European
- Sino-Tibetan
- Mon-Khmer
- Japanese and Korean
- Uralic and Altaic
- Dravidian
- Malayo-Polynesian
- African families
- Afro-Asiatic
- All other languages

MAJOR LANGUAGES

Above: A map of the world's main languages. About half of the world's people speak Indo-European languages. The second-largest group, the Sino-Tibetan, includes the various forms of Chinese. A little more than one-fifth of the world's people speak Sino-Tibetan languages.

Below: The most widely spoken languages belong to the Indo-European group. The diagram shows many of the Indo-European tongues, which originated in Europe, the USSR, parts of southwestern Asia, and in India. Some Indo-European languages, especially English, French, Russian, Spanish, German, Portuguese, and Italian, have spread around the world.

The Chinese people (above left) belong to the Mongoloid racial group. The North Chinese are mostly taller and more slender than the southern Chinese, who are of the Indonesian type of Mongoloids. North American Indians (left) like Eskimos and South American Indian also belong to the Mongoloid group.

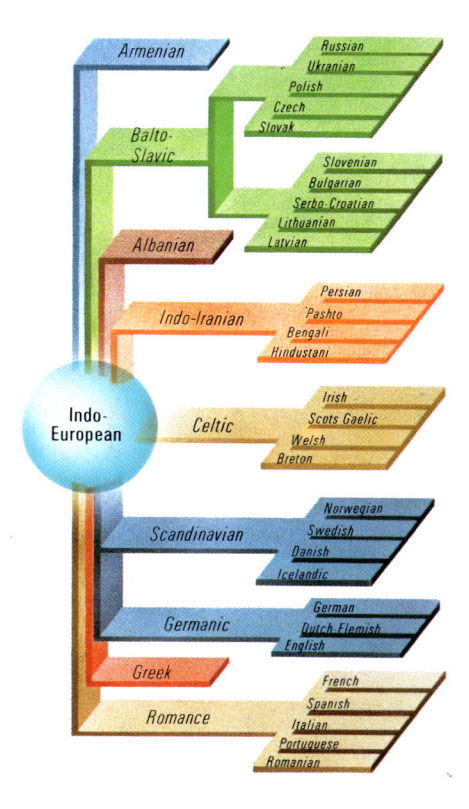

Indo-European:
- Armenian
- Balto-Slavic: Russian, Ukranian, Polish, Czech, Slovak, Slovenian, Bulgarian, Serbo-Croatian, Lithuanian, Latvian
- Albanian
- Indo-Iranian: Persian, Pashto, Bengali, Hindustani
- Celtic: Irish, Scots Gaelic, Welsh, Breton
- Scandinavian: Norwegian, Swedish, Danish, Icelandic
- Germanic: German, Dutch Flemish, English
- Greek
- Romance: French, Spanish, Italian, Portuguese, Romanian

51

Developed and Developing Countries

The world is divided into two main groups of nations: the developing countries, sometimes called the *have-nots*, and the developed nations, called the *haves*.

According to the United Nations, developing countries include most of Asia, apart from Japan and Israel; the Americas, with the exception of the USA and Canada; all of Africa, except South Africa; and Oceania, except for Australia and New Zealand. Most of Europe and the USSR are in the developed world.

Developing nations face many problems. The people often do not have enough food. Schools, doctors, and hospitals are in short supply. Many people cannot expect to live more than 26 to 30 years, whereas in developed nations people can expect to live until they reach their late 60s or 70s.

The populations of developing countries are increasing faster than those of the developed nations. So even though some developing nations are growing richer, their people are becoming poorer. Most people are farmers, producing only

A busy scene in Chicago, Illinois. Mechanized farming means that 1,000 farmers can feed 100,000 city dwellers. City workers in turn provide goods and services.

Above: Most people in Turkey have a low standard of living. Though manufacturing is developing, many people do not have jobs.

Above: In the United States, people enjoy high living standards. Shops sell a wide range of goods to make life more comfortable.

Below: A natural gas field in Algeria. Some developing countries are gaining wealth by developing their natural resources.

52

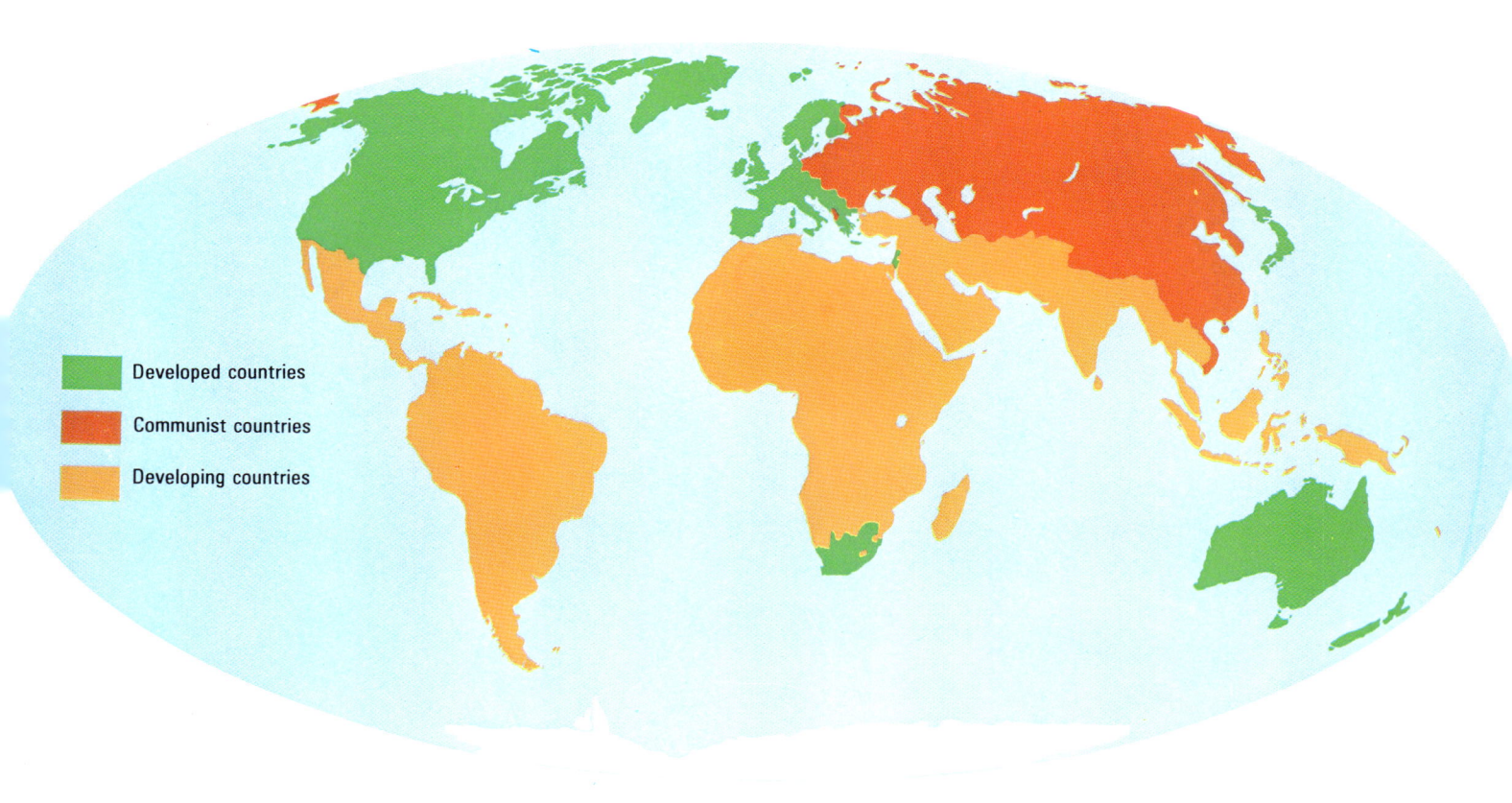

enough to feed their own families. If a drought occurs or pests destroy the crops, they starve. Most developing countries have few manufacturing industries, so to modernize farming methods they must buy such things as tractors and other farm equipment from developed nations.

Manufacturing industries are gradually being set up in the towns and cities of developing countries. People can make more money as factory workers than as farmers, so many people have deserted the land and moved into cities, causing problems of overcrowding and a shortage of housing.

Developed countries give aid to developing countries, and the United Nations helps in many ways. But many experts believe that because of the population increase, the poor of the developing nations are growing poorer.

Above: The map shows the three major groupings of the world's nations: the developed countries, most of which are in what is sometimes called the Western World; the developing countries, sometimes called the Third World; and the Communist countries, which include Russia, China, and their allies.

Below left: Textiles are woven in an Australian factory. The number of manufacturing industries possessed by a country is an important guide to whether it is a developed or developing nation.
Below: Traditional business remains unchanged in an African market, where traders still sell grain as they have for centuries.

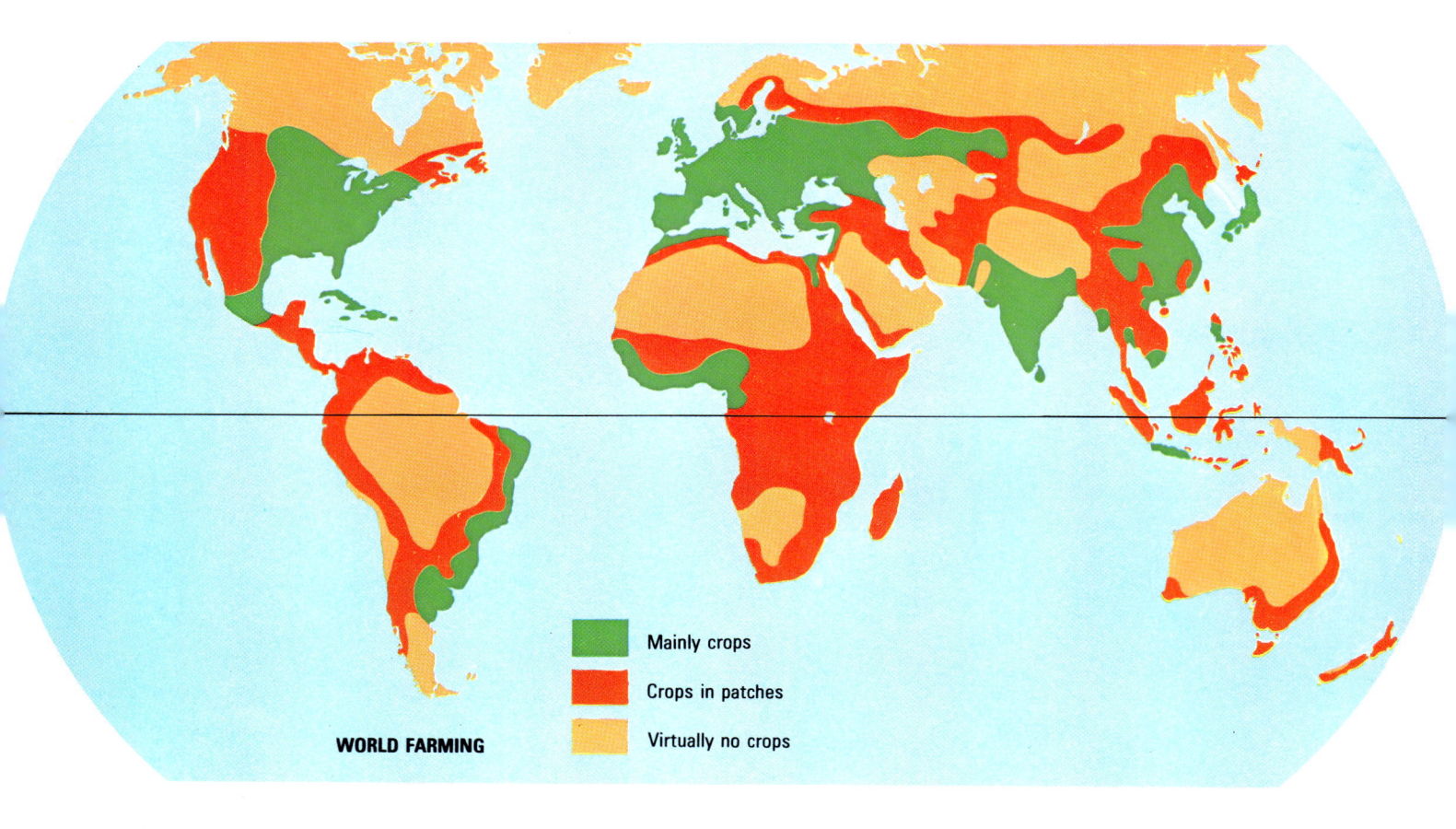

Above: The farming areas of the world.

Below: A cotton-picking machine harvests cotton bolls in Turkey. Cotton was once picked by hand, but the invention of cotton-picking machines made cotton-growing more profitable.

Food and Farming

Just over half of the world's people are farmers. Many are poor farmers in Asia and Africa who barely scratch a living from the soil. Others are wealthy farmers cultivating thousands of acres in Australia or the USA.

The chief group of food crops are cereals, or grains, such as wheat, rye, barley, maize, and oats. Other important crops include fruits and vegetables, oil crops (such as coconuts and olives), and fiber crops, such as cotton, flax, and hemp. Rubber, tobacco, tea, cocoa, and coffee are often grown on plantations – large farms specializing in a single crop.

Farming also includes the raising of livestock such as cows, sheep, pigs, poultry, and beef cattle. Today, many farm animals are carefully bred to produce more milk, meat, eggs, or wool. Many farms in Europe, the Americas, Australia, and New Zealand are mixed farms, where the farmers grow crops and raise livestock at the same time.

Farming methods vary greatly around the world. In developed countries, farming is usually mechanized – that is, most farms are well equipped with machinery and need few workers. But in developing countries in Africa, Asia, and Central and South America, most farming is done by hand and many people work on farms.

In Communist countries such as the USSR, small farms have been replaced by huge *collectives*, which are run by the government and employ many workers who receive wages.

Above: Irrigation canals lead water from the river Nile to farmland alongside the river. Irrigation is essential in dry countries. Today, about 95 percent of Egyptians live along the Nile valley. The rest of Egypt is desert.

Above: Combine harvesters in an Australian wheatfield. Mechanization has greatly increased farm production in developed countries.

Left: New varieties of crops help to combat starvation in developing countries. *Syntha*, a type of rice with weak stems (far left), often collapsed under the weight of the ripe grain, causing the crop to rot. A new variety of strong-stemmed rice (left) holds the grain upright.

Below: Women pick tea on a plantation in Sri Lanka.

IMPORTANT FOOD CROPS

Bananas are tropical fruits. Cooking bananas (plantains) are basic foods in parts of Africa, Asia, and the Americas.
Barley is a cereal, mostly used to feed animals, which is grown in temperate areas.
Cassava is a tropical root crop.
Maize is a cereal, grown as a human food in warm, moist parts of Africa and Asia, and as a human and animal food in North America.
Oats, a cereal, grow in cool, damp parts of the USSR, Europe, and North America.
Potatoes are a valuable starchy food, grown especially in cool temperate areas.
Rice, a cereal, is the basic food for about half of mankind. It grows in warm and wet areas.
Sorghum is a cereal grown in parts of Africa and Asia as a subsistence crop.
Sugar is made from sugar beet, which grows in cool temperate climates, and from sugarcane, which flourishes in the tropics.
Vegetable oils are produced from various plants, including coconuts, cotton seed, groundnuts (peanuts), maize, olives, soybeans, and sunflower seeds.
Wheat is an important cereal that grows in areas with moderately wet and not too severe winters, and warm, fairly dry summers.

Wealth from the Sea

People have been fishing the seas for thousands of years. Today, fishing is still important. But with shortages of food and other natural resources on land, we are turning more and more to the sea to supply these. Seawater contains many important minerals, and the seabed along continental shelves contains valuable deposits of oil and natural gas.

Magnesium is one important mineral that is extracted from seawater. Today, magnesium from seawater accounts for about two-thirds of the world's output. About one-fifth of the world's petroleum comes from operations on the continental shelves. Sand, gravel, and limestone are mined along coasts for use in the building industry. The extraction of salt from seawater is an ancient industry, dating back to biblical times.

Today, fishermen use many modern techniques, though fishing methods are still not as advanced as farming methods. Scientists have suggested that catches could be increased by "fish farming" – breeding young fish and releasing them in nutrient-enriched waters.

Below: Some fishing methods. From left to right: fish such as cod and haddock are caught by their gills in gill nets; in long-line fishing, baited hooks are attached to a long line; a purse seine net is drawn around a school of fish; lobsters are snared in traps; the otter trawl net is dragged over the seabed, trapping bottom fish. Also shown are such commercially important fish as tuna, sardines, herring, mackerel, and cod.

Above: About one-fifth of the world's petroleum is now pumped up from deposits that lie beneath the shallow seas on continental shelves, such as the North Sea and the Gulf of Mexico. Some of these deposits are also rich in natural gas, which is trapped in rock structures similar to those of petroleum.

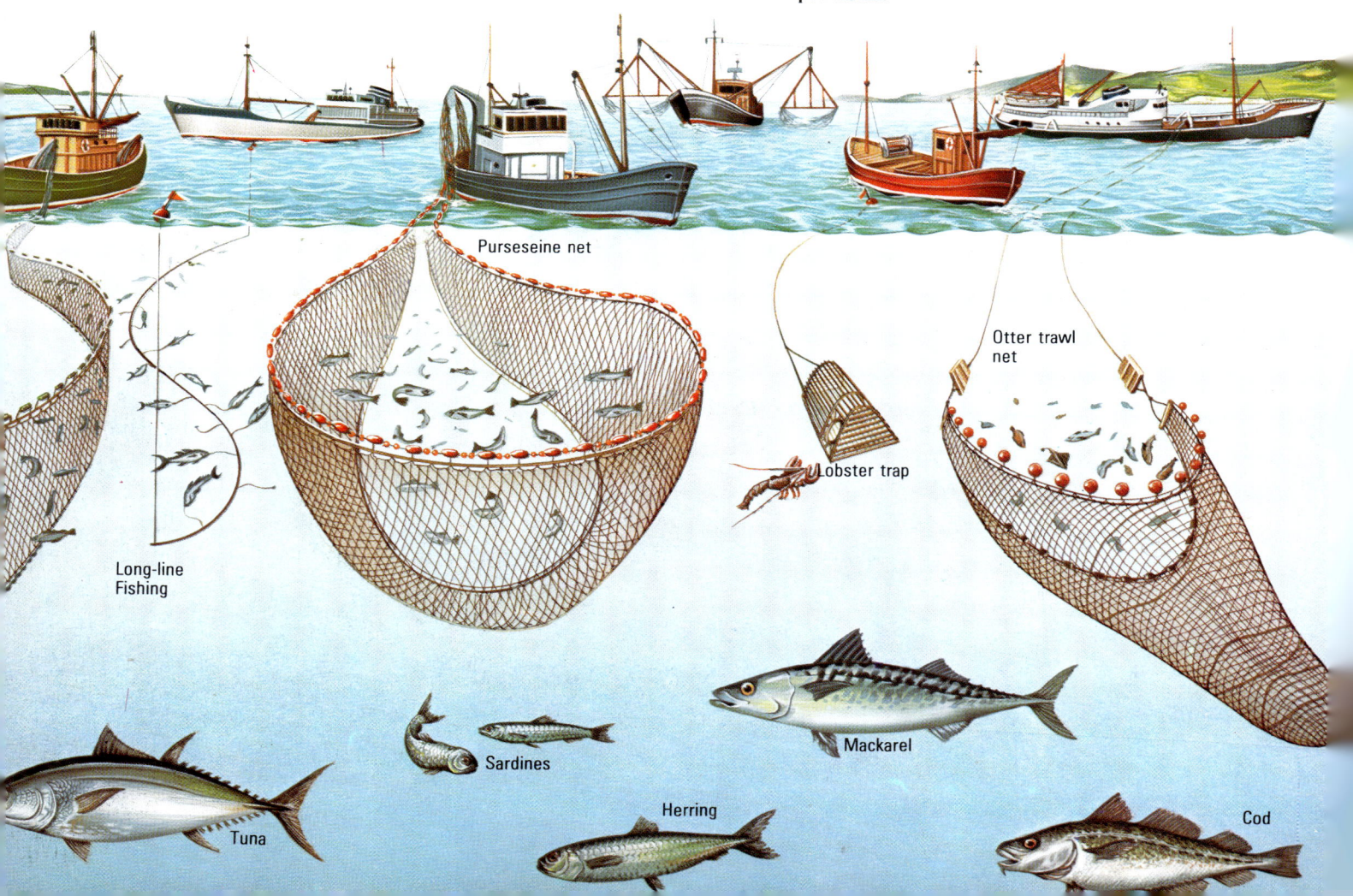

Right: Icelandic fishermen are rewarded with a large haul of fish that will fill more than a hundred of their baskets. Fishing today is chiefly carried out on the continental shelves of the Atlantic Ocean, the North Sea, and the Bering Sea. Relatively few fish are caught in deep waters.

Below: On average, one pound of ocean water contains half an ounce of dissolved material. The diagram shows that the two main elements are chlorine and sodium. Sodium chloride is common salt.

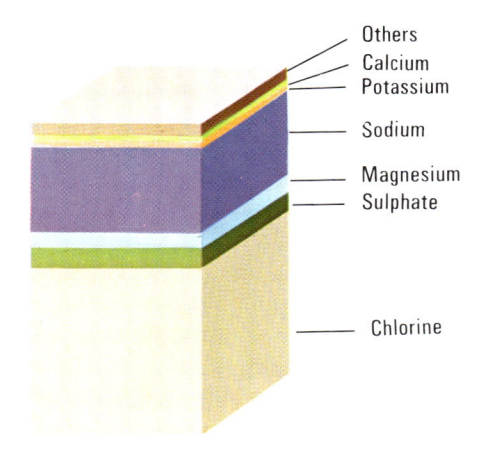

- Others
- Calcium
- Potassium
- Sodium
- Magnesium
- Sulphate
- Chlorine

Left: A British factory at Hartlepool produces magnesium from seawater. Magnesium is one of the many substances that are present in seawater in large quantities. But the extraction of other substances is very expensive and is unlikely until land supplies are used up.

Below left: A plant that makes fresh water from seawater is called a *desalination plant*. This process is still expensive, but it is important in desert areas lacking fresh water.

Below: A traditional way of producing salt is to flood coastal hollows, called *salt pans*, and let the Sun evaporate the water.

Wealth from the Earth

Early people used rocks and minerals for building materials and primitive tools and weapons. Today, mining the Earth's crust is still important. It provides metals used in manufacturing, sources of power such as coal and oil, and nonmetallic minerals, for building and other uses.

There are several methods of extracting minerals from the ground. Surface, or *open-cast*, mining is the cheapest, and is carried out when the ores are on or close to the surface. Underground mines reach layers of rocks that lie far below the surface. Coal is one important mineral that is mined underground. Petroleum and natural gas are extracted by drilling deep wells into underground deposits and pumping the minerals up to the surface.

Left: An iron and steel foundry. The production of steel is important because so many manufactured goods are made from it. The USA, the USSR, and Japan make more than half of the world's steel.

IMPORTANT MINERALS

Bauxite (aluminum ore) Main producers: Australia, Jamaica, Guinea.

Copper Main producers: the USA, the USSR, Chile.

Gold Main producers: South Africa produces most of the non-Communist world's new gold. The USSR, a Communist country, is the second largest producer.

Iron ore Main producers: the USSR, the USA, Australia.

Lead Main producers: the USA, the USSR, Australia.

Silver Main producers: the USSR, Canada, Peru.

Tin Main producers: Malaysia, Bolivia, Indonesia.

Uranium Main producers: the USA, Canada, South Africa.

Zinc Main producers: Canada, the USSR, Australia.

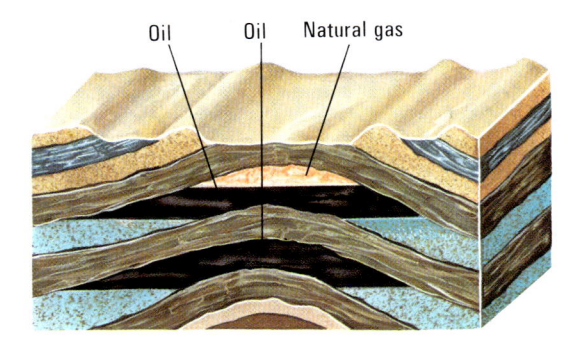

Left: The diagram shows the most common rock structure – an anticline, or upfold – in which natural gas and petroleum collect in a water-bearing rock layer, enclosed between impermeable rocks.

Left: Atomic reactors are producing an increasing amount of electricity in many countries, such as Britain, which gets 10 percent of its electricity from nuclear fuels.

Below: The map shows the distribution of metals around the world. Some developing countries have large mineral deposits, but in general the leading mining nations are the USA and the USSR, the two superpowers.

Above: Geiger counters are used by prospectors to locate deposits of radioactive rocks, such as uranium, which can be used as fuels in atomic power stations.

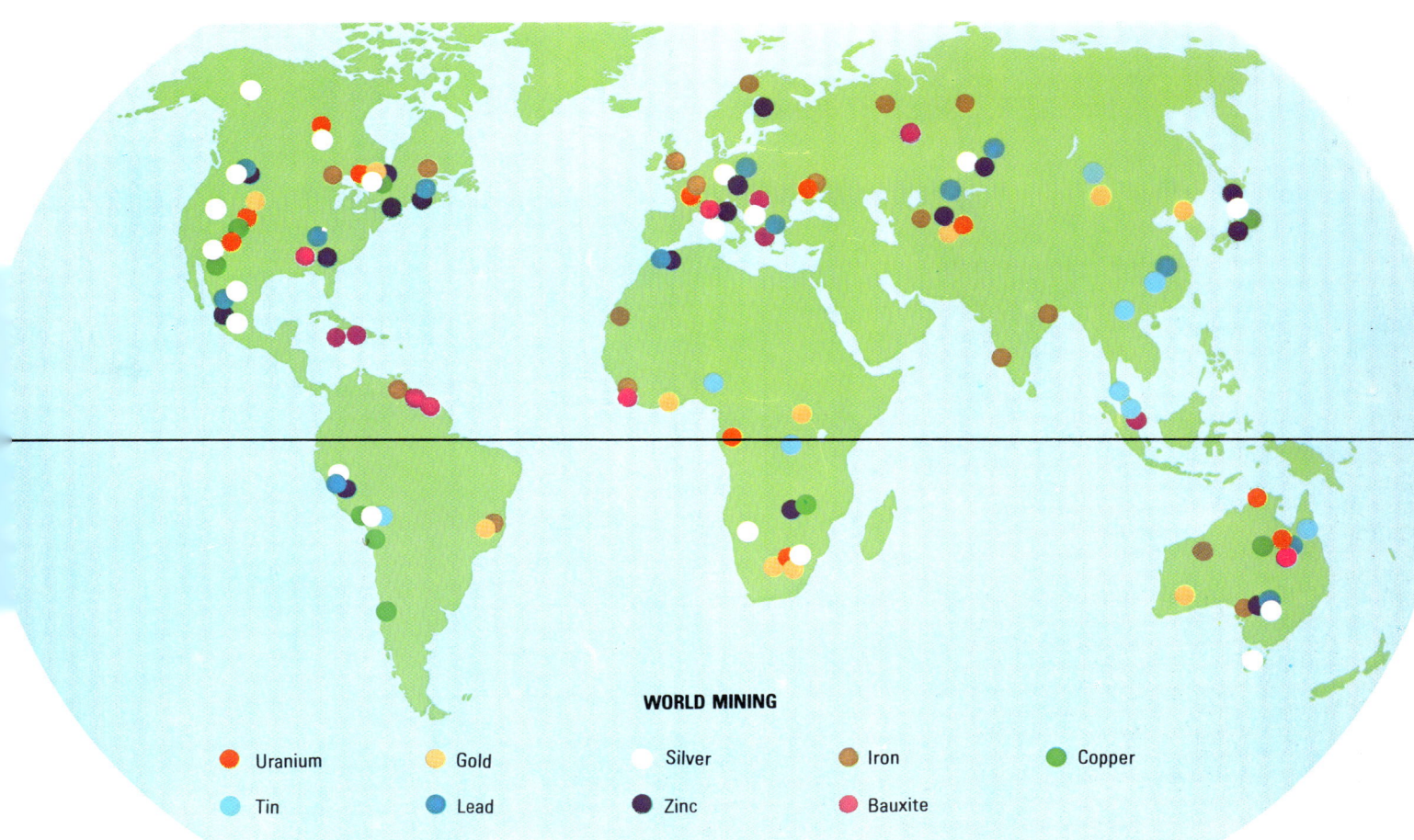

WORLD MINING

- ● Uranium
- ● Gold
- ● Silver
- ● Iron
- ● Copper
- ● Tin
- ● Lead
- ● Zinc
- ● Bauxite

59

The Continents

About 30 percent of the Earth's surface is covered by land. These land areas are divided into seven continents: Asia, Africa, Europe, North America, South America, Oceania, and Antarctica. Each continent includes large land masses and the islands nearby.

The biggest continent is Asia, and more than half the world's peoples live there. Asia includes China and India, which have the world's largest populations. Out of every 100 people in the world, about 36 are either Chinese or Indian.

Europe is even more thickly populated than Asia and has, on average, about 175 people to every square mile. Europe is a highly developed continent. It has many manufacturing industries and efficient farms. Other developed areas include the North American countries of Canada and the United States, and Australia and New Zealand in Oceania. Most of Africa, Latin America, and Asia, except for Israel and Japan, are less developed. Countries in these areas are called developing countries. Most of the people who live in developing countries are poor. On average, they do not live as long as people in developed countries.

One continent, Antarctica, has no people, although a few scientists and whalers spend brief periods there. The other continents also include large, almost empty areas, too dry or too cold for farming. In fact, most of the world's $4\frac{1}{2}$ billion people are crowded on only about one-tenth of the Earth's land surface.

FACTS AND FIGURES

The Earth's Area: 197,000,000 square miles. Land covers about 30 percent of the Earth's surface. Water covers the rest.

Areas of the Continents (sq mi)

Asia**	17,240,000
Africa	11,700,000
North America*	9,410,000
South America	6,860,000
Antarctica	5,405,000
Europe**	3,840,000
Oceania	3,290,000

*Includes Mexico, Central America and West Indies
**Includes part of the USSR

Populations of Continents (1988 est)

Asia	2,990,000,000
Europe	680,100,000
Africa	600,700,000
North America	407,300,000
South America	277,000,000
Oceania	25,000,000

Note: Antarctica has no permanent population

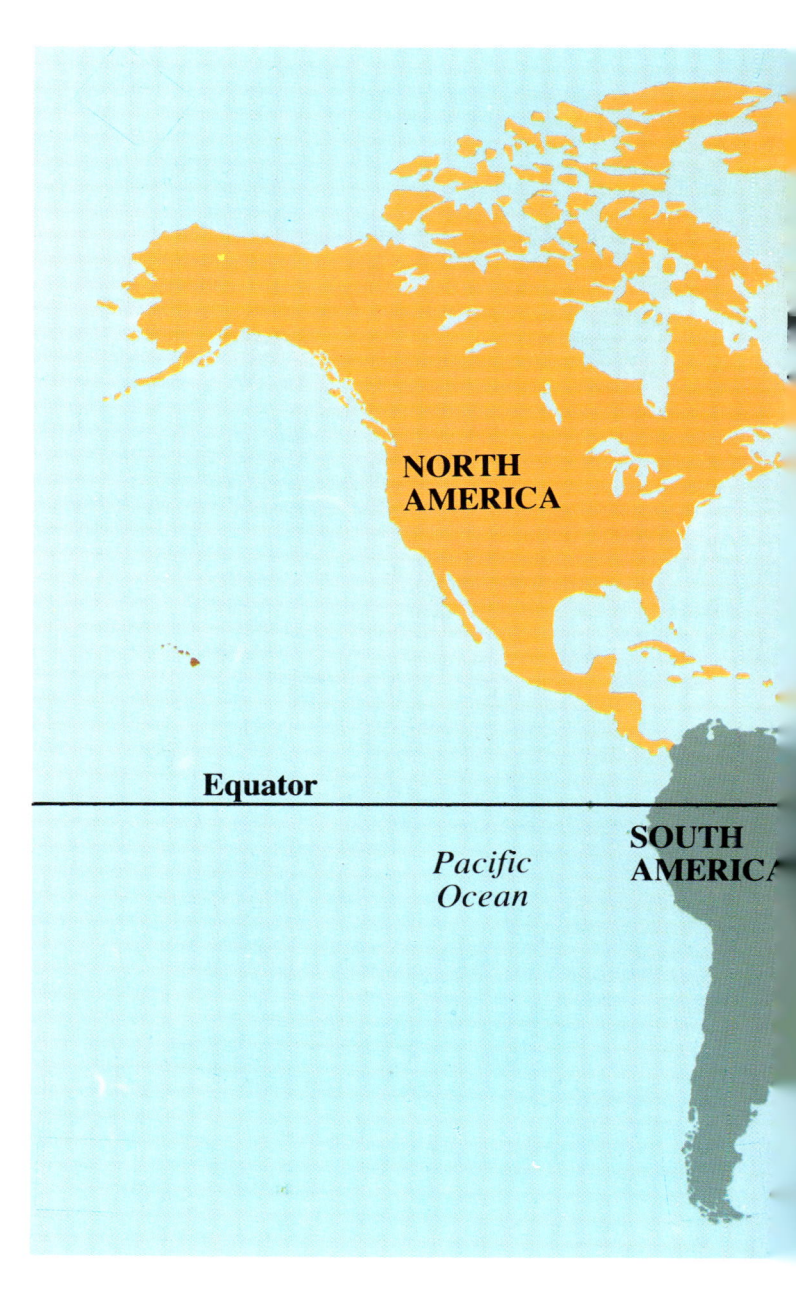

The Grand Canyon, in Arizona in the southwestern USA, was carved out by the Colorado River. Its magnificent scenery brings many tourists to admire it.

Machu Picchu is in the Andes Mountains of Peru. It is an ancient city built by the Inca of South America, who once ruled a vast mountain empire.

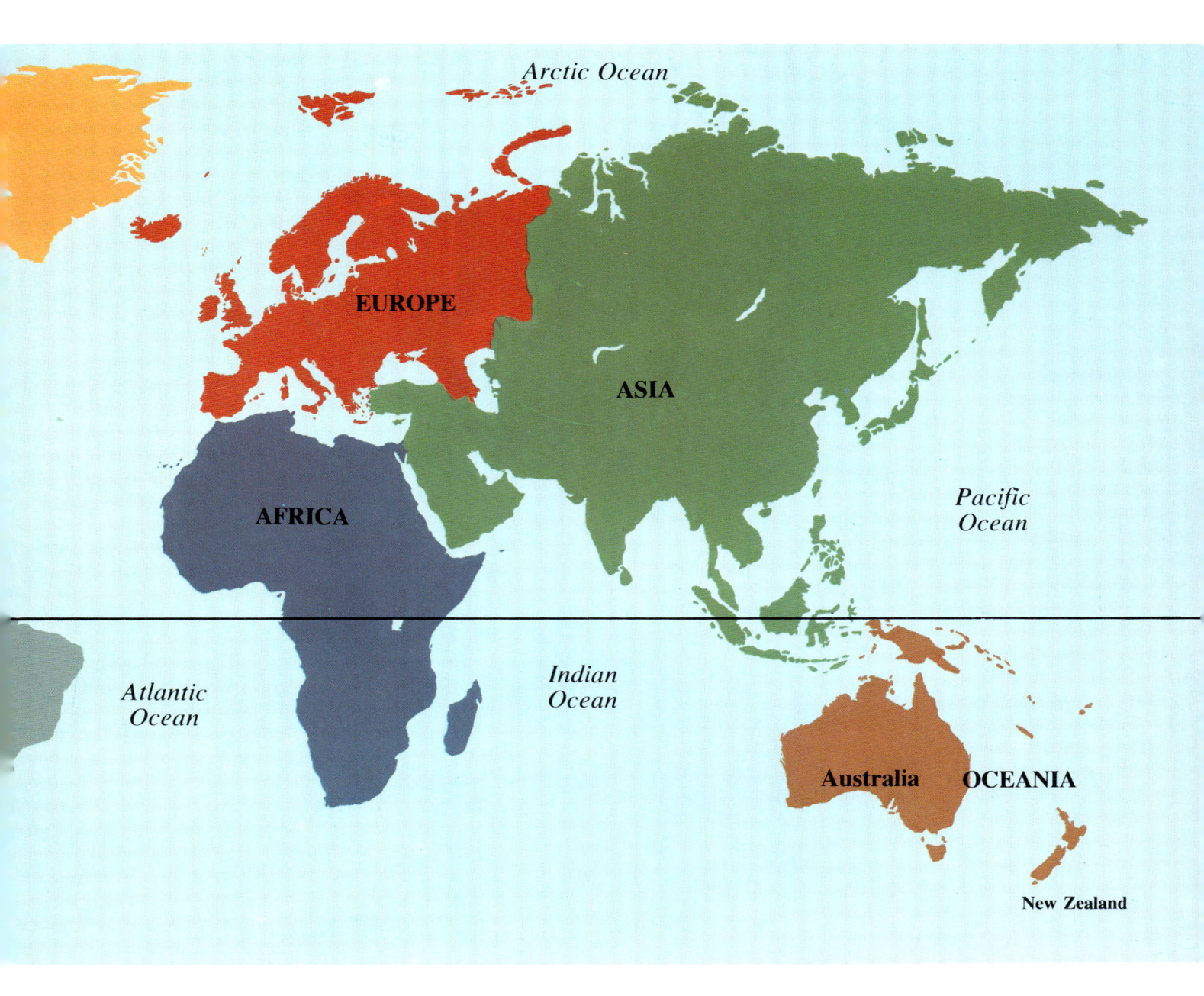

Arctic Ocean

EUROPE

ASIA

AFRICA

Pacific Ocean

Atlantic Ocean

Indian Ocean

Australia OCEANIA

New Zealand

A village in Zambia, in south central Africa. Most people in Africa are farmers. They grow food crops, and some rear cattle.

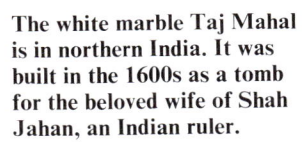

Switzerland, in south central Europe, is famous for its magnificent scenery. It includes part of the Alpine mountain range and has beautiful lakes.

The white marble Taj Mahal is in northern India. It was built in the 1600s as a tomb for the beloved wife of Shah Jahan, an Indian ruler.

New Zealand, in Oceania, where the climate is mild and pleasant. There are 56 million sheep in this country, and nearly 10 million cattle.

61

EUROPE

EUROPE

If you put the world's continents in order of size (largest first), Europe comes sixth. But if you put them in order of population (largest first), Europe comes second. One-seventh of the total world population lives in Europe. Only Asia, which is four times the size of Europe, has more people.

The Arctic regions in the far north of Europe are extremely cold. The countries by the Mediterranean Sea in the south are very warm. But most of Europe has a mild and pleasant climate – neither very hot nor very cold.

Western civilization began in Europe, and during the last 2,000 years, European ideas and culture have spread over the whole world. Today Europe is a wealthy continent. It has well-developed trade and industry and some of the best farmland in the world.

FACTS AND FIGURES

Area: 3,840,000 square miles, including about 25 percent of the USSR, and 3 percent of Turkey. *Greatest width:* 3,000 miles. *Greatest length:* 4,000 miles.

Population: 680,100,000

Population Density: 175 people per square mile. Europe is the most densely populated of all the continents, and only Asia has a greater total population.

Number of Countries: 34, including Turkey and the USSR. The largest country is the USSR and the smallest is the Vatican City.

Highest Peak: Mount Elbruz in the Caucasus Mountains of the European USSR, 18,481 feet above sealevel.

Largest Lake: The Caspian Sea, which is on the border between Europe and Asia, is 143,200 square miles.

Longest Rivers: The Volga, which flows 2,194 miles through the European USSR; the Danube, which flows 1,777 miles from West Germany to the Black Sea.

Northern Europe

Thousands of years ago the whole of northern Europe was covered by sheets of ice. This was the Ice Age. The scenery of the northern European countries – Denmark, Norway, Sweden, Iceland, Finland, and the northern USSR (see page 80) – was molded by this ice. For example, Denmark is covered by ice-worn material called *moraine*. Glaciers and ice sheets wore down the land to form *fjords* (sea inlets) in Norway and lake basins in Finland. Denmark, Norway, and Sweden are together known as Scandinavia.

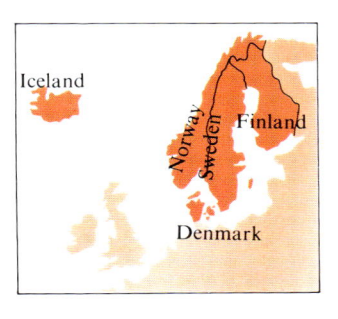

Left: Northern Europe includes Iceland, in the Atlantic Ocean.

Right: The famous statue of the Little Mermaid in Copenhagen, Denmark's capital.

DENMARK
Area: 16,633 square miles
Population: 5,110,000 (1988 est) **Capital:** Copenhagen
Government: Monarchy
Major Languages: Danish **Currency:** Krone

Denmark consists of about 500 islands and the Jutland peninsula, which is joined on to Germany. Copenhagen, the capital, is on the largest island, Sjaelland. The land in Denmark is very flat, and the highest point (in the center of Jutland) is only 567 feet above sealevel.

More than two-thirds of the land is fertile farmland. Denmark is a good country for farming because of the mild climate and because the moraine in the east forms fertile soils. The main farming products are bacon, butter, cheese, and eggs. Fishing is also an important occupation, since the seas around Denmark are rich in herring, cod, and plaice.

Denmark has many manufacturing industries. The most important ones are food processing, production of chemicals, machinery and engineering goods, and shipbuilding. Denmark imports many of the minerals and materials needed for these industries, since they are not available in the country itself. Denmark is particularly famous for the design of its manufactured goods, especially its silverware and furniture.

FINLAND
Area: 130,558 square miles
Population: 4,900,000 (1988 est) **Capital:** Helsinki
Government: Republic
Major Languages: Finnish, Swedish
Currency: Markka

Two-thirds of Finland is covered by forest, and there are about 35,000 lakes. The lakes were

Norway, like much of northern Europe, is rugged and forested. Its coast is jagged with deep fjords, worn by ice.

Lapps with their reindeer. These people follow the migrating reindeer herds as they move around northern Sweden.

formed when ice bored hollows in the ground or when moraine dammed rivers. Timber from the forests is used to make wood pulp (for paper) and other wood products. In the southwest, where the climate is milder, farmers grow food crops in summer.

ICELAND
Area: 39,769 square miles
Population: 200,000 (1988 est) **Capital:** Reykjavik
Government: Republic
Major Languages: Icelandic **Currency:** Krona

This cold country is an island in the northern Atlantic Ocean. It has enormous glaciers and a lot of ice as well as hot springs, steaming geysers, and volcanoes. Sometimes there are earthquakes. Most of the land is barren and not much farming can be done. So most Icelanders earn their living by fishing or working in fish-processing factories. The fishing industry has made them a prosperous people.

NORWAY
Area: 149,158 square miles
Population: 4,200,000 (1988 est) **Capital:** Oslo
Government: Monarchy
Major Languages: Norwegian **Currency:** Krone

Much of Norway is uninhabited. Part of it lies north of the Arctic Circle and is very cold. But the beautiful coast, with its many fjords (long sea inlets, worn out by glaciers during the Ice Age), has a milder climate. It is warmed by onshore winds that blow across the North Atlantic Drift, an extension of the warm ocean current called the Gulf Stream.

Norway has the world's third-largest fishing fleet, and there are many fishing villages in the sheltered fjords. There are farms in the lowlands, many of them near Oslo, but only 3 percent of Norway is farmland. There are huge forests that supply timber for paper and other industries. Norway also produces metal goods and canned foods.

The country's swift-flowing rivers drive hydroelectric stations, which provide power for the industries. The Norwegians are already prosperous but are becoming even wealthier through their sales of North Sea oil.

SWEDEN
Area: 173,780 square miles
Population: 8,400,000 (1988 est) **Capital:** Stockholm
Government: Monarchy
Major Languages: Swedish **Currency:** Krona

Sweden is another big country with a small population. Like Norway, Finland, and the northern USSR, it stretches into the Arctic Circle. The people who live here are the Lapps, and so the region is known as Lapland. The Lapps are nomads – they wander from place to place, following the herds of reindeer. Reindeer supply meat and skins for making clothes and tents, as well as pulling the Lapps' sledges.

Sweden has large forests and an important timber industry. In the milder south there are farms, especially in the lake region around the capital, Stockholm, and in Scania province in the far south. But most of Sweden's wealth comes from mining and manufacturing. There are large shipbuilding, machinery, and steel-making industries. The major industrial centers are Stockholm, Gothenberg, and Norrköping. The iron ore for the steel comes from the north, near the towns of Gällivare and Kiruna. Sweden does not have much coal, so hydroelectric stations provide its power.

Most Swedes live in towns and cities. Because of all this industry, they have one of the highest standards of living in the world.

British Isles

Right: The British Isles are part of northwest Europe.

UNITED KINGDOM
Area: 94,249 square miles
Population: 56,800,000 (1988 est) **Capital:** London
Government: Monarchy
Major Languages: English, Welsh, Gaelic
Currency: Pound sterling

Four countries – England, Northern Ireland, Scotland, and Wales – make up the United Kingdom of Great Britain and Northern Ireland. Sometimes it is called Great Britain or just Britain. It is thickly populated, especially in southeastern England, and is a major trading and manufacturing nation.

The United Kingdom has many different kinds of scenery, some of it very beautiful. There are uplands in Scotland, Wales, and Northern Ireland, and in northern and southwestern England. The highest peak (4,405 feet) is Ben Nevis in the Scottish Highlands. Elsewhere there are gentle hills, fertile valleys, and flat, marshy fens. The largest lake in the United Kingdom is Lough Neagh in Northern Ireland. The longest rivers are in England. They are the Severn and the Thames. The United Kingdom was the first country in the world to become an industrial power. Industrialization began in the late 1700s, made possible by the mining of coal and iron ore. Soon many factories had been built, especially in the north of England, and towns increased in size. Now, four out of five British people live and work in urban areas.

The largest cities in England are London (the capital), Birmingham, Leeds, Liverpool, Sheffield, and Manchester. Edinburgh, the capital of Scotland, is one of the biggest Scottish cities, and Glasgow is the other. The capital of Wales is Cardiff, and the capital of Northern Ireland is Belfast. These cities are centers of major industrial regions, although some industries, like coal-mining, have declined. In the 1960s oil and gas were discovered in the North Sea, and by the 1980s the United Kingdom was an important oil producer. Besides being an industrial center, London is also a center of world trade.

The farmers of the United Kingdom are very efficient, and much of the country's food is home-grown, though a good deal has to be imported as well. The mild, moist climate helps. The eastern parts of the country are drier, so most of the crops are grown there. Livestock are raised in the wet upland areas.

Although they form one kingdom, the four countries of the United Kingdom have very different cultures and traditions. About 20 percent of the Welsh people speak Welsh as well as English, for example. Not everyone likes being part of the United Kingdom. Many Scottish and Welsh people would prefer to have their own governments in their own countries. Some Roman Catholics in Northern Ireland would like to be united with the Republic of Ireland. But the Protestants, who are the majority, wish to remain British citizens. Because of these differences, there has been much bloodshed and unrest in Northern Ireland.

The Isle of Man, in the Irish Sea, is British but has limited self-government. Its area is 227 square miles and its capital is Douglas. Off the coast of France lie the British Channel Islands. They too have limited self-government. The largest islands are Jersey and Guernsey, and their total area is 75 square miles.

Grenadier Guards marching away from Buckingham Palace, London.

Above: Cricket at Worcester, the cathedral in the background. This is England's favorite summer sport.
Left: A Welsh woman at her spinning wheel.
Below: Digging peat in the Irish bogs. It is used as a fuel.

IRELAND, REPUBLIC OF

Area: 27,136 square miles
Population: 3,500,000 (1988 est) **Capital:** Dublin
Government: Republic
Major Languages: English, Irish **Currency:** Punt

At one time, the Republic of Ireland was part of the United Kingdom. However, in 1921, after many years of struggle, it became a separate country. It is a thinly populated country – there were more people living in Ireland in 1840 than there are now.

This is because people have emigrated, many in search of work. The Republic of Ireland does not have much industry – the chief occupation is farming. The wet climate helps to produce rich pastures that are good for rearing livestock. It is because of these beautiful green fields that the Republic of Ireland is known as the Emerald Isle. There are also mountains in the Republic, near the coast.

The Low Countries

Belgium, Luxembourg, and the Netherlands are called the Low Countries because most of their land is flat and near sealevel. The Ardennes plateau in southeastern Belgium and Luxembourg is the only upland. The Low Countries are the most thickly populated group of nations in Europe. They have close economical and political bonds. They helped to form the European Economic Community in 1958, and in 1960 they joined together in a full economic union.

Above: The elegant buildings in Antwerp's main square. Antwerp has many buildings like these. It is Belgium's main port.

Left: Belgium, Luxembourg, and the Netherlands are the Low Countries.

BELGIUM
Area: 11,781 square miles
Population: 9,900,000 (1988 est) **Capital:** Brussels
Government: Monarchy
Major Languages: Dutch, French
Currency: Franc

In many towns in Belgium, you will see street signs in two languages, Flemish and French. This is because the northern Belgians speak Flemish and the people in the south (the Walloons) speak French. There is also a small group in the southeast who speak German. There is sometimes conflict between the Flemish- and French-speaking peoples.

Belgium's manufacturing industries have made it a wealthy country. Iron and steel, glassware and textiles are all important exports. The old towns on the western plains, Bruges and Ghent, produce the textiles. The Sambre-Meuse valley in the southeast was the first great industrial region, based on a coalfield stretching from Mons to Namur and Liège. But now it is expensive to mine coal there, and the chief coalfield is the Campine district in the northeast. It is the center of many industries including ironworks and steelworks. There is also a wide range of industries in the port of Antwerp and in Brussels, Belgium's capital city.

Farmland covers about half of Belgium. Livestock farming is important, and most farmers grow cereals, potatoes, and sugar beet.

LUXEMBOURG

Area: 999 square miles
Population: 400,000 (1988 est)   **Capital:** Luxembourg
Government: Grand Duchy
Major Languages: Luxembourgish, French, German
Currency: Franc

Luxembourg is a tiny country, lying between Belgium, France, and West Germany. It has rich iron ore deposits, and so there are large ironworks and steelworks, and iron is the main export. Luxembourg's well-developed industries have helped to make it a very prosperous country. There is farmland in the southern lowlands. The north is part of the Ardennes plateau. Luxembourg, Belgium, and the Netherlands form a trade group called the Benelux.

Below: The 17th century was a time of great prosperity in Amsterdam, because of the Dutch trading empire. These merchants' houses were built then.

NETHERLANDS

Area: 15,892 square miles
Population: 14,600,000 (1988 est)   **Capital:** Amsterdam
Government: Monarchy
Major Languages: Dutch
Currency: Gulden

The Netherlands is the most densely populated of the Low Countries, with about 900 people to every square mile.

At high tide, nearly half the Netherlands is below sea level, and for hundreds of years the Dutch people have fought a battle against the sea. They have gradually pushed it back by building strong sea walls called *dykes*. Every time there is a bad flood – there have been 140 in the last 700 years – the people rebuild the dykes and reclaim the land.

The dykes enclose large areas of rich farmland called *polders*. More than 60 percent of the country is farmland. Most of the farms are small and highly specialized. The Netherlands is famous for its flowers and bulbs, but there are other important crops. These include potatoes, sugar beet, and wheat. Many farmers breed livestock, and butter, cheese, and eggs are major products.

The Dutch export food, but much of their wealth depends on their manufacturing industries. The most important industries are textiles, china, and earthenware; radio and television sets; shipbuilding; and oil-refining. The Netherlands does not have any minerals of its own so it has to import them. The capital, Amsterdam, and Rotterdam are the chief industrial centers. Rotterdam claims to be the world's busiest port.

Below: For many years, the Dutch have been gradually reclaiming land from the sea. They built sea walls (dykes) and dams around polders (the flooded areas). They then drained the land and made the soil fertile by removing the salt. Then they dug canals to drain the low-lying land. But, during bad storms, the sea may still flood large areas.

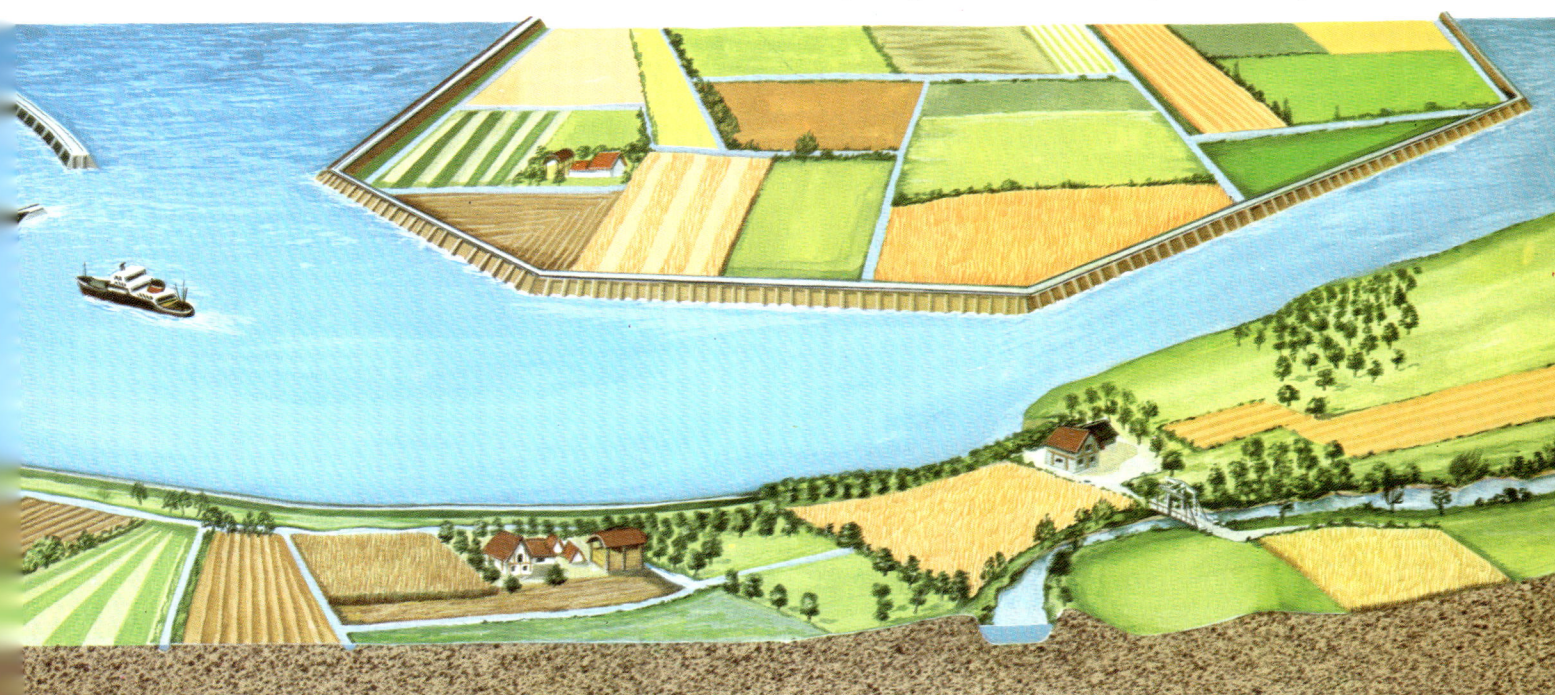

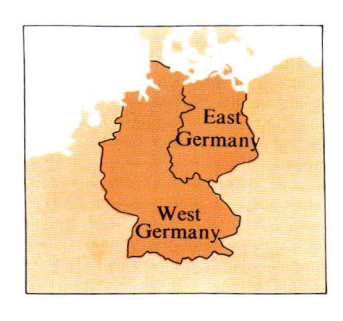

Germany

Since 1945, Germany has been divided in two.

In 1945, at the end of the Second World War, the Allied armies defeated Germany. The Allies divided the country into four zones – American, British, French, and Russian. Large areas in the east were given to Poland. Berlin, the former capital, now lay in the Russian zone, and it too was divided into four zones. The American, British, and French zones in the west had joined together by 1948. But the Russian zone remained separate with a separate (Communist) government. So today there are two Germanies: West Germany, or the Federal Republic of Germany, and East Germany, or the German Democratic Republic. East Berlin is the capital of East Germany and West Berlin remains part of West Germany.

Below: Hamburg, almost destroyed in the Second World War, has been completely rebuilt. The German economy has made a similar recovery.

WEST GERMANY
Area: 96,016 square miles
Population: 61,480,000 (1988 est)   **Capital:** Bonn
Government: Federal Republic
Major Languages: German   **Currency:** Deutsche Mark

After the Second World War, West Germany was in ruins. But with the help of the United States it began to rebuild old industries and set up new ones. It soon began to produce manufactured goods and is now the leading industrial nation in Europe. It is a founder member of the European Economic Community.

The main industrial region in West Germany is the Ruhr, named after a tributary of the river Rhine, which is an important transport route. The Ruhr is based on a coalfield. Cities there include Essen, Dortmund, and Duisberg – all major industrial centers. Nearby on the Rhine are the manufacturing cities of Dusseldorf and Cologne. Farther south the cities of Frankfurt, Munich (München), Nuremburg (Nürnberg), and Stuttgart are important manufacturing centers, as are the Hanover-Brunswick (Braunschweig) region in the northern plains and the ports of Hamburg and Bremen.

West German farmers cannot produce enough food to feed all the people. About a third has to be imported. The soils in the northern plains are generally infertile and the chief crops there are potatoes and rye. In the more fertile southern uplands, especially in the highlands that border the Rhine, there are flourishing crops of cereals, fruits, hops, sugar beet, tobacco, and grapes from which wine is produced. In the far south, where the land rises toward the Alps, there is a good deal of pasture.

EAST GERMANY
Area: 41,768 square miles
Population: 16,725,000 (1988 est)   **Capital:** Berlin (East)
Government: Republic
Major Languages: German   **Currency:** Mark

Before the Second World War the area that is now East Germany was mostly farmland. But the Russians encouraged the East Germans to set up industries, and the country has developed rapidly. In the south the land contains lignite (poor-grade coal) and potash, and chemical factories were set up to use these reserves. East Germany now gets 60 percent of its income from manufacturing. The major industrial centers include Leipzig, Dresden, Karl-Marx-Stadt, Magdeburg, and Erfurt. The richest farming regions are in the south.

71

Above: The Hôtel des Invalides in Paris, the capital of France. It covers Napoleon's tomb. Paris is a lovely city, with fine buildings, parks and broad avenues.

Left: One of the many artists who live in Paris.

Right: Grapes are grown in many parts of France, mostly for wine-making.

France

Right: France is the biggest nation in Western Europe. Andorra and Monaco, two tiny principalities, lie on its borders.

Area: 211,208 square miles
Population: 55,600,000 (1988 est)   **Capital:** Paris
Government: Republic
Major Languages: French   **Currency:** Franc

France is the largest country in Europe with the exception of the USSR. It is twice the size of the United Kingdom. It is bordered by the Atlantic Ocean in the west and the Mediterranean Sea in the south. It has several mountain regions – the French Alps in the southeast, the Pyrenees in the southwest, the Vosges in the northeast, and the Central Massif in south central France. The highest mountain is Mont Blanc in the Alps near Italy. It is 15,771 feet above sea level. Tourists flock to France, attracted by the elegant capital, Paris, the southern beaches, and the many ancient towns and magnificent *châteaux* (castles).

France has very well-developed industries. They include cars, chemicals, iron and steel goods, machinery, textiles, and luxury goods such as perfumes. There is plenty of iron ore and some coal, oil, and natural gas (but these fuels have to be imported as well). Hydroelectric power stations in the mountains supply some energy, and so does tidal power. The river Rance tidal power station in Britanny was the first to use the tide to make electricity. It was opened in 1966.

The population of the French cities is growing; five cities, with their suburbs, have more than 500,000 people. Paris is one of the world's largest cities. There are many industries there and it is the fashion capital of the world. Other important industrial centers are Lille, on the northwest coalfield, and Lyon in the southeast, which is famous for its textiles. The main ports are Marseille on the Mediterranean and Bordeaux on the Atlantic.

ANDORRA
Area: 175 square miles
Population: 48,000 (1988 est)   **Capital:** Andorra la Vella
Government: Principality
Major Languages: Catalan, Spanish, French
Currency: French franc, Spanish peseta

Nestling in the Pyrenees, the range of mountains between France and Spain, is the small country of Andorra. It is supposed to be ruled by the French president and the Spanish Bishop of Urgel, who appoint delegates to represent them. But really Andorra is ruled by an elected council. The country is a winter skiing center, and most Andorrans look after the tourists or work on farms.

MONACO
Area: 0.6 square miles
Population: 28,000 (1988 est)   **Capital:** Monaco
Government: Principality
Major Languages: French, Italian   **Currency:** French franc

Monaco is on the Mediterranean Sea, southeast of France. It is a tiny country ruled by a prince. It is famous as a resort. The district of Monte Carlo is known for its gambling casino and international car rally.

In the Middle Ages, many great stone cathedrals and churches were built in Europe, their soaring splendor a monument to the faith of their builders. Notre Dame cathedral, Paris, was begun in 1163 and was a model for many later French churches.

Above: The summers in Provence in southeast France are dry and sunny. Here you can see a large field of fragrant lavender bushes, whose flowers are used in making perfume.

France has many fertile plains, and farming is very important. About 13 percent of the working population works in farming, fishing, and forestry. More than half the country is covered by farmland; the most important areas are the Paris basin, the Loire valley, the Aquitaine basin in the southwest, and the Rhône-Saône valley in the southeast. Important crops are wheat, barley, oats, flax, and sugar beet. Many farmers breed livestock, including dairy cattle. France is famous for its cheeses and its high-quality wines. Many of these are named after districts where they were produced, such as the sparkling wine called *champagne*, which comes from the Champagne region in eastern France.

Most of the people speak French. However, in the northeast in Alsace, they speak German as well. The Breton people of the northwest have their own Celtic language. In some areas along the Pyrenees Mountains, Basque and Catalan are spoken, and some people in the southeast speak Provençal.

Mountain Countries

Right: Austria, Liechtenstein, Switzerland, and Yugoslavia.

Austria, Switzerland, Yugoslavia, and the tiny principality of Liechtenstein are all in southern Europe. They are all mountainous and have very beautiful scenery. Millions of tourists from all over the world visit them. Yugoslavia has a coastline, but the other three nations are landlocked.

AUSTRIA
Area: 32,377 square miles
Population: 7,600,000 (1988 est)   **Capital:** Vienna
Government: Federal Republic
Major Languages: German   **Currency:** Schilling

About three-quarters of Austria is covered by Alpine ranges. This makes the tourist industry, particularly winter sports, very important. The land in the north of the country is comparatively low-lying, and the chief farming region is in the river valley of the Danube. The farmers grow cereal, sugar beet, and vines, and breed livestock. Timber from the forests, which cover 40 percent of the land, is used in manufacturing. There are iron ore and lignite mines, which provide the raw materials for the iron and steel industries. Vienna, the old and gracious capital city on the river Danube, is the largest city and the chief manufacturing center.

SWITZERLAND
Area: 15,943 square miles
Population: 6,600,000 (1988 est)   **Capital:** Bern
Government: Federal Republic
Major Languages: German, French, Italian
Currency: Franc

Switzerland is a small country with few natural resources of its own. However, it is one of the most prosperous countries in the world. Nearly half its people work in manufacturing and construction industries such as chemicals, glassware, machinery, metal products, and textiles. The Swiss are famed for their manufacture of precision products such as watches and scientific instruments. Three-quarters of the people live in the central plateau, which is the chief farming region. Not many of the Swiss work on farms, but main farming products

Switzerland's mountains attract climbers in summer and skiers in winter.

are cheese, butter, sugar, and meat. Zurich is an important world banking center and one of the largest cities. Other large cities are Basel, an industrial center; Geneva, which is the base of many international organizations; and Bern. Three languages are spoken in Switzerland – French, German, and Italian.

LIECHTENSTEIN
Area: 62 square miles
Population: 28,000 (1988 est)   **Capital:** Vaduz
Government: Principality
Major Languages: German   **Currency:** Franc

Liechtenstein is ruled by a prince and has close links with Switzerland. Farming was once the basis of this tiny country's economy, but now manufacturing is more important.

YUGOSLAVIA
Area: 98,766 square miles
Population: 23,400,000 (1988 est)   **Capital:** Belgrade
Government: Federal Republic
Major Languages: Serbo-Croatian, Slovenian, Macedonian
Currency: Dinar

Yugoslavia is a Communist country, but it is independent of the USSR and China. Central Yugoslavia is a poor mountainous area. Inland are broad fertile plains, cold in winter. Here are the two largest cities, Belgrade, the capital, and Zagreb. Many tourists come to the coast, which is bordered by long narrow islands. Farming used to be the most important activity, but now the mining and manufacturing industries are growing.

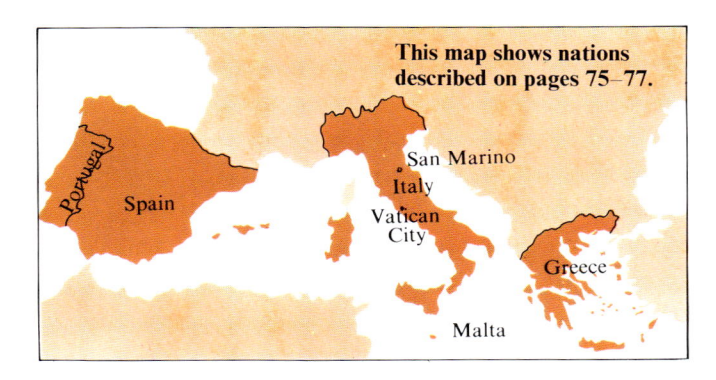

Mediterranean Lands

Except for Portugal, which is on the Atlantic Ocean, the other countries of southern Europe are on the edges of the Mediterranean Sea. The summers here are hot and dry, and most of the rain falls during the mild winters. Tourists come from northern Europe, attracted by the sunshine and the beaches. In Greece and Italy they can also see the ruins of two of the world's greatest classical civilizations, those of Ancient Greece and of Ancient Rome.

GREECE
Area: 50,944 square miles
Population: 10,000,000 (1988 est) **Capital:** Athens
Government: Republic
Major Languages: Greek **Currency:** Drachma

Greece is made up of many beautiful islands (of which the largest is Crete) and the southern part of the Balkan peninsula. This peninsula is divided almost in two by two gulfs (sea inlets), which are joined by the artificial Corinth Canal (4 miles long). The mainland and most of the islands are mountainous. Mount Olympus, the highest peak (9,570 feet), is on the mainland.

Many Greeks are peasant farmers, although farming is only possible on one-third of the land. They grow citrus fruits, grapes, olives, tobacco, and wheat. The chief farming areas are Macedonia and Thrace in the northeast and the Thessaly plain in the east. The most valuable exports are manufactured goods, many of which are processed farm products, because there are few minerals. The Greek merchant navy is one of the largest in the world and provides a valuable source of income.

Above: A Portuguese fishing boat comes in. About 30,000 Portuguese men and boys fish, for sardines in particular. Canned sardines are exported.

Many tourists visit Greece to see the remains of its temples and cities, particularly the Acropolis at Athens, the capital, and the sacred city of Delphi on the mainland. On Crete are ruins from the even earlier Minoan civilization. Other tourists visit the beaches, where many modern hotels are being built to cater to this new industry.

Below: Grapes are grown all over Crete, a large Greek island in the Mediterranean Sea. Crete's main products are wine, citrus fruits, and olive oil.

ITALY

Area: 116,319 square miles
Population: 57,400,000 (1988 est)   **Capital:** Rome
Government: Republic
Major Languages: Italian   **Currency:** Lira

Many of the 30 million tourists who visit Italy each year go for the summer sunshine and the beaches. They also go to visit the many historic cities. In the capital, Rome, they can see the Vatican City (see page 77) and the ruins of the old capital of the Roman Empire. Pompeii is another old Roman city, buried in AD 79 in volcanic ash from the erupting volcano Vesuvius. Vesuvius is still active, as is another Italian volcano on the island of Sicily, Mount Etna. Many of Italy's most beautiful cities, such as Florence and Venice, were built in the Middle Ages. In them there are impressive art galleries, museums, and churches.

To the north, Italy is bordered by the Alps, including Monte Rosa, which rises to 15,217 feet above sea level. South of the Alps lies the broad Lombardy plain, through which flows the Po, Italy's longest river. Here maize, wheat, rice, and vines are grown. Mulberry trees are also important – their leaves are fed to silkworms. Italy is Europe's leading silk producer. The Italian peninsula, south of the Lombardy plain, juts into the Mediterranean Sea. Besides the Apennine Mountains there are fertile valleys and plains here, where fruits, vines, olives, cereals, and vegetables are grown. But this part of Italy is poorer than the north. More than 70 islands, including Sicily, Sardinia, and Elba, also form part of Italy.

Although farmland covers two-thirds of the country, most of its income depends on manufacturing. Its industries include textiles, chemicals, and motor vehicles. Four Italian cities have populations of over a million. They are Rome;

A market square in Rome, the capital of Italy. St. Peter's Basilica (the domed building) can be seen in the distance.

Mediterranean lands are mostly hilly. But the hillsides and coastal plains are covered by farms, vineyards, and olive groves. Tourists flock to the sunny beaches.

Milan, a commercial and industrial city; Turin, which produces motor vehicles; and Naples, a big port.

European art and culture owe a great debt to Italy. Many of the greatest painters were Italian, among them Leonardo da Vinci and Michelangelo. The country is also famous for being the birthplace of opera, which started in the 1600s. Great Italian operatic composers include Giuseppe Verdi, Giacomo Puccini, and Gioacchino Rossini. La Scala in Milan is one of the world's great opera houses.

MALTA

Area: 122 square miles
Population: 400,000 (1988 est)   **Capital:** Valletta
Government: Republic
Major Languages: English, Maltese
Currency: Pound

Malta is the name both of the group of islands south of Sicily and of the largest island in the group. It became independent from Britain in 1964. Farming, fishing, and tourism are all important sources of income.

PORTUGAL

Area: 35,516 square miles
Population: 10,300,000 (1988 est)   **Capital:** Lisbon
Government: Republic
Major Languages: Portuguese   **Currency:** Escudo

Portugal, which used to rule a large empire, is now one of Europe's poorest countries. In the center are tablelands bordered by coastal plains. It depends a good deal on farming, fishing, and forestry, and exports cork, sardines, wine, and wood pulp. There are some minerals in Portugal, and industries – especially textiles and iron and steel – are developing in some of the towns, including the capital, Lisbon.

SAN MARINO

The capital of San Marino has the same name. The country covers only 24 square miles and has a population of 23,000. It is an ancient republic enclosed in Italy. Its main exports are building stone, textiles, and wine.

SPAIN

Area: 194,882 square miles
Population: 39,000,000 (1988 est)   **Capital:** Madrid
Government: Monarchy
Major Languages: Spanish, Catalan   **Currency:** Peseta

Most of Spain is a tableland between 1,970 and 2,950 feet above sea level. This is bordered by mountain ranges, including the Sierra Nevada in the south and the Pyrenees in the north. The capital and largest city, Madrid, is in the center of the tableland. There is some manufacturing in the cities, and many Spaniards work in the tourist industry, for Spain attracts millions of tourists every year. But the majority of Spaniards work on the land. The main crops are barley, fruits, grapes (for wine), olives, potatoes, wheat, and vegetables. The fertile plains around the coast, such as the Andalusian plain in the southwest, are well irrigated. Barcelona and Valencia are two of the main coastal towns.

VATICAN CITY

The Vatican City is the home of the Pope and houses the government of the Roman Catholic Church. It is in Rome, covers only 0.2 square miles, and has about 1,000 residents.

Eastern Europe

Right: The USSR and its Communist neighbors.

There are nine countries in Eastern Europe – USSR, Albania, Bulgaria, Czechoslovakia, Hungary, Poland, Romania, East Germany (see page 70), and Yugoslavia (see page 74). All these countries have Communist governments, which, with the exception of the government of the USSR, were set up after the Second World War. Yugoslavia and Albania are independent but the others are all strongly influenced by the USSR. In Communist countries, most land and industries are owned by the state.

ALBANIA
Area: 11,100 square miles
Population: 3,100,000 (1988 est)   **Capital:** Tirana
Government: Republic
Major Languages: Albanian   **Currency:** Lek

Albania is a mountainous country, and only about 40 percent of the land is used for farming. But most of the people work on farms on the coast and in inland basins. They grow cereals, grapes, mulberry leaves, and olives. Albania used to be an ally of China, which helped it to set up some industries.

BULGARIA
Area: 42,823 square miles
Population: 9,300,000 (1988 est)   **Capital:** Sofia
Government: Republic
Major Languages: Bulgarian   **Currency:** Lev

Bulgaria is on the edge of the Black Sea and has many attractive tourist centers there. It is one of the main tourist centers in Eastern Europe. It is a mountainous country with the Balkans in the north and the Rhodope Mountains in the south. Sofia, the capital, lies in a fertile mountain basin. The land along the river Danube in the far north is low-lying. The central lowlands are the chief farming region. The farms produce fruits, mulberry leaves, roses for scent-making, sugar beet, tobacco, and wines. The Bulgarians mine lignite, copper, iron ore, and oil, and their industrial products include cement, iron and steel products, and textiles.

Above: Blowing glass in a factory in Czechoslovakia. Czechoslovakia's most valuable products are manufactured goods.

Right: The warm, sunny summers in Bulgaria are good for growing tobacco. Here a woman threads leaves together.

Left: Hungarian girls in national costume at a festival.

CZECHOSLOVAKIA
Area: 49,378 square miles
Population: 15,600,000 (1988 est)   **Capital:** Prague
Government: Federal Republic
Major Languages: Czech, Slovak   **Currency:** Koruna (crown)

Two groups of people live in Czechoslovakia: the Czechs, who live in Bohemia and Moravia in the west and center; and the Slovaks, who live in the upland region in the east. The capital, Prague, is in thickly populated Bohemia. Bohemia is mostly upland, but the Elbe River valley is fertile. There is more farmland in Moravia. About 15 percent of the people work on farms. Some are collective farms where the workers share the produce; others are state farms where they receive wages. The main crops are barley, hops, rye, sugar beet, and wheat. Czechoslovakia is rich in coal. Since 1945 it has expanded its state-owned manufacturing industries, and today these provide the bulk of the country's exports.

POLAND
Area: 120,728 square miles
Population: 37,800,000 (1988 est)   **Capital:** Warsaw
Government: Republic
Major Languages: Polish   **Currency:** Zloty

The Poles are a proud, independent people, although twice in the past, in 1795 and 1939, Poland has been divided up between its neighbors. In 1945 Poland became a country again, but many of the Poles resent the influence of the USSR. Unusually for a Communist country, about 80 percent of the people are practicing Roman Catholics. The Poles opposed the Communist government when it tried to set up state and collective farms, and today four-fifths of the land is privately owned.

The Poles' dissatisfaction with Russian influence showed itself in riots in 1956 and 1970. There was more unrest in the late 1970s and early 1980s. This led to a change of government and permission to form a trade union, Solidarity. In December 1981 a military government took control of Poland, and many leading Solidarity members were imprisoned.

Poland borders the Baltic Sea. Most of the land is flat except for a tableland in the south. This is where Poland's main farming areas, mines, and industrial centers are. Mining and manufacturing are now more important than farming in Poland. Warsaw (Warszawa), the capital, Lodz, and Cracow (Krakow) are major manufacturing centers.

HUNGARY
Area: 35,921 square miles
Population: 10,700,000 (1988 est)   **Capital:** Budapest
Government: Republic
Major Languages: Hungarian   **Currency:** Forint

The Hungarian people are called Magyars. Their country is mostly a low, flat plain, although there is an upland region in the northeast on the Czechoslovakian border. Hungary has no coastline, but the great river Danube and its tributaries run through it. Budapest, the capital and the largest city, stands on the Danube. Like other East European countries, Hungary has state-owned collective and state farms that produce maize, rye, sugar beet, wheat, and grapes for making wine. But industry is more important than farming. Hungary has to import many of the raw materials used in manufacturing, but it does produce some coal and other minerals. Budapest is the main industrial city.

ROMANIA
Area: 91,699 square miles
Population: 23,000,000 (1988 est)   **Capital:** Bucharest
Government: Republic
Major Languages: Romanian, Hungarian   **Currency:** Leu

Romania has been under the influence of the USSR since the Second World War, but in the 1970s the Romanians started to reduce this influence by encouraging trade with China, the UK, and the USA. In the west and south, Romania has fertile plains that are good for farming. About nine-tenths of the farmland is state-owned, and about two-fifths of Romanians work on the land. They grow barley, grapes, maize, potatoes, sugar beet, sunflower seeds (for oil), and tobacco. In the center of the country is a mountainous area, rich in forests and minerals. Romania produces natural gas and oil, coal, iron, and other minerals. Nearly 40 percent of the people work in the manufacturing and building industries.

Union of Soviet Socialist Republics

Area: 8,600,383 square miles
Population: 284,000,000 (1988 est)   **Capital:** Moscow
Government: Union of Soviet Socialist Republics, including 15 republics in all
Major Languages: Russian and other Slavic languages
Currency: Ruble

The Union of Soviet Socialist Republics, the USSR, is a huge country extending nearly halfway around the Earth from the Baltic Sea in the west to the Bering Sea in the east. It covers one-sixth of the world's land area and is $2\frac{1}{2}$ times the size of the USA. But large areas of it are very thinly populated, especially the cold north tundra and the less developed east.

West of the Ural Mountains and the Caspian Sea is the European part of the USSR. It covers 2,150,974 square miles – only about 25 percent of the total area of the country. But more than 70 percent of the Soviet people live there. Most of the USSR's manufacturing centers are there, and so is the best farmland, the steppes in the south. Eleven cities in the European USSR have populations of over a million, including the capital, Moscow, and Leningrad. In the Asian part of the USSR there are only two cities of this size.

People often call the USSR Russia, but Russia is only one of the 15 republics. It covers about three-quarters of the country, stretching across Europe into Asia. There are nine smaller republics in the European USSR and five partly or wholly in Asia. Russian is the most important of the 60 languages used in the USSR.

The USSR is now one of the world's two superpowers. But before 1917 Russia was a very poor country and less developed than most other European nations. The two World Wars and a civil war in 1917 caused much destruction in the country. In 1917 there was a revolution and the Communist Party gained power. Communists took control of all property and drew up plans to raise production levels. Any opposition to Communist policies was firmly and often cruelly put down. The USSR developed rapidly. Between 1913 and 1973, coal and iron ore output increased by 23 times and electricity output by 480 times.

Today the USSR is the world's leading producer of chromium, iron, lead, and manganese; and only the USA produces more coal, oil, and natural gas. In 1913 about 75 percent of the people worked on the land. But by 1973, although the area of farmland had doubled, only 25 percent of the people were farm workers. The system of state owned collective and state farms is not, however, as successful as the mining and manufacturing industries.

Bulgaria, Czechoslovakia, East Germany, Hungary, Poland, and Romania are all part of the *Soviet bloc*, and the USSR has exerted great influence on them since World War II. But it is not on friendly terms with the other great Communist power, China.

Left: May Day (May 1) in Red Square, Moscow. This is one of the USSR's most important holidays, and there is always a military parade.

Above: A mechanic in a Moscow car factory.

Right: Part of the Kremlin, once the home of the Tsars and now the seat of the Communist government.

Below: Inside GUM, Moscow's huge department store.

Below right: A gas pipe under construction in western Siberia.

NORTH AMERICA

NORTH AMERICA

North America stretches from Greenland, northern Canada, and Alaska in the frozen north to the tropical forests of Panama. The countries south of Mexico are also known as Central America. The West Indian islands in the Caribbean Sea are also part of North America.

Canada, wealthy and thinly populated, is the largest country in North America. But the United States, the richest of the North American countries, has, on average, ten times as many people to each square mile as has Canada. It is one of the two world superpowers – the USSR is the other. To the south are Mexico, the countries of Central America, and the West Indies, whose people are much poorer than those living farther north.

FACTS AND FIGURES

Area: 9,410,000 square miles. *Greatest width:* 4,909 miles. *Greatest length:* 5,126 miles.
Population: 407,300,000
Population Density: 42 per square mile. The average population density is lowest in the north, increasing southward.
Countries: North America is sometimes taken to be Greenland (a Danish county), Canada, the United States, and Mexico. Here, it also includes Central America and the West Indies.
Highest Peak: Mount McKinley in Alaska, 20,320 feet above sea level.
Lowest Point on Land: 282 feet below sea level in Death Valley, California.
Largest Lake: Lake Superior, one of the Great Lakes, is also the world's largest freshwater lake. It covers 31,820 square miles.
Longest Rivers: The Mackenzie River, 2,635 miles long, is North America's longest river. The Mississippi River is the continent's second longest and measures 2,348 miles.

Canada

Right: Canada is in the northern part of the continent of North America.

CANADA
Area: 3,831,033 square miles
Population: 25,900,000 (1988 est)   **Capital:** Ottawa
Government: Monarchy, with federal system
Major Languages: English, French   **Currency:** Dollar

Canada is about the same size as the whole of Europe. It is the second-largest country in the world – only the USSR is bigger. One-third of all the fresh water on Earth is in Canada, and it has some of the world's largest lakes.

It is thought that the first inhabitants of Canada came from Asia across the 53-mile Bering Strait about 28,000 years ago. Their descendants are known as Indians. Today about 276,000 Indians live in Canada. Later more people came from Asia. They were the ancestors of the Eskimos who hunted fish, walruses, and caribou (deer). Today there are about 17,000 Canadian Eskimos.

Canada may have been discovered by the Vikings, but the first recorded European landing was made by an Italian, John Cabot. He led an English expedition to eastern Canada in 1497. For the next few hundred years, first the French and then the British settled in Canada and became its rulers. People tended to settle within 200 miles of the southern border with the United States because farther north it is so cold.

Because of its mixed population, Canada has two official languages – French and English. About 45 percent of Canadians are descended from British people, 29 percent from French, and 6 percent from German. Canada's 10 million Roman Catholics form the largest single religious group, and more than half of them live in the province of Quebec. Most people in Quebec speak French, which is the official language of the province. Some *Quebecois* are in favor of an independent Quebec, but polls held in the late 1970s showed a strong feeling for national unity throughout Canada, including Quebec.

Canada has rich mineral deposits. No other country produces more asbestos, nickel, and zinc, and it is also a major producer of copper, gold, iron, lead, silver, sulphur, uranium, and oil. However, most of Canada's prosperity is due to its manufacturing industries. The St. Lawrence River valley is the main industrial area, together with the lowlands around the Great Lakes. The St. Lawrence Seaway, extending 189 miles from Montreal to Lake Ontario, carries a great deal of traffic. It is the world's longest artificial seaway.

Below: The lofty Rocky Mountains in western Canada (far left). There are huge forests. Much of the central plain is farmland. Near the Great Lakes in the east there are large cities.

PROVINCES AND TERRITORIES OF CANADA

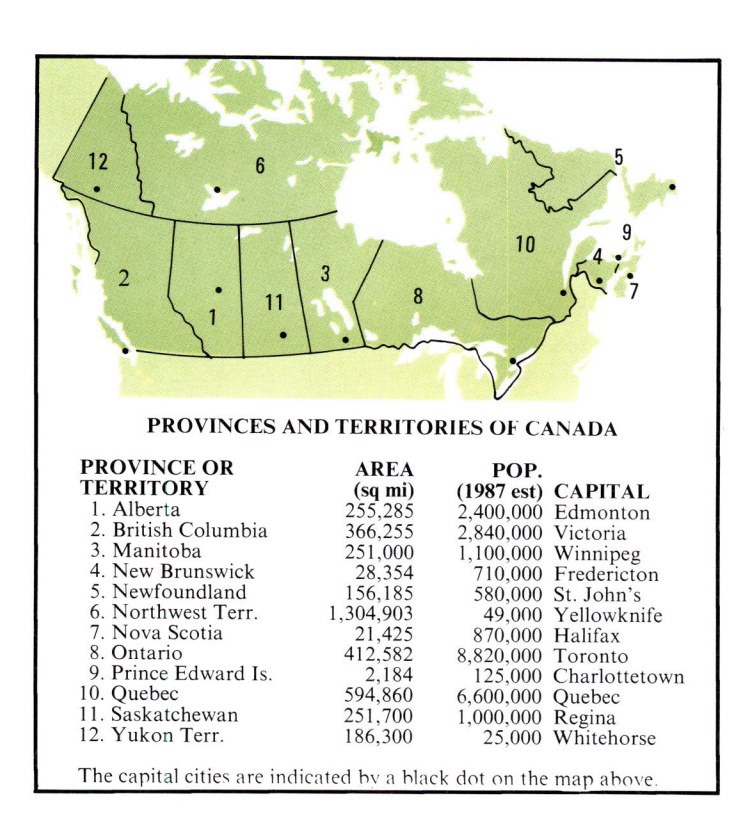

PROVINCE OR TERRITORY	AREA (sq mi)	POP. (1987 est)	CAPITAL
1. Alberta	255,285	2,400,000	Edmonton
2. British Columbia	366,255	2,840,000	Victoria
3. Manitoba	251,000	1,100,000	Winnipeg
4. New Brunswick	28,354	710,000	Fredericton
5. Newfoundland	156,185	580,000	St. John's
6. Northwest Terr.	1,304,903	49,000	Yellowknife
7. Nova Scotia	21,425	870,000	Halifax
8. Ontario	412,582	8,820,000	Toronto
9. Prince Edward Is.	2,184	125,000	Charlottetown
10. Quebec	594,860	6,600,000	Quebec
11. Saskatchewan	251,700	1,000,000	Regina
12. Yukon Terr.	186,300	25,000	Whitehorse

The capital cities are indicated by a black dot on the map above.

Right: Log booms float down the Campbell River in British Columbia. Canada is the third largest producer of coniferous softwoods.

Less than a tenth of Canadian land is farmed, but the country is one of the leading producers of barley, oats, wheat, rye, and timber. There is also livestock ranching, dairy farming, and fruit growing. On the coasts, especially off British Columbia in the west and Newfoundland in the east, large fishing industries flourish.

The United States of America

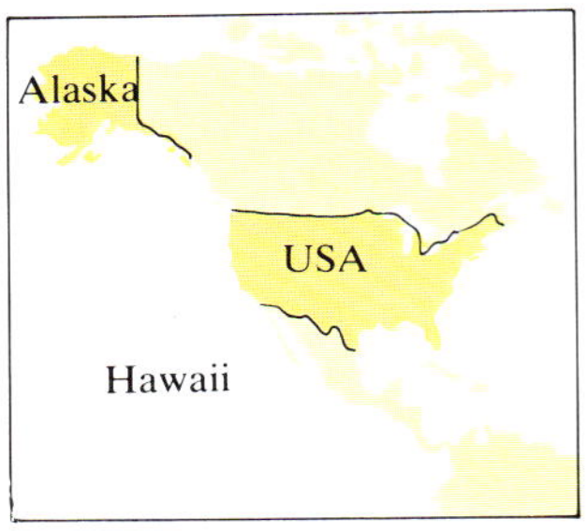

Right: The USA, which includes Alaska and Hawaii, is the third-largest nation in the world.

Area: 3,679,201 square miles
Population: 243,800,000 (1988 est) **Capital:** Washington, D.C.
Government: Federal Republic (50 states and the small District of Columbia, which contains the capital)
Major Languages: English   **Currency:** Dollar

Above: A ranch in Oregon, one of the three Pacific Coast states of the USA. Cowboys are needed to look after the cattle, which can wander vast distances on the ranches.

The United States is the third-largest country in the world. It has the fourth-largest population. Forty-eight of the 50 states lie between Canada and Mexico. Alaska, the 49th and largest state, is in the northwestern corner of North America. Hawaii, a group of volcanic and coral islands in the middle of the Pacific Ocean, is the 50th state. These last two both became states in 1959.

The scenery and climate of the USA are very varied. Alaska in the north is icy cold, Florida in the southeast is warm and sunny. There are huge prairies, arid deserts, and high snow-topped mountains. These latter include the lovely Appalachians in the east, which reach 6,683 feet above sea level. To the west are the Sierra Nevada-Cascade range and the Rocky Mountains, many of which are over 13,900 feet high. There is much spectacular and breathtaking scenery in the USA – for example, the Grand Canyon in Arizona, the Great Lakes on the Canadian border, and Death Valley in California.

The American Indians were the first people to settle in this area. They originally came overland from Asia. When Europeans began to settle, the Indians suffered. Many of them died from European diseases and many others were killed while fighting against the Europeans. As they were forced to change their way of life, their numbers dwindled, and by 1890 only about 248,000 were left. Now there are a few more – about 600,000.

At first the USA was a colony of Britain, but in 1776 it declared independence. By that time there were many black slaves from Africa in the country. Slavery ended in 1865. The 22 million black Americans who form 11 percent of the population today are descendants of those slaves. About 178 million Americans are of European origin, and there are also groups of Chinese, Japanese, Filipino, and Mexican descendants.

The USA is the most industrialized nation in the world, producing half the world's industrial goods. It makes a third of the world's cars and a quarter of its steel. American technology triumphed in 1969 with the landing of the first men on the Moon.

The extensive mineral resources of the USA have helped the development of industry. The USA is the leading producer of copper, oil and natural gas, sulphur, uranium, and phosphates, and it is a major producer of iron ore, lead, and coal.

American farming is highly mechanized and efficient, and farmland covers nearly half the country. The USA is among the world's top

Below: Canoeist at a camp in the woods of New Hampshire.

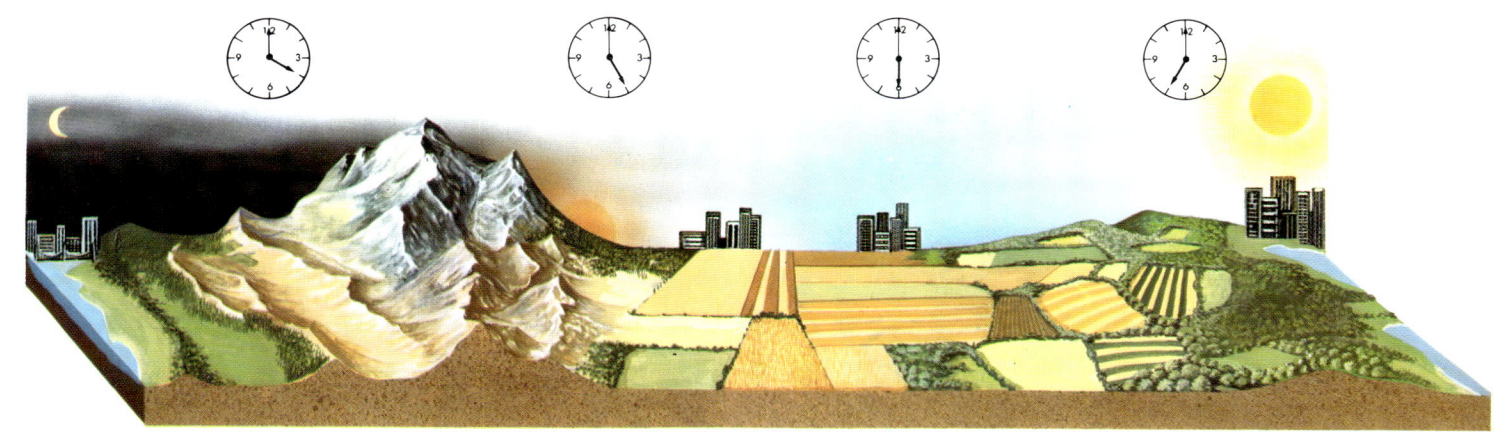

Above: The great width of the USA means that it has several time zones. The Sun rises in the east, and so when it is 7 AM in New York City, it is 6 AM in St Louis, 5 AM in Denver, and 4 AM in San Francisco. In the far west of Alaska, it is even earlier in the day, 1 AM.

Cable cars are used to climb many of the steep hills in San Francisco. This city, in the state of California, is a major port on the West Coast of the USA.

livestock producers. Important crops are wheat, fruits, oats, maize; cotton, soybeans, tobacco, and sugar beet. Timber is also important.

The capital of the USA is Washington. D.C., but the largest city is New York, which is one of the largest cities in the world (Tokyo is the largest). Huge skyscrapers (tall buildings) dominate the skyline of New York and many other modern American cities. The Sears Tower in Chicago is the tallest building in the world.

87

THE 50 STATES

STATE	CAPITAL	AREA (sq mi)	POPULATION (1984 est)	STATE BIRD	STATE FLOWER
1. Alabama	Montgomery	51,705	3,980,000	Yellowhammer	Camellia
2. Alaska	Juneau	591,004	470,000	Willow ptarmigan	Forget-me-not
3. Arizona	Phoenix	114,000	2,965,000	Cactus wren	Saguaro (Giant cactus)
4. Arkansas	Little Rock	53,187	2,295,000	Mockingbird	Apple blossom
5. California	Sacramento	158,706	25,500,000	California valley quail	Golden poppy
6. Colorado	Denver	104,091	3,160,000	Lark bunting	Rocky Mountain columbine
7. Connecticut	Hartford	5,019	3,185,000	Robin	Mountain laurel
8. Delaware	Dover	2,044	605,000	Blue hen chicken	Peach blossom
9. Florida	Tallahassee	58,664	10,920,000	Mockingbird	Orange blossom
10. Georgia	Atlanta	58,910	5,765,000	Brown thrasher	Cherokee rose
11. Hawaii	Honolulu	6,471	1,015,000	Néné (Hawaiian goose)	Hibiscus
12. Idaho	Boise	83,566	980,000	Mountain bluebird	Syringa (Mock orange)
13. Illinois	Springfield	57,871	11,465,000	Cardinal	Native violet
14. Indiana	Indianapolis	36,413	5,455,000	Cardinal	Peony
15. Iowa	Des Moines	56,275	2,900,000	Eastern goldfinch	Wild rose
16. Kansas	Topeka	82,280	2,440,000	Western meadow lark	Sunflower
17. Kentucky	Frankfort	40,409	3,670,000	Kentucky cardinal	Goldenrod
18. Louisiana	Baton Rouge	47,751	4,475,000	Brown pelican	Magnolia
19. Maine	Augusta	33,265	1,140,000	Chickadee	White pine cone and tassel
20. Maryland	Annapolis	10,460	4,300,000	Baltimore oriole	Black-eyed Susan
21. Massachusetts	Boston	8,284	5,815,000	Chickadee	Arbutus (Mayflower)
22. Michigan	Lansing	97,102	8,995,000	Robin	Apple blossom
23. Minnesota	St. Paul	86,614	4,175,000	Common loon	Pink and white lady's-slipper
24. Mississippi	Jackson	47,690	2,555,000	Mockingbird	Magnolia
25. Missouri	Jefferson City	69,697	4,975,000	Bluebird	Hawthorn
26. Montana	Helena	147,049	810,000	Western meadow lark	Bitterroot
27. Nebraska	Lincoln	77,355	1,595,000	Western meadow lark	Goldenrod
28. Nevada	Carson City	110,560	945,000	Mountain bluebird	Sagebrush
29. New Hampshire	Concord	9,279	970,000	Purple finch	Purple lilac
30. New Jersey	Trenton	7,787	7,490,000	Eastern goldfinch	Purple violet
31. New Mexico	Santa Fe	121,593	1,400,000	Roadrunner	Yucca
32. New York	Albany	52,735	17,735,000	Bluebird	Rose
33. North Carolina	Raleigh	52,669	6,115,000	Cardinal	Flowering dogwood
34. North Dakota	Bismarck	70,703	680,000	Western meadow lark	Wild prairie rose
35. Ohio	Columbus	44,786	10,800,000	Cardinal	Scarlet carnation
36. Oklahoma	Oklahoma City	69,956	3,290,000	Scissor-tailed flycatcher	Mistletoe
37. Oregon	Salem	97,073	2,660,000	Western meadow lark	Oregon grape
38. Pennsylvania	Harrisburg	46,043	11,865,000	Ruffed grouse	Mountain laurel
39. Rhode Island	Providence	1,213	965,000	Rhode Island Red	Violet
40. South Carolina	Columbia	31,112	3,260,000	Carolina wren	Carolina jessamine
41. South Dakota	Pierre	77,116	690,000	Ring-necked pheasant	American pasqueflower
42. Tennessee	Nashville	42,144	4,695,000	Mockingbird	Iris
43. Texas	Austin	266,807	16,070,000	Mockingbird	Bluebonnet
44. Utah	Salt Lake City	84,899	1,625,000	Sea gull	Sego lily
45. Vermont	Montpelier	9,614	520,000	Hermit thrush	Red clover
46. Virginia	Richmond	40,766	5,595,000	Cardinal	Flowering dogwood
47. Washington	Olympia	68,138	4,325,000	Willow goldfinch	Coast rhododendron
48. West Virginia	Charlestown	24,231	1,950,000	Cardinal	Rhododendron
49. Wisconsin	Madison	66,215	4,810,000	Robin	Wood violet
50. Wyoming	Cheyenne	97,809	525,000	Meadow lark	Indian paintbrush

Each state's capital city is indicated by a black dot on the map below.

New York is the world's second largest city.

Central America and the West Indies

The tropical part of North America consists of Mexico, Central America, and the West Indies. But often much of this region is included in Latin America, together with most of South America. The chief languages of Latin America are Portuguese, Spanish, and French – all descendants of ancient Latin. There are no English-speaking countries in Latin America. Most Latin Americans are Roman Catholic and have Europeans, Negroes, or Indians (the original people) as their ancestors.

BAHAMAS
These are a group of about 700 islands and more rocky islets southeast of Florida in the USA. One of them, San Salvador, was the first landing place of Columbus in 1492. The main industry of the Bahamas is tourism, and Nassau, the capital, is a major resort.

BARBADOS
This is the most easterly West Indian island. The pleasant climate makes it popular with tourists. Sugar farming is the main industry.

BELIZE
Belize, in Central America, used to be called British Honduras and was a British colony. In 1981 it became independent. Sugar is the main crop and export.

COSTA RICA
Costa Rica, famous for its coffee, is one of Central America's more prosperous republics. Most of the people who live there are descended from the early Spanish pioneers.

Nassau, the capital and major tourist center of the Bahamas.

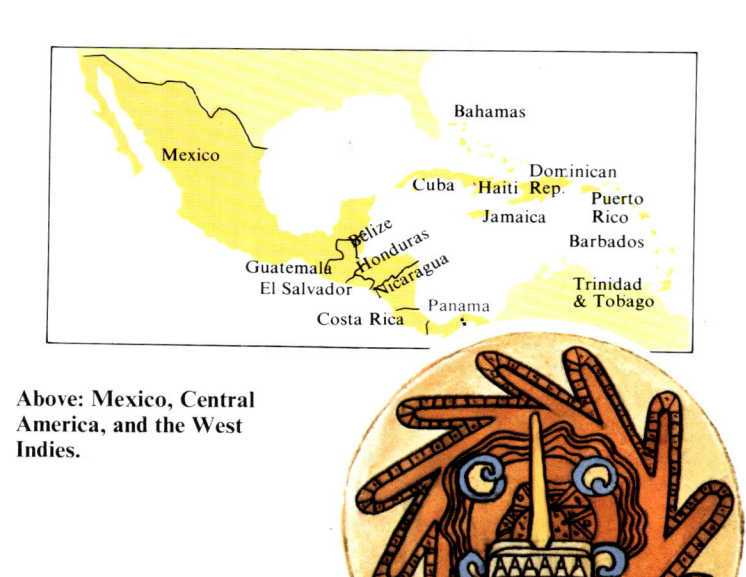

Above: Mexico, Central America, and the West Indies.

Right: The Aztecs, who ruled Mexico from the 1200s to the early 1500s, made masks like this one.

CUBA
Columbus visited Cuba in 1492 and until 1898 it was ruled by Spain. Then it came under the influence of the USA. In 1959 Fidel Castro led a Communist force to seize power, and Cuba became an ally of the USSR. Cuba, the largest island in the West Indies, is a leading producer of sugarcane. Tobacco, rum, and nickel are other major products.

DOMINICAN REPUBLIC
The Dominican Republic is in the eastern part of the West Indian island of Hispaniola. Its people are of European and African descent. The main activity is farming, mostly of sugarcane.

EL SALVADOR
El Salvador, in Central America, is a mountainous country with some volcanic peaks. Most of the people are farmers, producing coffee, cotton, and sugarcane. But in the late 1970s and early 1980s there was fighting between the ruling right-wing government and left-wing rebels, causing much suffering.

GUATEMALA
This is the most northerly of the countries in Central America. The largest group of people are the American Indians; most others are of mixed Spanish and Indian origin. There are frequent earthquakes. Most people are poor farmers, and coffee is the chief crop.

HAITI
Haiti is the western part of the West Indian island of Hispaniola. Most of its people are of black

African descent. It is a poor country. The chief products are coffee and bauxite.

HONDURAS
Another Central American nation, Honduras is thinly populated by people of mixed Spanish and Indian origin. It is a mountainous land, but farming is important, with bananas the main crop.

JAMAICA
Many tourists come to this mountainous West Indian island, attracted by the scenery and climate. Most of the people are of black African or mixed African and European origin. The main crops are bananas and sugar, and the country is the second-largest producer of bauxite (aluminum ore) in the world.

MEXICO
Mexico is a large republic and a neighbor of the USA. It was the home of the Aztec Indians, and tourists can see the ruins of their civilization. From 1521 to 1822, Spain ruled Mexico. Most Mexicans are of Indian and Spanish origin. Much of the country is mountainous although there is a fertile plateau between the two main Sierra Madre ranges. This is where most Mexicans live. The Yucatan peninsula in the southeast is the largest lowland. Mexico leads the world in silver mining. There are also other minerals, and the main industries are textiles and steel. Maize is the main crop. Mexico City, Guadalajara, and Monterrey are the largest cities, each with a population of over 2 million.

NICARAGUA
Nicaragua is the largest country in Central America. Most of the people are of Indian and Spanish descent and there are some blacks. The main activity is farming, and the chief export is cotton.

PANAMA
This country is the farthest south in Central America. Bananas, sugarcane, shrimp, and oil products are its chief exports.

Sugar is the chief industry of Martinique in the West Indies, an island settled by the French in 1635.

PUERTO RICO
This West Indian island is a self-governing commonwealth of the USA. The people are descended from black Africans and Spaniards. Sugar-processing, tourism, and farming are important.

TRINIDAD AND TOBAGO
The islands of Trinidad and Tobago in the West Indies together form a republic. It is the leading producer of natural asphalt. It also manufactures oil products, which are more valuable. Farming and tourism are important.

COUNTRY	CAPITAL	AREA (sq mi)	POPULATION (1988 est)	GOVERNMENT	MAJOR LANGUAGES	CURRENCY
Bahamas	Nassau	5,382	235,000	Monarchy (Independent 1973)	English	Dollar
Barbados	Bridgetown	166	253,000	Monarchy (Independent 1966)	English	Dollar
Belize	Belmopan	8,866	169,000	British colony	English, Spanish	Dollar
Costa Rica	San José	19,730	2,715,000	Republic	Spanish	Colon
Cuba	Havana	44,218	10,222,000	Republic	Spanish	Peso
Dominican Republic	Santo Domingo	18,704	6,790,000	Republic	Spanish	Peso
El Salvador	San Salvador	8,124	5,110,000	Republic	Spanish	Colon
Guatemala	Guatemala City	42,042	8,600,000	Republic	Spanish	Quetzal
Haiti	Port-au-Prince	10,714	5,870,000	Republic	Creole, French	Gourde
Honduras	Tegucigalpa	43,277	4,650,000	Republic	Spanish	Lempira
Jamaica	Kingston	4,244	2,300,000	Monarchy (Independent 1962)	English	Dollar
Mexico	Mexico City	761,604	81,710,000	Republic	Spanish	Peso
Nicaragua	Managua	50,193	3,350,000	Republic	Spanish	Cordoba
Panama	Panamá	29,762	2,230,000	Republic	Spanish	Balboa
Puerto Rico	San Juan	3,515	3,280,000	Commonwealth of the USA	Spanish, English	US Dollar
Trinidad and Tobago	Port-of-Spain	1,980	1,205,000	Republic (Independent 1962)	English, Spanish	Dollar

SOUTH AMERICA

SOUTH AMERICA

South America is the fourth-largest continent. Most of it belongs to Latin America – only English-speaking Guyana and Dutch-speaking Surinam do not.

The original inhabitants of South America were known as Indians. One group, called the Inca, had a huge empire in the Andes Mountains, extending from Ecuador and Peru in the north to Chile in the south. Later South America was colonized by Portugal and Spain, then by Britain and the Netherlands. African slaves were imported to some areas, such as Brazil. Modern South Americans are descendants of three races – Indians, Europeans, and Africans. Many are very poor, but the continent is developing rapidly, and towns and cities are growing fast.

FACTS AND FIGURES

Area: 6,860,000 square miles. *Greatest width:* 3,200 miles. *Greatest length:* 4,753 miles.
Population: 277,000,000
Population Density: 38 per square mile.
Countries: 13. The largest country, Brazil, covers nearly half of South America. The smallest country is French Guiana.
Highest Peak: Mount Aconcagua in Argentina, near the border with Chile, 22,831 feet above sea level. It is the highest peak in the Western Hemisphere.
Largest Lake: Lake Maracaibo in Venezuela. Lake Titicaca on the Peru-Bolivia border is the world's highest large lake.
Highest Waterfall: Salto Angel in Venezuela. With a total drop of 3,212 feet, it is the world's highest waterfall.
Longest River: The river Amazon is 3,902 miles long. In length, the Amazon is third only to the Nile and the Yangtze among the world's rivers, but the Amazon has a greater flow of water than any other river in the world.

Northern South America

Six of South America's 13 countries are in the northern part of the continent. All six countries have hot tropical climates, and the Equator passes through Ecuador and southeast Colombia. It is pleasanter to live in the high valleys of the Andes (the range of mountains in the west) because they are so much cooler than the plains. All the northern countries except Venezuela are poor.

Left: The countries in northern South America.

Below: Bogotá is the capital and largest city of Colombia. In a basin in the Andes Mountains, it is 8,661 feet above sea level.

COLOMBIA
Area: 439,737 square miles
Population: 30,000,000 (1988 est)   **Capital:** Bogotá
Government: Republic
Major Languages: Spanish   **Currency:** Peso

Colombia, named after Christopher Columbus, was ruled by Spain from 1536 to 1819. More than two-thirds of the present population are *mestizos* (of mixed Indian and European origin). Others are direct descendants of Europeans, American Indians, or Africans.

Colombia is bordered by the Pacific Ocean in the west and the Caribbean Sea to the north. The coastlands are very hot, so most people live in the high fertile valleys of the northern Andes, where it is much cooler. There are three cities, Bogotá, the capital, Medellín, and Cali, all in the uplands. They each have more than a million people. In eastern Colombia the *llanos* (grasslands) give way to the rain forests of the Amazon basin. Only Brazil produces more coffee than Colombia. It is grown in the uplands and is the chief export. Other exports are emeralds, meat, cotton, and oil.

ECUADOR
Area: 109,483 square miles
Population: 9,650,000 (1988 est)   **Capital:** Quito
Government: Republic
Major Languages: Spanish, Quechua   **Currency:** Peso

'Ecuador' is the Spanish word for Equator. It is a small country on the edge of the Pacific Ocean. The coastal plains are very hot with an average temperature of 80°F. The Andes range is inland and so the temperature is cooler. Quito, the capital, which is about 9,350 feet above sea level, has an average temperature of 55°F. There are active volcanoes in the highlands. The hot Amazon basin lies to the east. Most of the people are American Indians with their own languages, although the official language is Spanish. Other people are of European and African origin. Farming is an important occupation, and cocoa, coffee, and bananas are the main exports. About 66 percent of the people are farmers.

FRENCH GUIANA
Area: 35,135 square miles
Population: 85,700 (1988 est)   **Capital:** Cayenne
Government: Republic
Major Languages: French   **Currency:** French franc

French Guiana, on the edge of the Atlantic Ocean, is a small, hot country. It is an overseas department (district) of France. A lot of the land is covered with forests. There is some farmland, and the farmers grow rice, cassava, bananas, sugarcane, and maize. There are some valuable mineral resources, including gold. Many of the people are of African descent. Inland live the American Indians. The French set up penal colonies to which

Quito, the capital of Ecuador, has a 17th-century cathedral. De Belalcazar, a lieutenant of Pizarro, designed the city along typical Spanish lines in the 1530s.

criminals from France were transported. The most famous was Devil's Island, near Cayenne. These hindered the country's development but were closed by 1947.

GUYANA
Area: 83,000 square miles
Population: 800,000 (1988 est)   **Capital:** Georgetown
Government: Republic
Major Languages: English   **Currency:** Dollar

Guyana used to be British Guiana, but it became independent in 1966. There are some American Indians in the country, but the origins of most of the people are Indonesian, African, Chinese, or European. Most people live on the hot Atlantic coast, where the main crop is sugarcane. There are huge forests, and grasslands on the highlands in the south. After diamonds, sugar, and gold, the most valuable export is bauxite (aluminum ore).

SURINAM
Area: 63,037 square miles
Population: 400,000 (1988 est)   **Capital:** Paramaribo
Government: Republic
Major Languages: Dutch, Creole   **Currency:** Gulden (guilder)

Surinam used to belong to the Netherlands but became independent in 1975. There are large areas of forest there, and the timber industry is important. The only farms are on the Atlantic coast; they grow fruits, sugarcane, and rice. About half the people have African ancestors. Others are American Indians or of Indonesian, Indian, Chinese, and European descent.

VENEZUELA
Area: 325,144 square miles
Population: 17,790,000 (1988 est)   **Capital:** Caracas
Government: Republic
Major Languages: Spanish   **Currency:** Bolivar

Venezuela is one of the richest countries in South America. In the Lake Maracaibo basin in the northeast there are valuable oilfields, and Venezuela is the fifth-largest oil producer in the world. A steel industry, based on local ore, has been set up in the Orinoco lowlands.

The Venezuelans have used their oil money to build cities and roads into the interior and to develop industries. In the coastal lowlands they grow tropical crops like bananas, sugarcane, and cocoa. The most valuable crop in the Andes region is coffee. Maize is also grown there. In the *llanos* (grasslands) of the river Orinoco basin they raise cattle. Venezuela gained independence from Spain in 1811. Some Venezuelans are of European or African descent but most are *mestizos*, of mixed Indian and Spanish origin. A few Indians live in the interior.

Below: Venezuela's main oil wells in Lake Maracaibo.

Brazil, Peru, and Bolivia

Right: The three nations of central South America.

There are three large countries in central South America, Brazil (fifth largest in the world), Peru, and Bolivia. The vast Amazon basin stretches from Brazil into the other two countries. Parts of the Andes range, which runs down western South America, also dominate each country.

BRAZIL
Area: 3,265,075 square miles
Population: 143,300,000 (1988 est)   **Capital:** Brasilia
Government: Republic
Major Languages: Portuguese   **Currency:** Cruzeiro

The Amazon forest in northern Brazil is the largest rain forest in the world. Once only a few American Indians lived there. Now people are trying to open up the area and are building a new road, the Trans-Amazon Highway. Many of the Indians are having to give up their traditional way of life, and

Above: The elegant city of Rio de Janeiro, Brazil's second-largest city and once its capital. It is an important port and manufacturing center. The sharp increase in population has led to the development of slums, as in other Brazilian cities.

Below: The llama is an important beast of burden in the Andes, which rise in the western part of central South America. East of the Andes, the land falls to the vast hot basin of the river Amazon, which supports the world's largest rain forests.

some suffer even more – they have no resistance to European diseases. There is also a danger that if too much of the Amazon forest is removed, the ozone layer of the atmosphere will be unbalanced. In central and southern Brazil there are uplands, plateaus, and a developed coastal strip. This area is healthy and fertile, and there are minerals in the highlands.

The Portuguese ruled Brazil from the 1500s until 1822. About 75 percent of the people are descended from the Portuguese and other European settlers. There are also many of mixed Indian, African, and European descent, and some pure Indians and blacks. The population increases by more than 3 million people a year. About 56 percent of Brazilians live in towns and cities. Sao Paulo, Rio de Janeiro, Belo Horizonte, Recife, and Salvador all contain over a million people. Since 1960 Brasilia, a modern city in the highlands, has been the capital.

Brazil is the leading world producer of coffee and bananas. It also produces a great deal of veal and beef, cotton, maize, cocoa, soybeans, tobacco, and sugarcane. Nearly 50 percent of the people are farmworkers. Much of Brazil's great mineral wealth has not yet been exploited. Manufacturing is important. The chief exports are sugar, coffee, cotton, iron ore, and pinewood.

PERU
Area: 496,224 square miles
Population: 20,210,000 (1988 est)   **Capital:** Lima
Government: Republic
Major Languages: Spanish, Quechua   **Currency:** Sol

Peru is the third-largest South American country. In the east of the country is the Amazon basin, and the high Andes Mountains rise behind the narrow plain on the dry coast. In the mountains are ruins of old Inca cities, destroyed when Spain conquered the area between 1531 and 1533. Peru became independent from Spain in the 1820s. Most of the people are American Indians, mestizos, or direct descendants of Spanish settlers. About 25 percent of the people speak only Indian languages. Nearly 50 percent are farmers, growing cotton, coffee, and sugarcane, and getting wool from sheep, llamas, and alpacas. Manufacturing industries are growing up, and Peru is also a leading fishing nation, most of the catch being made into fishmeal for cattle food. The greater part of Peru's income comes from mining. Minerals include copper, iron, silver, lead, zinc, and oil.

A market in La Paz, Bolivia. Although La Paz is Bolivia's seat of government, Sucre is the official capital.

BOLIVIA
Area: 424,164 square miles
Population: 6,300,000 (1988 est)   **Capital:** Sucre
Government: Republic
Major Languages: Spanish, Quechua   **Currency:** Peso

Bolivia is the poorest country in South America. It has no coastline and is divided into two main regions. There is a central plateau, bounded by the Andes in the southwest, which is rich in minerals. In the northeast is the Amazon basin. From 1532 to 1825 Bolivia was ruled by Spain. The country is named after Simón Bolívar, the Venezuelan general who eventually freed it. More than half the people are American Indians and a third are mestizos. The rest are descended from Europeans. Seven-tenths of the people are farmworkers, but the most valuable industry is mining. Bolivia is the world's second-largest producer of tin. It also produces oil and natural gas, copper, antimony, lead, silver, and wolfram (tungsten ore).

Left: Asunción, the capital of Paraguay, founded in 1537. It is the nation's largest city and chief cultural center. The leading occupations are trade and manufacturing.

Below: Some people in the rural areas of Uruguay are poor. Nearly all Uruguayans have European ancestors.

A group of gauchos, the cowboys who ride the pampas of Argentina and Uruguay.

Southern Lands

Most of the countries in southern South America have a temperate climate. This is because most of the region lies outside the tropics, and the southern tip of the continent is only about 600 miles from icy Antarctica. There is a British colony off the southeastern coast of South America – the Falkland Islands, which are claimed by Argentina.

Left: The four countries in southern South America. On the whole, their climate is temperate.

ARGENTINA
Area: 1,068,301 square miles
Population: 31,200,000 (1988 est)   **Capital:** Buenos Aires
Government: Republic
Major Languages: Spanish   **Currency:** Peso

Argentina, the second-largest country in South America, is a major farming area. The country gets much of its wealth from crops and livestock, and is among the world's leading producers of wheat, fruits, millet and sorghum, wool, beef, and veal. The chief farming region is northwest and south of Buenos Aires, the capital. It is called the *pampas* (plains). Here there are enormous farms, and rich pasture feeds millions of cattle and sheep. The manufacturing industries in the cities process farming products. Most of the mines are in the parched western region near the Andes. Here is Mount Aconcagua, South America's highest peak. In the north the tropical forests are undeveloped, and the south, Patagonia, is semidesert. Argentina was ruled by Spain from 1535 to 1810. Most of the people are descendants of European settlers. About 8 percent are mestizos, and there are about 20,000 pure Indians.

CHILE
Area: 292,135 square miles
Population: 12,265,000 (1988 est)   **Capital:** Santiago
Government: Republic
Major Languages: Spanish   **Currency:** Peso

Chile is a long, thin country – about 2,800 miles long and only 249 miles wide. On the southern coast there are many islands and deep inlets. Not many people live in the south, which is wet and covered with forests. The dry north includes the Atacama Desert, an important mining area. The center has warm, dry summers and moist, mild winters. Most people live there, around Santiago, the capital, and the port of Valparaiso. Chile's most valuable resources are minerals, especially copper, iron, oil, and nitrates. About 20 percent of the working people are in manufacturing industries, which are also important. Farming products include barley, fruits, wheat, maize, and wines. Some pure Indians live in the south, but most people are mestizos.

PARAGUAY
Area: 157,048 square miles
Population: 4,120,000 (1988 est)   **Capital:** Asunción
Government: Republic
Major Languages: Spanish, Guarani   **Currency:** Guarani

Paraguay, on the Tropic of Capricorn, is a landlocked country. Most Paraguayans are poor mestizos. Their main industry is farming, most of the farms being east of the Paraguay River. The grasslands provide grazing for nearly 6 million cattle, and meat products are the chief exports. Major crops are cotton, maize, rice, soybeans, tobacco, and wheat. Timber is an important product, and manufacturing industries process farm products.

URUGUAY
Area: 68,037 square miles
Population: 2,950,000 (1988 est)   **Capital:** Montevideo
Government: Republic
Major Languages: Spanish   **Currency:** Nuevo peso

Uruguay is one of the smallest countries in South America, and 90 percent of the land is farmed. Crops, mainly rice, maize, and wheat, are grown on one-tenth and the other eight-tenths is pasture. There are more than 8 million cattle and 20 million sheep. In both Uruguay and Argentina the cowboys who look after the livestock are called *gauchos*. Uruguay's chief exports are meat and meat products, wool, and textiles. Most Uruguayans are descended from European settlers; two-fifths of them live in Montevideo, the only large city.

A Roman Catholic church overlooks a busy street market in Chile. The scene could be Spanish. The influence of Spain is strong here; the official language is Spanish, and about 90 percent of the people are Roman Catholic. They are mostly mestizos, of mixed South American Indian and European descent.

ASIA

ASIA

Asia, the world's largest continent, has a larger population than any of the others. But the population is not as dense as that of Europe; on average, Europe has 15 more people to every square kilometre. There are two reasons for this. One is that parts of Asia are uninhabitable – northern Asia is very cold and there are mountains and rain forests in the south. Asia has fewer manufacturing industries than Europe, the only really industrialized nation being Japan.

FACTS AND FIGURES

Area: 17,240,000 square miles, including 75 percent of the USSR and 97 percent of Turkey. *Greatest width:* 5.996 miles. *Greatest length:* 5,406 miles.
Population: 2,990,000,000
Population Density: 166 per square miles.
Countries: 39 independent countries. China is the largest nation wholly in Asia. Macao is the smallest territory.
Highest Peak: Mount Everest, in the Himalayas, 29,028 feet above sea level, the world's highest.
Lowest Point on Land: 1,299 feet below sea level, on the shore of the Dead Sea, Israel – the world's lowest point.
Largest Lake: Caspian Sea.
Longest Rivers: The Yangtze River, China, is 3,915 miles long. The Amur, Hwang Ho, Lena, Mekong, Ob, and Yenisey are each more than 2,500 miles long.

China

Area: 3,630,747 square miles
Population: 1,063,000,000 (1988 est)   **Capital:** Peking (Beijing)
Government: Republic
Major Languages: Chinese, Mongolian, Turkish

Of all the countries in the world, China has the largest population. It is also the world's fourth-largest country. Its history goes back 3,500 years, and it once had a great civilization. Since 1912 it has been a republic. In 1949, Communist forces led by Mao Tse-tung took control of the country. Since then all property has been taken over by the government, including land, factories, and mines. Villages have come together in groups to share work and share the produce. They are called *communes*. China has concentrated on developing its farming.

About two-thirds of the people are farmers. China is the leading producer of millet, rice, tobacco, and sorghum. It is also a major producer of cotton, silk, tea, groundnuts, timber, wheat, barley, and maize. It has enormous numbers of livestock, including pigs, cattle, goats, and sheep, and a large fishing industry.

China has also expanded its mining and manufacturing industries, although some of its large mineral reserves are still untapped. It is a major producer of antimony, asbestos, coal, iron ore, mercury, and tungsten. Its oil production is also increasing. The main industrial areas are Manchuria, the Szechwan basin, and the larger cities like Shanghai, Peking (the capital), and Tientsin. Iron and steel are the main manufacturing products.

The summers in northeast China are warm, but the winters are extremely cold. The climate in southeast China is subtropical. There are mountain ranges, deserts, and the Tibetan plateau in the west, or Outer China, as it is sometimes called.

Below: This map shows the positions of China, Taiwan, Hong Kong, Macao, and Mongolia.

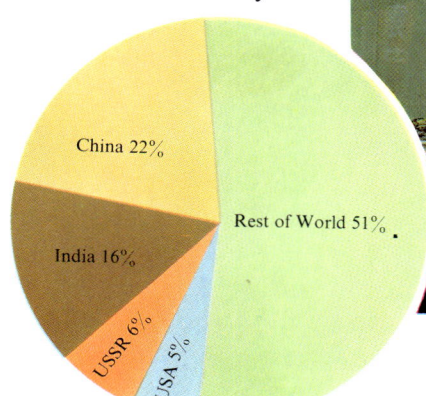

Above: A fair in Canton in southern China.

Left: This diagram shows that China has just over one-fifth of the world's total population.

Mount Everest is on China's border with Nepal. Most people live in the east, in the fertile river valleys of the Hwang Ho and the Yangtze and along the coast.

China's population is increasing by about 12 million a year. One person out of every five in the world is a Chinese citizen. The country is trying to control population growth in several ways, one being to encourage people to marry later than their parents did.

Thirty years ago, China was a backward farming country. Starvation was common. Today it is becoming one of the greatest industrial powers in the world.

TAIWAN

Area: 13,900 square miles
Population: 19,600,000 (1988 est)   **Capital:** Taipei
Government: Republic
Major Languages: Chinese   **Currency:** New Taiwan dollar

Taiwan used to be called Formosa. In 1949, when the Communists took over China, their opponents, the Nationalists, set up a government on this island. The United Nations did not recognize Communist China till 1971, so Taiwan repre-

Above: A Ch'ing dynasty vase (1644–1911) and a Ming dynasty ginger jar (1368–1644).

Left: The Great Wall of China. It was built in the 200s BC.

sented the country at the United Nations. Taiwan is prosperous due to farming, forestry, mining, and manufacturing industries.

HONG KONG
Area: 410 square miles
Population: 5,420,000 (1988 est) **Capital:** Victoria
Government: British colony
Major Languages: Chinese, English
Currency: Dollar

This small, wealthy British colony is on the southeastern coast of China. It has many manufacturing industries and is an important port and trading center.

MACAO
Area: 6 square miles
Population: 434,000 (1988 est) **Capital:** Macao
Government: Portuguese territory
Major Languages: Chinese, Portuguese
Currency: Pataca

Macao is a tiny Portuguese territory. It is near Hong Kong at the mouth of the Canton River. It is an important center for trade.

A Chinese funeral in Taiwan, where many of the traditional ways of life that have been abandoned in Communist China are still carried on. Funerals there involve many complicated ceremonies, music, and dancing.

MONGOLIA
Area: 604,250 square miles
Population: 1,943,000 (1988 est) **Capital:** Ulan Bator
Government: Republic
Major Languages: Mongolian **Currency:** Tugrik

Mongolia is a thinly populated country between China and the USSR. It has a Communist government, and the USSR is its main trading partner. A bleak desert covers much of the country, and nomadic herdsmen wander around it. Some of the people work in mining and manufacturing industries that are developing in Ulan Bator (the capital) and other towns.

A street in Tokyo today. Japan is the only highly industrialized country in Asia.

Japan and Korea

Japan and the Korean peninsula are in northeast Asia. The northern parts of both regions have very cold winters. The summers are hot, especially in the southern areas. In 1910, Japan, already an industrialized country, seized Korea. It helped to set up industries there, especially in the north.

The map shows the positions of Japan, North Korea, and South Korea.

JAPAN
Area: 145,834 square miles
Population: 121,410,000 (1988 est) **Capital:** Tokyo
Government: Monarchy
Major Languages: Japanese **Currency:** Yen

Japan lacks many natural resources, but it is the most developed and prosperous country in Asia. The hardworking Japanese have built up many manufacturing industries. At first their products were considered cheap and of poor quality when compared with those made in Western countries. Now, however, they are highly respected, and Japan competes with Western industrial countries.

Japan is made up of many islands – four large ones, Hokkaido, Honshu, Shikoku, and Kyushu, and about 3,000 smaller ones. Most of the land is mountainous and many of the volcanoes are active. Mount Fuji, which last erupted in 1707, is revered as a sacred mountain. There are about 1,500 earthquakes every year, but many are not really noticeable. However, every few years there is a serious one. In 1923 the most destructive earthquake ever recorded destroyed much of Tokyo and Yokohama.

Mountains and forests cover 70 percent of the country, and so there is very little farmland in Japan. But in the 15 percent of land that is cultivated, the yields are high. The chief crop is rice, which grows on nearly half of the farmland. Barley, fruits, soybeans, and wheat are also important crops. There are about $3\frac{1}{2}$ million cattle, but as there is little grazing land, there are not many goats or sheep. Fish is the chief animal food, and Japan is the world's leading fishing and whaling nation.

Although many minerals, including coal and copper, are mined in Japan, there are not enough to supply the manufacturing industries. So many are imported, including iron ore. About a quarter of the working population works in the many light and heavy industries. Japan is the leading producer of motorcycles, merchant ships, radios, and television sets, among other products. Only the USA manufactures more motor vehicles, and only the USA and USSR produce more electrical energy.

Most of Japan's factories are in the large cities. Ten cities have populations of over a million. Tokyo, the capital, is the largest city in the world. Osaka, Yokohama, Nagoya, and Kyoto are other large cities. Like the Chinese, most Japanese people are Mongoloid. But on Hokkaido there are about 15,000 Caucasoids, the Ainu. These stocky bushy-haired people are the *aborigines* (original people) of Japan.

NORTH KOREA

Area: 46,540 square miles
Population: 20,550,000 (1988 est)   **Capital:** Pyongyang
Government: Republic
Major Languages: Korean   **Currency:** Won

The Korean peninsula is joined to China and the USSR. Japan used to occupy this country, but after the Second World War the USSR invaded the northern part and it became Communist. Until 1949 the USA occupied South Korea. Between 1950 and 1953 North and South Korea were at war. Eventually they agreed upon the present boundary. North Korea has extensive mineral resources, and 80 percent of the people work in manufacturing industries. North Korea, once dependent on South Korea for food, has recently raised its own food production.

SOUTH KOREA

Area: 38,025 square miles
Population: 43,300,000 (1988 est)   **Capital:** Seoul
Government: Republic
Major Languages: Korean   **Currency:** Won

When Korea was one country, the south was the main farming region. It grew rice and other grains. But since the country has been divided the South has established various manufacturing industries with the help of the USA. Many of these are based around the capital, Seoul.

In 1972 the two Koreas agreed to reunite, but very little progress has been made since then.

Japanese Kabuki drama began in the 16th century as a form of light-hearted entertainment. It is now a serious art form.

Japan is a chain of volcanic islands. In winter, the volcanoes may have snow on them. Forests cover Japan's mountain slopes and hills. Fish is a major food, and only about 15 percent of the land is farmed.

105

Southeast Asia

Southeast Asia is covered with mountains and forests. It has the ideal weather for growing rice – hot and rainy. Although it has some minerals, it has not developed many manufacturing industries. Buddhism and Islam are the main religions, although most Filipinos are Christians.

BURMA
Area: 261,228 square miles
Population: 37,650,000 (1988 est)   **Capital:** Rangoon
Government: Republic
Major Languages: Burmese, English   **Currency:** Kyat

There are mountains in the north of Burma, but the plains in the south are fertile, especially in the valleys of the Sittang and Irrawaddy rivers. The delta of the latter is a major rice-growing area. Seventy-five percent of the people are farmers. Main exports are rice, jute, rubber, and teak.

CAMBODIA
Area: 69,898 square miles
Population: 6,400,000 (1988 est)   **Capital:** Phnom Penh
Government: Republic
Major Languages: Khmer, French   **Currency:** Riel

Cambodia (Kampuchea), a mostly flat country, has a hot, wet climate. Farming, fishing, and forestry are important, and rice is the main crop. But there has been much unrest and upheaval in Cambodia. It became a Communist republic in 1975, and in 1979 it was invaded by Vietnam.

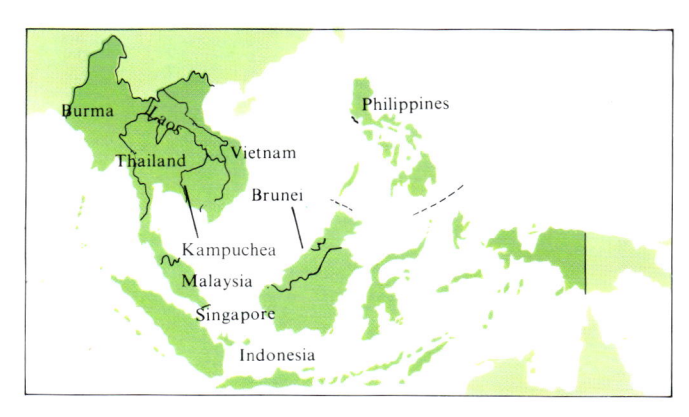

In Southeast Asia, India, Sri Lanka, and Indonesia, elephants are used as working animals.

LAOS
Area: 91,429 square miles
Population: 3,700,000 (1988 est)   **Capital:** Vientiane
Government: Republic (since 1975)
Major Languages: Lao, French   **Currency:** Kip

This poor country is mountainous and landlocked. There are large areas of forest. Tin is mined and chief farming crops are rice, maize, tobacco, and cotton. Once a monarchy, it became a Communist republic in 1975.

THAILAND
Area: 198,115 square miles
Population: 52,440,000 (1988 est)   **Capital:** Bangkok
Government: Monarchy
Major Languages: Thai, Chinese   **Currency:** Baht

Three-fifths of Thailand (formerly Siam) are covered by forest. Mountains surround the fertile Chao Phraya River valley and to the east there is a dry plateau. The chief exports are rice, maize, tapioca products, rubber, and tin. There was some fighting in the north in the 1970s, but Thailand has remained a monarchy.

VIETNAM
Area: 127,242 square miles
Population: 62,000,000 (1988 est)   **Capital:** Hanoi
Government: Republic
Major Languages: Vietnamese   **Currency:** Dong

France used to rule all of Vietnam. In 1946 fighting broke out between the two countries and in 1954 France withdrew. Vietnam was divided in two, the Communist North and the non-Communist South. In 1975, after some years of fighting, North Vietnam occupied the South. A Communist government was set up to unify the country, which had suffered much in the wars. The main occupation in Vietnam is farming, and the chief crop is rice. In the north, coal and other minerals are mined. There are some manufacturing industries.

A river market in Thailand. Thailand (once called Siam) is a hot, tropical country, with enormous forests.

BRUNEI
Area: 2,226 square miles
Population: 240,000 (1988 est) **Capital:** Bandar Seri Begawan
Government: Sultanate
Major Languages: Malay, English **Currency:** Dollar

Brunei, formerly a British protectorate, lies on the north coast of Borneo. Its chief product is oil.

INDONESIA
Area: 741,101 square miles
Population: 176,800,000 (1988 est) **Capital:** Djakarta
Government: Republic
Major Languages: Indonesia, Chinese **Currency:** Rupiah

Above: Tapping rubber in Malaysia, which leads the world in producing natural rubber.

Indonesia is the large *archipelago* (group of islands) that lies between Malaysia, the Philippines, and Australia. There are thousands of islands. The biggest land areas are Kalimantan (part of Borneo), Sumatra, West Irian (part of New Guinea), Sulawesi (Celebes), and Java, which is the most thickly populated island. Most of Indonesia became independent in 1949. In 1962 West Irian was added, and in 1976, Portuguese Timor.

Indonesia has more active volcanoes than any other country; in recent times over 70 have erupted. Forestry and mining are important; there are large deposits of bauxite (aluminum ore), coal, oil, and tin. But most of the people are farmers. They export coffee, copra (from coconuts), palm oil and kernels, rubber, tea, and tobacco. The main food is rice. Most Indonesians are Muslims. There are also large Christian, Hindu, and Buddhist minorities.

MALAYSIA
Area: 128,430 square miles
Population: 15,840,000 (1988 est) **Capital:** Kuala Lumpur
Government: Monarchy, with federal system
Major Languages: Malay, Chinese **Currency:** Ringgit

Malaysia is a hot, humid country. It is made up of the southern part of the Malay peninsula (excluding Singapore), and Sabah and Sarawak, territories on the island of Borneo. Four-fifths of the people live in the Malay peninsula; about 53 percent of them are Malays, 35 percent of Chinese

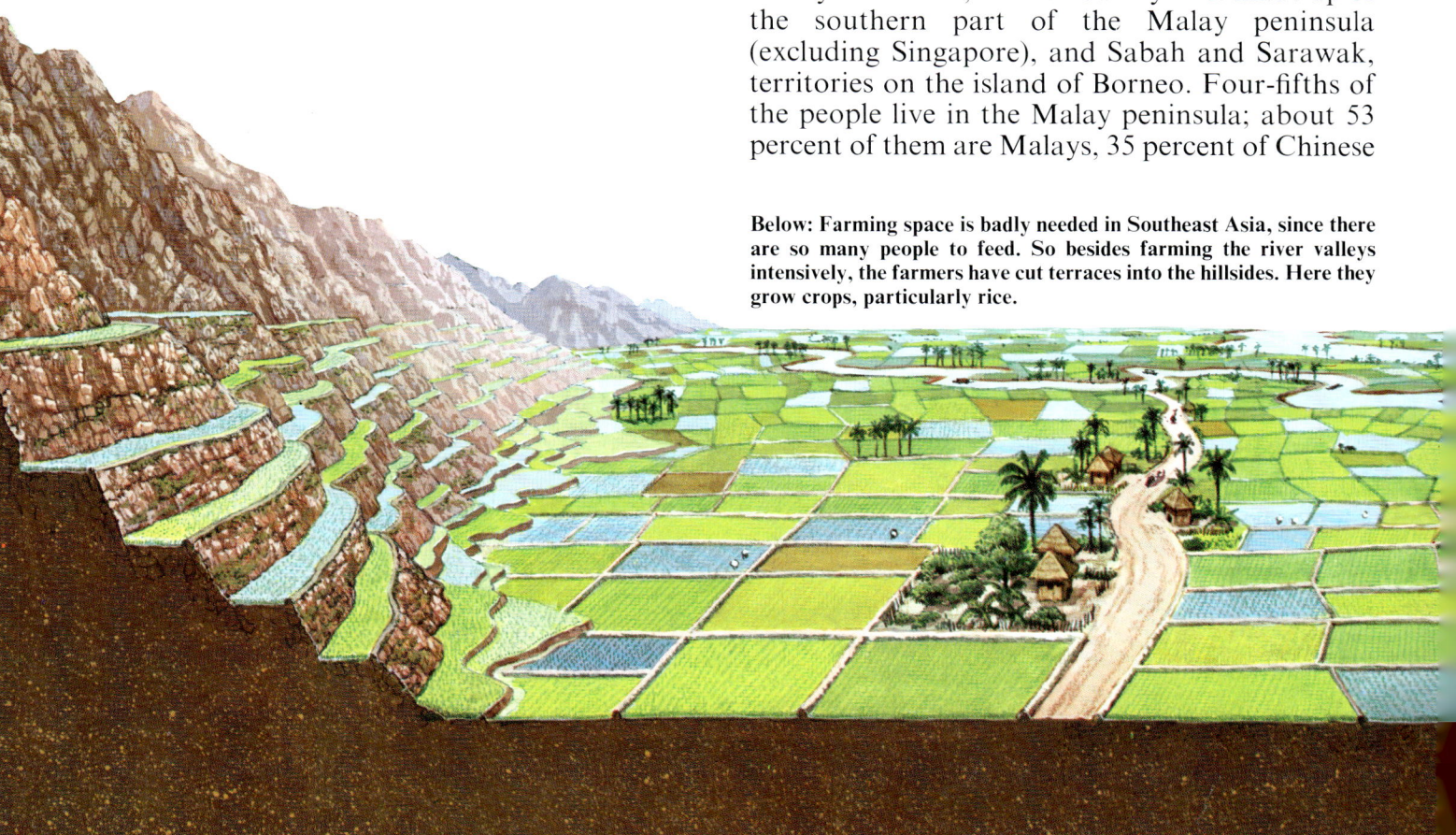

Below: Farming space is badly needed in Southeast Asia, since there are so many people to feed. So besides farming the river valleys intensively, the farmers have cut terraces into the hillsides. Here they grow crops, particularly rice.

The Buddhist shrine in Borobudur in Java. It was built in about AD 800. It has a square base with five square terraces above. On top are three round terraces crowned by a bell-shaped *stupa* (a building containing a relic of the Buddha or a Buddhist saint). Around it are 72 small stupas, each containing a figure of the Buddha.

origin, and 11 percent Indian or Pakistani. The official language is Malay. Tribal groups, such as the Dyaks, once famous for head-hunting, live in Sabah and Sarawak.

Malaysia is one of the more prosperous countries in Southeast Asia. It is the world's leading producer of rubber, tin, and palm oil. Tropical hardwoods from the huge rain forests are another important export. Malaysia also produces pepper, tea, oil, and some manufactured goods. Most of the people are farmers, and rice is the chief food crop.

PHILIPPINES

Area: 115,831 square miles
Population: 58,100,000 (1988 est) **Capital:** Quezon City
Government: Republic
Major Languages: Pilipino, English **Currency:** Peso

The Philippines is another archipelago. About one-tenth of its 7,000 islands are inhabited. Some are large and mountainous and have volcanoes, while others are tiny coral outcrops. The largest islands are Luzon and Mindanao.

Spain ruled the Philippines from the 1500s to 1898. During that time, many people became Christians, and today the Philippines is the only Christian nation in Asia. From 1898 to 1946, when the country became an independent republic, it was controlled by the USA. Most of the people are farmers, and timber, copra, coconut oil, sugar, bananas, and oil are the chief exports. Copper is mined, and the Filipinos are building up manufacturing industries, especially around the largest city, Manila (which is also the leading port).

SINGAPORE

Area: 224 square miles
Population: 2,590,000 (1988 est) **Capital:** Singapore
Government: Republic
Major Languages: Chinese, Malay, English, Tamil
Currency: Dollar

This small territory is the wealthiest in Southeast Asia because of its trading and manufacturing industries, which include shipbuilding and petrochemicals. Singapore is one of the largest ports in the world. There is little farming or fishing, and food is imported. Singapore was a British colony, and between 1963 and 1965 it was part of Malaysia. But differences with the Malaysian government made it break away. Singapore has a mixed population of Chinese (76 percent), Malays (15 percent), Indians, and others. So it has four official languages.

India and its Neighbors

India, Bangladesh, and Pakistan are three of the most densely populated countries in the world. About 19 out of every 100 people in the world today are citizens of one of these countries. They were once all one country, India, which was part of the British Empire until it became independent in 1947. Then it was divided in two: India, mainly Hindu; and Pakistan, mainly Muslim. Pakistan was in two parts, East and West, separated by the width of India. In 1971 they fought a civil war, and East Pakistan finally became the independent nation of Bangladesh.

Right: A map of India and its neighbors.

Left: A statue of the Buddha (Enlightened One). The Buddha was born in what is now Nepal.

Below: A busy street in Delhi, capital of India.

BANGLADESH
Area: 55,598 square miles
Population: 104,250,000 (1988 est)   **Capital:** Dacca
Government: Republic
Major Languages: Bangla, English   **Currency:** Taka

Most of the people of Bangladesh are very poor. This flat, wet country lies around the delta of the Ganges, Brahmaputra, and other rivers. When storm winds drive the sea inland, there are sometimes floods, which cause starvation and disease. Most of the people are farmers – about two-thirds of the land is farmland. The main food is rice and the main cash crop is jute.

The stupa at Sanchi is one of the most famous Buddhist monuments in India. It was built by the Emperor Ashoka in the 3rd century BC and later enlarged.

BHUTAN
Area: 18,147 square miles
Population: 1,450,000 (1988 est)   **Capital:** Thimphu
Government: Monarchy
Major Languages: Tibetan dialects
Currency: Ngultrum, Indian rupee

Bhutan is a small kingdom between northeastern India and China (Tibet). It has no coastline. The chief occupations are farming and forestry, and there are some craft industries. Foreign affairs are handled by India.

INDIA
Area: 1,237,061 square miles
Population: 784,000,000 (1988 est)   **Capital:** New Delhi
Government: Republic
Major Languages: Hindi and other Indo-Aryan languages, English   **Currency:** Rupee

India is the seventh-largest country in the world, but only China has a larger population. The

Right: Oxen are used to plow a field of rice in India.

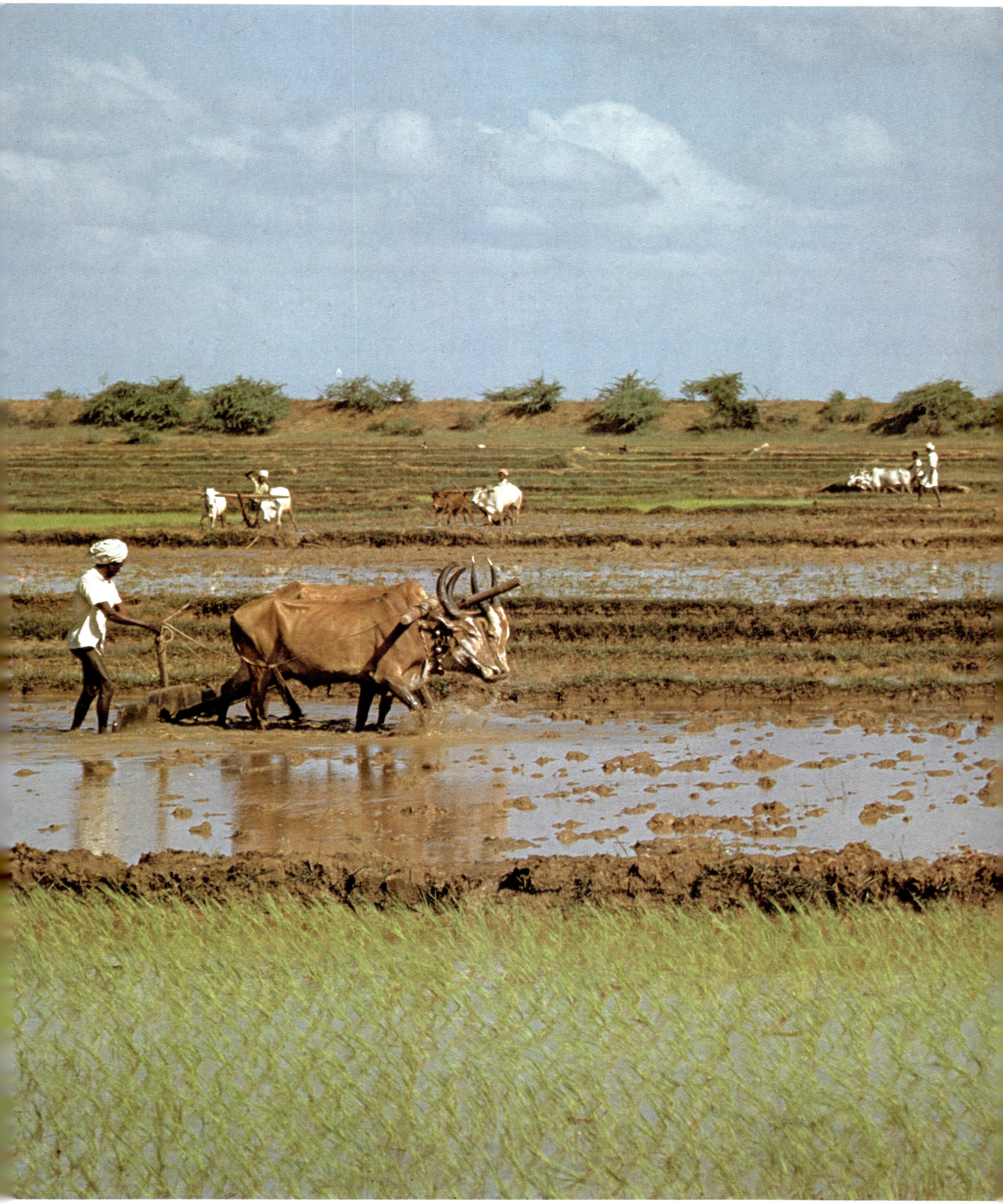

population is increasing by about 13 million every year and there is not enough food for all the people.

In the north is the magnificent Himalayan mountain range. The highest peak in India is Nanda Devi, 25,646 feet above sea level. Three rivers rise in the Himalayas: the Indus, the Ganges, and the Brahmaputra. The Indus flows into Pakistan, and the other two flow over broad plains in India and Bangladesh. Much of the triangular peninsula that is southern India consists of a tableland, the Deccan plateau. It is bordered by mountains, the Western and Eastern Ghats, which give way to coastal plains.

Between them, the Indian people speak more than 800 languages and dialects. Hindi was once the official language, but there were riots against the government by people who did not speak it. So English was made a second official language. About 83 percent of Indians are Hindus and 11 percent are Muslims. There are also Christians, Jains, and Sikhs. India and Pakistan are often in conflict. For example, they fought over the state of Kashmir in the northwest. Now the boundary divides Kashmir between India and Pakistan.

Farming, particularly rice-growing, is important in India. The wet tropical monsoon climate is suited to it. Other crops are cotton, millet, sugarcane, jute, tea, and wheat. About 70 percent of the people earn their living by farming. There are millions of cattle and water buffalo, but Hindus are forbidden by their religion to kill them. Although India has coal and other minerals, mining is not highly developed. Textiles are the chief manufactures. The main exports are jute products, cotton goods, tea, iron ore, and leather. Nine cities have populations of over a million. The largest cities are Calcutta, Bombay, Delhi, and Madras.

The Jagmandir Palace is built on an island in Pichola Lake, Rajasthan, in northwestern India. The 17th-century Mughal Emperor Shah Jahan was given shelter here when he was rebelling against his father, and its decorations are thought to have inspired his later buildings in Delhi.

MALDIVE ISLANDS
Area: 115 square miles
Population: 180,000 (1988 est)   **Capital:** Malé
Government: Republic
Major Languages: Divehi, Arabic   **Currency:** Rupee

In the Maldive Islands, southwest of India, fishing and coconut products are the most important industries. The islands became independent in 1965.

NEPAL
Area: 56,135 square miles
Population: 17,430,000 (1988 est)   **Capital:** Katmandu
Government: Monarchy
Major Languages: Nepáli   **Currency:** Rupee

The founder of Buddhism, Gautama Buddha, was born in Nepal. It is a landlocked kingdom between India and China. In the north is Mount Everest. Farming and forestry are the main activities.

PAKISTAN
Area: 319,867 square miles
Population: 101,860,000 (1988 est)   **Capital:** Islamabad
Government: Republic
Major Languages: Urdu, English   **Currency:** Rupee

In north and west Pakistan there are mountains and tablelands. Although there are river valleys, including that of the Indus, Pakistan is a dry country. Most people depend on farming, and the land has to be irrigated. The main crops are cotton, maize, sugarcane, rice, and wheat. The main industry is textiles, especially cotton goods. Karachi, on the coast, and Lahore, in the north, are the largest cities. Most Pakistanis are Muslims. In the 1960s the capital was moved from Rawalpindi to the new city of Islamabad.

A distant view of the Himalayas, the highest mountains in the world. As India moved north and collided with the rest of Asia, these great walls of rock were pushed up.

SRI LANKA
Area: 24,962 square miles
Population: 16,640,000 (1988 est)   **Capital:** Colombo
Government: Republic
Major Languages: Sinhala, Tamil   **Currency:** Rupee

Sri Lanka used to be called Ceylon. It is an island southeast of India. There are mountains in the center and lowlands, and plains around the coast. Sri Lanka has a mixed population, the largest groups being the Sinhalese and the Tamils. Tea, rubber, and coconut products are the chief exports, and the chief mineral is graphite.

These statues of Buddha at Polonnawura in Sri Lanka date from the 11th century. For some time part of this island was under Indian rule.

Southwest Asia

There are 17 countries in Southwest Asia. Twelve of them have Arab populations and Arabic is their official language. There are also some Arabs in Israel, but most Israelis are Jews. Afghanistan, Iran, and Turkey are not Arab countries, but most of their people are Muslims (followers of the Arab religion, Islam). In Cyprus and Lebanon, there are large groups of Christians. This area of Asia produces most of the world's oil. There is much conflict between the Arab countries and Israel, and there were Arab-Israeli wars in 1948, 1956, 1967, and 1973.

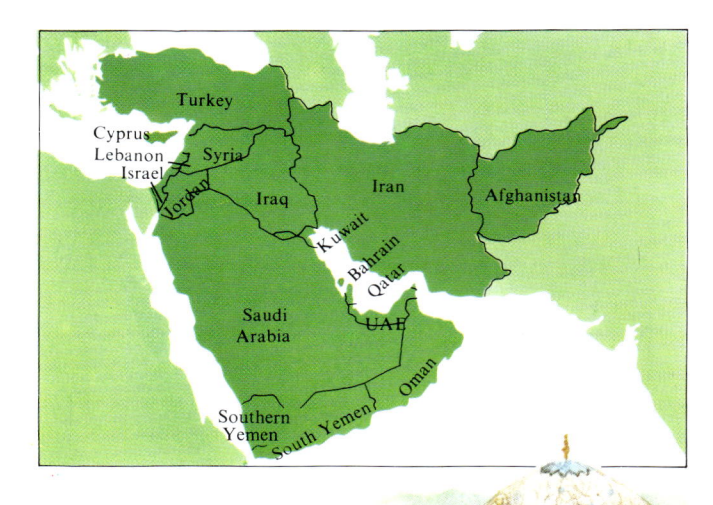

Above: There are 17 nations in Southwest Asia.

Right: A mosque in Isfahan, Iran. In 14 of the 17 Southwest Asian countries, the majority of the population is Muslim.

AFGHANISTAN
Area: 250,000 square miles
Population: 15,100,000 (1988 est) **Capital:** Kabul
Government: Republic
Major Languages: Dari (Persian), Pushtu
Currency: Afghani

Most of this landlocked country is covered by mountains. About 2½ million people are nomads who rear sheep and goats. Most of the people are farmers, although manufacturing is slowly growing. They produce cereals, cottons, fruits, vegetables, and wool. Karakuls (Persian lambskins) and some natural gas are exported. The country has been in confusion since 1979 when, despite worldwide protest, the USSR invaded and occupied it. The Russians began a withdrawal in 1988.

IRAN
Area: 636,296 square miles
Population: 46,610,000 (1988 est) **Capital:** Tehran
Government: Islamic Republic
Major Languages: Farsi, Turkish dialects **Currency:** Rial

Iran, formerly Persia, has enormous oil reserves and is the world's fourth-largest oil producer. This means that it is a very wealthy country. The revenue from the oil sales is helping to improve industry and living conditions. It is a dry, mountainous country; only 10 percent of the land is suitable for farming although half the people are farmers. In 1979, Iran's ruler, the Shah, was deposed and Iran became an Islamic republic. An eight-year war with neighboring Iraq began in 1980, causing heavy casualties and much destruction on both sides.

IRAQ
Area: 167,925 square miles
Population: 16,020,000 (1988 est) **Capital:** Baghdad
Government: Republic
Major Languages: Arabic, Kurdish **Currency:** Dinar

Much of Iraq is desert, so the Tigris and Euphrates rivers, which flow into the Persian Gulf, are vital to the irrigation of farmland. Their valleys once contained the ancient civilizations of Babylon and Assyria. Most people are farmers, producing cotton, dates, rice, tobacco, wheat, and wool. Iraq is the sixth-largest oil producer in the world, but the country suffered heavily from the war with Iran.

SAUDI ARABIA
Area: 830,000 square miles
Population: 11,520,000 (1988 est) **Capital:** Riyadh
Government: Monarchy
Major Languages: Arabic **Currency:** Riyal

Saudi Arabia is in the Arabian peninsula, bounded by the Red Sea in the west and the Gulf in the east. Most of the country is desert so there is little farming, except near oases. It is famous for its holy Muslim cities of Mecca and Medina. It is also the world's third-largest oil producer and exports more oil than any other country. This means it has money to develop its industries, farming, and services.

COUNTRY	CAPITAL	AREA (sq mi)	POPULATION (1988 est)	GOVERNMENT	MAJOR LANGUAGES	CURRENCY
Bahrain	Manama	256	443,000	Monarchy	Arabic	Dinar
Kuwait	Kuwait	6,880	1,772,000	Monarchy	Arabic	Dinar
Oman	Muscat	82,030	1,272,000	Monarchy	Arabic	Rial
Qatar	Doha	4,247	306,000	Monarchy	Arabic	Riyal
Southern Yemen	Aden	128,560	2,280,000	Republic	Arabic	Dinar
United Arab Emirates	Dubai	32,278	1,330,000	Monarchy	Arabic	Dirham
Yemen	San'a	75,290	6,340,000	Republic	Arabic	Riyal

BAHRAIN
Bahrain is a group of low islands in the Gulf. It is a hot, dry country. Its people are Muslims. The capital, Manama, is on the largest island, also called Bahrain. In 1932, oil was discovered, and it is now the chief resource.

KUWAIT
Kuwait is an Arab country. It is ruled by an emir, and so is called an emirate. It is one of the world's leading producers of oil. Kuwait is a hot and dry country at the head of the Gulf.

OMAN
Oman, a sultanate (a country ruled by a sultan), is in the southeast corner of the Arabian peninsula. Oil is its most important resource, since much of the land is desert.

QATAR
Qatar, another emirate, is on a peninsula that juts out from Arabia into the Gulf. A few of the people are nomads but most live in and around Doha, the capital. Oil has made Qatar wealthy.

SOUTHERN YEMEN
This poor country in the southwestern corner of the Arabian peninsula is officially the People's Democratic Republic of Yemen. The main occupations are farming and fishing.

UNITED ARAB EMIRATES
The seven United Arab Emirates used to be called the Trucial States. Abu Dhabi and Dubai are the largest. Both are rich in oil.

YEMEN
Yemen has no oil and is a poor country, although it has the best farmland in the Arabian peninsula. It lies in a mountainous region on the shore of the Red Sea. Chief products are cotton, coffee, and hides.

Most of the Arab peoples of Southwest Asia used to be poor, wandering herdsmen. The discovery of oil has changed all that. Southwest Asia produces over a third of the world's oil.

Above: Jerusalem, the capital of Israel. To Christians, Muslims, and Jews, it is a holy city. The Dome of the Rock is in the center of the picture.

CYPRUS

Area: 3,572 square miles
Population: 674,000 (1988 est) **Capital:** Nicosia
Government: Republic
Major Languages: Greek, Turkish **Currency:** Pound

Cyprus is an island nation in the eastern Mediterranean Sea. It gained independence from Britain in 1960. The chief occupations are mining and farming. About 80 percent of the people are Christian Greeks and 20 percent are Muslim Turks. These two groups have often fought against each other and made progress for Cyprus difficult.

A Cypriot woman weaves a basket. The people of Cyprus live like southern Europeans, although Cyprus is geographically part of Asia. Some are Christian Greeks and others Muslim Turks.

ISRAEL

Area: 7,848 square miles
Population: 4,210,000 (1988 est) **Capital:** Jerusalem
Government: Republic
Major Languages: Hebrew, Arabic **Currency:** Shekel

In 1948, part of the country that was once called Palestine was established as a homeland for Jews. This was Israel, and today about one in five of the world's Jews live there. They form about 80 percent of the population, but there is a large Arab minority. Israel's Arab neighbors opposed the establishment of Israel and there has been conflict ever since. During three short wars Israel took land from Egypt, Jordan, and Syria. However, in the late 1970s and early 1980s, there were peace moves in which Egypt was prominent. Despite the conflict, Israel has become prosperous. Irrigation has turned desert to farmland, and the chief farming products are cereals, fruits, sugar, and vegetables. Many of these are exported, but the mining and manufacturing industries are even more valuable. More than 86 percent of the population lives in cities and towns. Others live in farming settlements called *kibbutzim*.

JORDAN

Area: 35,135 square miles
Population: 2,760,000 (1988 est)   **Capital:** Amman
Government: Monarchy
Major Languages: Arabic   **Currency:** Dinar

Most of this landlocked Arab nation is desert. The highlands receive the most rainfall and so are the most fertile areas; but Israel seized the western uplands. Cereals, fruits, and vegetables are the chief farming products. Phosphate, a mineral used to make fertilizers, is the most valuable export. There is little manufacturing.

LEBANON

Area: 4,015 square miles
Population: 2,700,000 (1988 est)   **Capital:** Beirut
Government: Republic
Major Languages: Arabic, French   **Currency:** Pound

Although Lebanon is an Arab nation, about 40 percent of the people are Christians. There is conflict between Christians and Muslims, and in the mid-1970s a bitter civil war broke out. The climate is warm and pleasant, and in the winter, when the mountains are covered by snow, many tourists used to visit the country in peaceful times. Most of the country's wealth comes from trade, although farming is also important, but trading and farming have both suffered in the fighting.

SYRIA

Area: 71,498 square miles
Population: 11,000,000 (1988)   **Capital:** Damascus
Government: Republic
Major Languages: Arabic, French   **Currency:** Pound

For thousands of years Syria has been a trading nation, through which goods traveled between Europe and Asia. The irrigated river valleys provide rich farmland, and cotton is the main crop. Syria has oil, and mining and manufacturing industries are being built up. Most Syrians are Arabs. But there are some Kurds, a people who also live in Iran, Iraq, Turkey, and the USSR.

TURKEY

Area: 300,948 square miles
Population: 51,820,000 (1988 est)   **Capital:** Ankara
Government: Republic
Major Languages: Turkish, Kurdish   **Currency:** Lira

Part of Turkey is in Europe, part in Asia. The waterway that connects the Mediterranean and Black seas is the dividing line. Istanbul, the largest city, is also in both continents. Anatolia (Asian Turkey) is mostly mountains or high tablelands and contains the chief farming regions. Exports are cottons, fruits, and tobacco. The manufacturing industries are developing, and Turkey is a major producer of chromium.

The cemetery of the Muradiye Mosque in Bursa in Turkey. This was the capital of the early Ottoman sultans before they took over Constantinople in 1453. It contains the tombs of Osman and Orhan, the founders of the Ottoman dynasty.

Mediterranean Sea
Tunis
Sfax
TUNISIA
Constantine
Algiers
Oran
Tangier
Rabat
Casablanca
Fès
Marrakech
MOROCCO
ATLAS MOUNTAINS
Tripoli
Benghazi
Alexandria
Cairo
Suez
Canary Is
Las Palmas
El Aaiun
WESTERN SAHARA
ALGERIA
LIBYA
EGYPT
Nile
SAHARA DESERT
Aswan
MALI
MAURITANIA
Nouakchott
NIGER
Agadez
CHAD
Red Sea
Dongola
Timbuktu
Senegal
Dakar
SENEGAL
GAMBIA
Banjul
Bissau
GUINEA-BISSAU
GUINEA
Conakry
Freetown
SIERRA LEONE
LIBERIA
Monrovia
Bamako
BURKINA FASO
Ouagadougou
Niamey
Kano
NIGERIA
Niger
L. Chad
N'Djamena
Khartoum
SUDAN
DJIBOUTI
Djibouti
Addis Ababa
ETHIOPIAN HIGHLANDS
ETHIOPIA
IVORY COAST
GHANA
TOGO
BENIN
Ibadan
Abidjan
Accra
Lomé
Porto-Novo
Lagos
CENTRAL AFRICAN REPUBLIC
Bangui
CAMEROON
Yaoundé
Malabo
EQUATORIAL GUINEA
SAO TOME & PRINCIPE
Libreville
GABON
CONGO
Equator
UGANDA
Kampala
KENYA
Mt Kenya
SOMALI REPUBLIC
Mogadishu
Congo Basin
Kigali
L. Victoria
Nairobi
RWANDA
Bujumbura
BURUNDI
Mt Kilimanjaro
Mombasa
INDIAN OCEAN
Brazzaville
Kinshasa
Cabinda
Zaire
ZAIRE
L. Tanganyika
Tabora
Dodoma
Zanzibar
Dar es Salaam
TANZANIA
ATLANTIC OCEAN
Luanda
L. Malawi
MALAWI
COMORO IS
Benguela
Huambo
ZAMBIA
Lusaka
Lilongwe
MOZAMBIQUE
ANGOLA
Zambezi
Harare
ZIMBABWE
Beira
Tananarive
NAMIBIA
Madagascar
BOTSWANA
Walvis Bay
Windhoek
Namib Desert
Kalahari
Gaborone
Limpopo
Pretoria
Maputo
Johannesburg
Mbabane
SWAZILAND
Orange
Maseru
LESOTHO
Durban
SOUTH AFRICA
DRAKENSBERG
East London
Cape Town
Port Elizabeth
0
500
1000 miles
0
500
1000
1500 kilometers
Capital Cities

AFRICA

Most of Africa is in the tropics. It has enormous rain forests, where the trees block most of the sunlight from the forest floor, and huge deserts, including the world's largest, the Sahara. Many different kinds of wild animals roam over the vast areas of savanna (tropical grassland). The tablelands in the center of the continent have a pleasant climate, although the coasts are, on the whole, hot and humid.

The people of Africa fall into two main groups, divided by the Sahara. The Arabs, or Berbers, in the north are Muslims. To the south, many of the people are black Africans, some of whom have their own religions. There are also some places, such as South Africa, where many people are of European origin.

FACTS AND FIGURES

Area: 11,700,000 square miles. *Greatest width:* 4,698 miles. *Greatest length:* 5,002 miles.
Population: 600,700,000.
Population Density: 44 per square mile.
Countries: 57 (including offshore islands).
Highest Peak: Mount Kilimanjaro in Tanzania, 19,340 feet above sea level.
Lowest Point on Land: Lake Assal in Djibouti is 509 feet below sea level.
Largest Lakes: Lake Victoria in Kenya, Tanzania, and Uganda covers 26,293 square miles. Lake Tanganyika, Africa's second-largest lake, is also the world's longest freshwater lake.
Longest Rivers: The river Nile is 4,145 miles long. It is the world's longest. Other great African rivers are the Zaire (formerly called Congo), 2,610 miles long; the Niger, 2,585 miles long; and the Zambezi, 1,653 miles long.

Northern Africa

Much of northern Africa is covered by the barren Sahara. There are oases (water holes) and river valleys at the edges of the desert, and this is where most people live.

ALGERIA

Area: 919,595 square miles
Population: 22,820,000 (1988 est)   **Capital:** Algiers
Government: Republic   **Independent:** 1962
Major Languages: Arabic, French   **Currency:** Dinar

More than 75 percent of Algeria is covered by the Sahara. The most valuable product is oil, which accounts for four-fifths of the country's exports. Natural gas is also found. There is farmland in the northern Atlas Mountains and on the fertile plains near the Mediterranean Sea. Most Algerians live here; they are farmers and grow barley, fruits, grapes, olives, vegetables, and wheat. In the uplands, they breed livestock. Algeria gained independence from France in 1962, when many people of French origin who had settled there left the country.

EGYPT

Area: 386,643 square miles
Population: 50,530,000 (1988 est)   **Capital:** Cairo
Government: Republic   **Independent:** 1922
Major Languages: Arabic   **Currency:** Pound

Most Egyptians live in the fertile valley of the river Nile, since the rest of the land is mostly desert. It was here that the great civilization of Ancient Egypt, which reached its peak in 1500 BC, was based. It left behind pyramids and other monuments.

Most people in Egypt are poor farmers who grow cotton for export and many food crops. But Egypt also has more manufacturing industries than any other North African country. These include cement, chemicals, plastics, steel, sugar, and textiles. The Egyptian economy has been weakened by wars with Israel. Egypt has been a leading country in trying to secure Arab-Israeli peace.

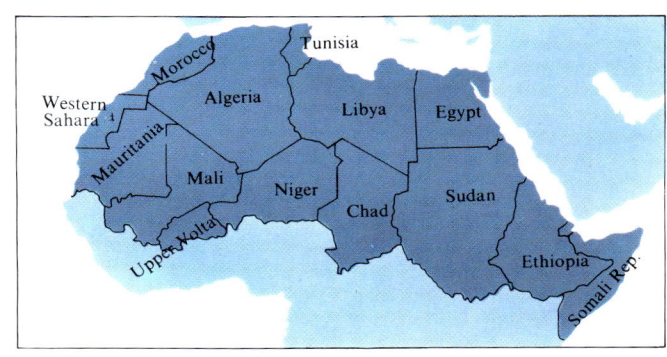

Above: The map shows the nations of northern Africa.

Below: The Great Pyramid and Sphinx near Giza in Egypt.

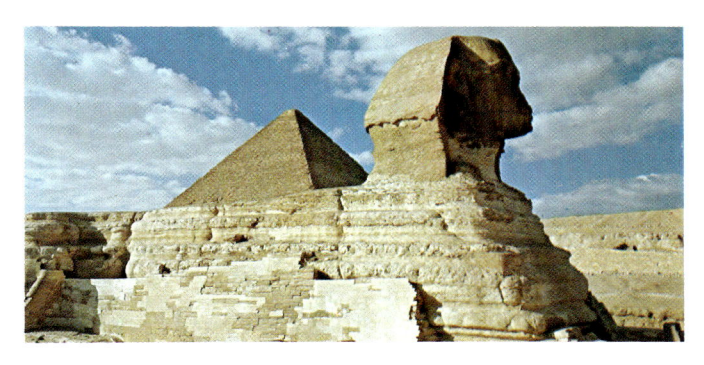

In the burning-hot Sahara, it is only possible to live around oases or in the Nile valley. The camel, which can go for days without water, is called *ship of the desert*.

LIBYA

Area: 679,362 square miles
Population: 3,880,000 (1988 est) **Capital:** Tripoli
Government: Republic **Independent:** 1951
Major Languages: Arabic **Currency:** Dinar

Libya used to be one of the poorest nations in the world. The only parts that can be used for farming are two narrow coastal regions in the northwest and northeast, since the rest of the land is hot desert. Main products are wheat, barley, fruits, olives, and vegetables. But since 1961, Libya has produced oil in the Sahara. Oil is now the country's chief source of wealth and has made it possible to expand the economy and improve standards of living.

MOROCCO

Area: 172,414 square miles, not including part of Western Sahara taken in 1976
Population: 23,670,000 (1988 est) **Capital:** Rabat
Government: Monarchy **Independent:** 1956
Major Languages: Arabic, Berber **Currency:** Dirham

Morocco is a mountainous country. One of the mountains in the high Atlas range, Djebel Toubkal, is 13,665 feet above sea level. In the east the dry Sahara borders the mountains, but north of the mountain ranges are farming areas. Here barley, wheat, grapes, and other crops are grown. Fishing and tourism are important industries.

Morocco's most valuable products are phosphates, which are used to make fertilizers. In 1976, Morocco divided its neighbor, Western Sahara, with Mauritania, and in 1979 it took over the whole country. Western Sahara contains the world's largest phosphate deposits. However, the Saharans are opposed to Morocco and are demanding independence. Algeria is supporting their claim.

Tunisian women wear long, loose cotton clothes to protect them from the sun.

TUNISIA

Area: 63,170 square miles
Population: 7,430,000 (1988 est) **Capital:** Tunis
Government: Republic **Independent:** 1956
Major Languages: Arabic, French **Currency:** Dinar

Many tourists visit the fine beaches on Tunisia's Mediterranean coast. Few people live in the dry south of the country, but in the north are fertile farmlands. Most people are farmers, chief products being olive oil, dates, cereals, fruits, and vegetables. There are many craftsmen. Oil and phosphates are mined.

WESTERN SAHARA

Area: 102,703 square miles
Population: 150,000 (1988 est) **Capital:** El Aaiún
Government: Western Sahara was divided between Morocco and Mauritania in 1976. Saharan tribesmen opposed this act and declared their country an independent republic.
Major Languages: Arabic
Currency: Mauritanian ouguiya, Moroccan dirham

Spain used to rule Western Sahara, a bleak country with a small population. But Morocco now controls it. The Saharans, most of whom are nomads, oppose Morocco. With the backing of Algeria, they claimed independence, and in 1981 renamed their country the Democratic Saharan Arab Republic.

CHAD

Area: 495,755 square miles
Population: 4,600,000 (1988 est)　**Capital:** N'Djamena
Government: Republic　**Independent:** 1960
Major Languages: French, native languages
Currency: CFA franc

Chad is a landlocked country in the heart of north central Africa. It is very poor, and most of the people are Muslim nomads. To the west is Lake Chad, which is in a low inland drainage basin. There are rivers flowing into the lake but none flowing out. Most of the north is desert. In the south there are farms where the people (who are black Africans) grow cotton, the main export, and food crops. There is some unrest in the country because of differences between the nomadic northerners and the black southerners.

DJIBOUTI

Area: 8,880 square miles
Population: 300,000 (1988 est)　**Capital:** Djibouti
Government: Republic　**Independent:** 1977
Major Languages: Arabic, French　**Currency:** Franc

This small, hot, dry country used to be the Territory of Afars and Issas. It is on the shore of the Red Sea. Until 1977, France ruled the country. The capital, Djibouti, is an important port, and about half of the population lives there. Those who do not are mostly nomads.

Below left: This mosque, at Mopti in Mali, was built by slapping mud onto wooden scaffolding.

Below center: Most Ethiopians are farmers or herdsmen.

ETHIOPIA

Area: 472,434 square miles
Population: 46,000,000 (1988 est)　**Capital:** Addis Ababa
Government: Republic
Major Languages: Amharic, Arabic　**Currency:** Birr

Ethiopia, in eastern Africa, is a mountainous country; the highest peak is Ras Dashen (15,157 feet above sea level). In the center of the country are moist, cool tablelands where the Christian Hamitic people live. They grow coffee and food crops and raise livestock. The hot, dry plains that surround the tablelands are peopled by nomadic Muslims. In 1962, Eritrea, an area in the northeast that was an Italian colony, became part of Ethiopia. But many Eritreans wanted independence. The Somali-speaking Muslims in the southeast want their lands to be united with the neighboring Somali Republic. In 1977 there was fighting between them and the Ethiopians.
fighting between them and the Ethiopians. During the late 1980s the country suffered years of drought and famine.

MALI

Area: 478,766 square miles
Population: 8,400,000 (1988 est)　**Capital:** Bamako
Government: Republic　**Independent:** 1960
Major Languages: French, Bambara　**Currency:** Franc

Mali is a large, landlocked country. The north is mostly desert; the south is irrigated by the river Niger, which is a valuable source of fish. Mali is thinly populated. Nomadic Berber people called Tuaregs live in the north, and Negroid people live in the south. They are farmers and produce cotton, millet, groundnuts, and oil seed. They also breed livestock, but in the early 1970s there were terrible droughts in which many animals died.

Below: Winnowing grain in Ethiopia. Barley, durra (sorghum), maize, teff (a kind of millet), and wheat are all important foods. But the most valuable crop is coffee.

A caravan of camels, laden with salt, at Bilma in Niger. The camel, with its ability to cross the desert from one oasis to the next, has played a very important part in northwestern African trade.

MAURITANIA
Area: 397,955 square miles, not including part of Western Sahara taken in 1976
Population: 2,000,000 (1988 est) **Capital:** Nouakchott
Government: Republic **Independent:** 1960
Major Languages: Arabic, French **Currency:** Ouguiya

Mauritania, on the edge of the Atlantic Ocean in northwest Africa, is a hot, dry country. Most of the people are Arab or Berber Muslims, though some in the far south are black Africans. Mauritania is Africa's second-largest producer of iron ore. The only farmland is in the south, and most people live by breeding cattle, goats, and sheep.

NIGER
Area: 489,191 square miles
Population: 7,000,000 (1988 est) **Capital:** Niamey
Government: Republic **Independent:** 1960
Major Languages: Hausa, Arabic **Currency:** Franc

Niger is a landlocked country and one of the poorest nations in the world. The north is mostly desert, although there are moister upland regions. These provide pasture for the livestock kept by the nomadic Tuaregs. In the late 1960s and early 1970s, severe droughts killed many animals. The people in the far south, who are mostly black Africans, are farmers, producing groundnuts for export, and millet. Islam is Niger's chief religion.

SOMALIA
Area: 246,200 square miles
Population: 7,700,000 (1988 est) **Capital:** Mogadishu
Government: Republic **Independent:** 1960
Major Languages: Somali **Currency:** Shilling

Somalia is in the Horn of Africa. The people in the dry and mountainous north keep livestock. In the south there are farms that grow, among other things, bananas for export. There are also Somali-speaking people in Djibouti, Ethiopia, and Kenya, many of whom want to join together to form one Somali nation.

SUDAN
Area: 967,500 square miles
Population: 23,000,000 (1988 est) **Capital:** Khartoum
Government: Republic **Independent:** 1956
Major Languages: Arabic, native languages **Currency:** Pound

Sudan is the largest country in Africa. Most of the people are farmers, producing livestock and cotton that they grow in irrigated land near the White and Blue Nile rivers. The north is hot and dry, but the south is wetter. There are Muslims in the north and black Africans in the south. In the late 1980s the country suffered from severe economic problems and famine.

BURKINA FASO
Area: 105,869 square miles
Population: 7,100,000 (1988 est) **Capital:** Ougadougou
Government: Republic **Independent:** 1960
Major Languages: French, native languages
Currency: Franc

Burkina Faso is perhaps the poorest country in the world. The average income per person in 1983 was only $150 per year. The country has no coastline, and most of the soils are not fertile. There are often severe droughts. In the 1970s, years of drought caused widespread famine. The people, mostly black Africans, keep livestock or grow food crops. Cotton and groundnuts are sold. Only one out of every five people is Muslim – the rest have their own traditional religions.

West Africa

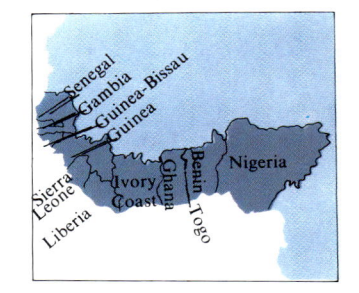

The map at right shows the West African countries, around the Gulf of Guinea.

Right: Students at Ibadan University in Nigeria.

The climate of West Africa is hot and tropical. There are wet plains covered with rain forest on the coast. The forests gradually give way to savanna (tropical grassland) in the center, where the climate is drier.

In Nigeria alone 250 languages are spoken, and there are many more in the rest of the area. So when the West African countries became independent, they could not choose an African language to be the official one. Most educated Africans spoke the language of the European nation that had ruled their country. So English, French, and Portuguese became official languages.

BENIN
Benin used to be called Dahomey. Most of its people are farmers, and the chief products and exports are palm oil and kernels. There are about 50 different language groups.

GAMBIA
This small country is about 250 miles long (from east to west) and 31 miles wide. Gambia is very poor. It exports groundnuts.

GHANA
Ghana, formerly the Gold Coast, is the world's leading producer of cocoa. About 70 percent of the people are farmers, most of them growing food crops such as cassava, millet, maize, and yams. The wet southwest, which contains valuable forests, is also the main farming region. The people in the savanna lands in the center and north rear livestock. There are gold, diamond, manganese, and bauxite mines, and the manufacturing industries are developing.

GUINEA
The main resource of this poor country is bauxite (aluminum ore). There are mountains in the interior, which is cooler and drier than the hot humid coast. Most of the people are farmers. Main exports are coffee, palm products, and bananas.

GUINEA-BISSAU
Guinea-Bissau used to be Portuguese Guinea but became independent in 1974. Most of the people work on the land, and the main exports are palm products and groundnuts.

Accra, capital of Ghana, was built in the 1600s around European trading posts.

COUNTRY	CAPITAL	AREA (sq mi)	POPULATION (1988 est)	GOVERNMENT	MAJOR LANGUAGES	CURRENCY	INDEPENDENCE
Benin	Porto Novo	43,484	4,300,000	Republic	French	Franc	1960
Gambia	Banjul	4,361	800,000	Republic	English	Dalasi	1965
Ghana	Accra	92,100	14,000,000	Republic	English	Cedi	1957
Guinea	Conakry	94,926	6,500,000	Republic	French	Syli	1958
Guinea-Bissau	Bissau	13,948	900,000	Republic	Portuguese	Peso	1974
Ivory Coast	Abidjan	123,847	10,800,000	Republic	French	Franc	1960
Liberia	Monrovia	43,000	2,500,000	Republic	English	U.S. dollar	1847
Nigeria	Lagos	356,669	108,700,000	Republic	Hausa	Naira	1960
Senegal	Dakar	75,955	7,200,000	Republic	French	Franc	1960
Sierra Leone	Freetown	27,925	4,000,000	Republic	English	Leone	1961
Togo	Lomé	21,925	3,300,000	Republic	Native languages	Franc	1960

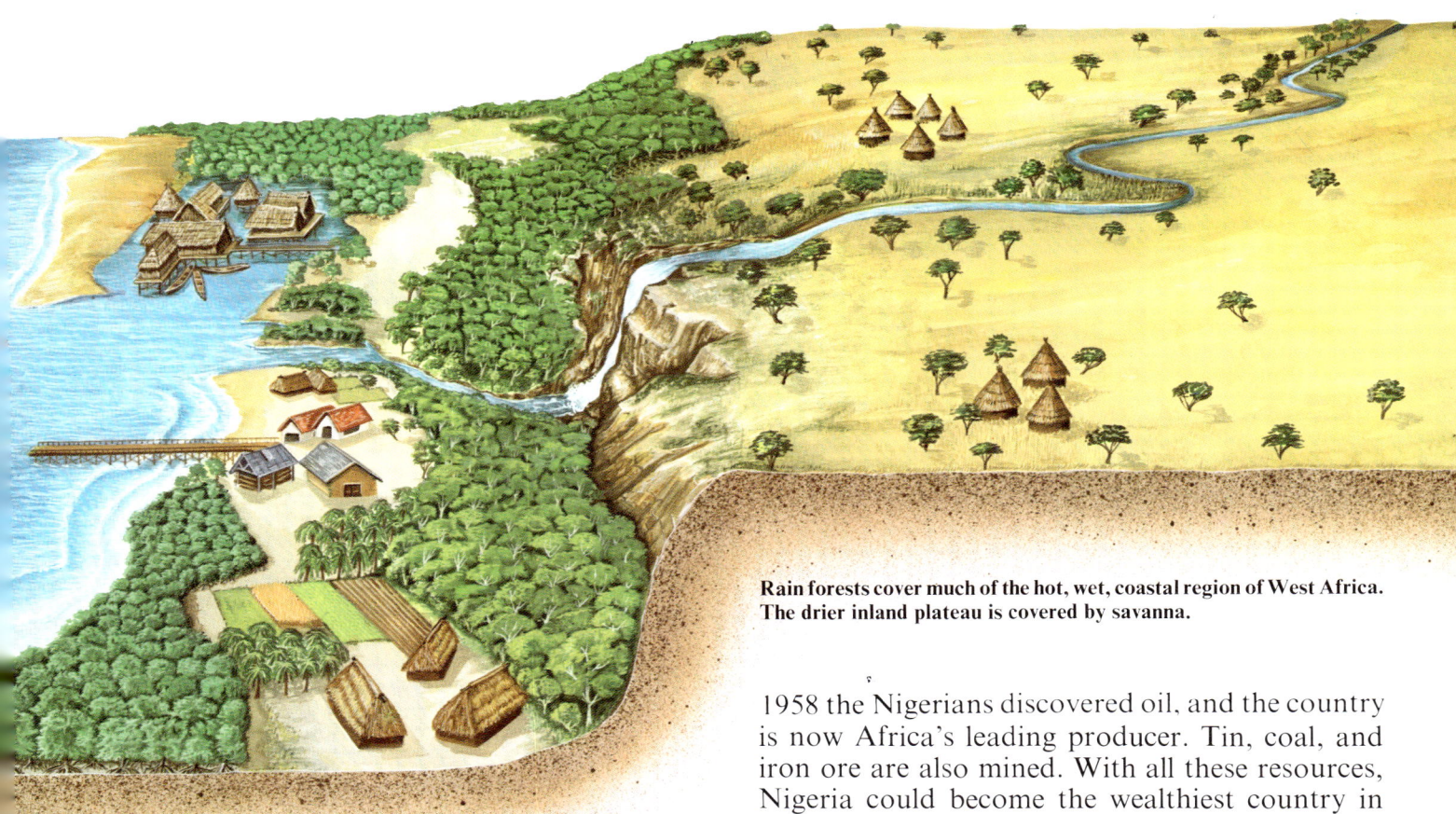

Rain forests cover much of the hot, wet, coastal region of West Africa. The drier inland plateau is covered by savanna.

IVORY COAST

Ivory Coast is one of the better-off of the West African countries. It is a major producer of coffee and cocoa, and timber is also important. The capital is Abidjan, which is the center for various manufacturing industries. Most of these are foreign-owned.

LIBERIA

There are about 50,000 people called Americo-Liberians in Liberia who run the country. They are descendants of freed American slaves who landed at Monrovia in 1822. But local people are becoming more involved in government. In 1980, Liberia's constitution was suspended following a military coup. The chief resources of this poor country are iron ore and rubber. It also derives much of its income from its large merchant navy.

NIGERIA

Nigeria has the largest population of all the countries in Africa. There are about 250 different groups of people. The largest are the Muslim Hausa and Fulani in the north, the Yoruba in the southwest, and the Ibo in the southeast. In 1967 the Ibo, afraid of northern domination, tried to set up their own country (Biafra). There was civil war until 1970, when Biafra surrendered.

Nigeria's landscape is very varied, from the semidesert far north to the rain-forested south. In 1958 the Nigerians discovered oil, and the country is now Africa's leading producer. Tin, coal, and iron ore are also mined. With all these resources, Nigeria could become the wealthiest country in Africa. Manufacturing is growing quickly, but most people are farmers. Farming products include rubber, timber, palm kernels, cocoa, and groundnuts.

SENEGAL

Senegal encloses Gambia. The two have not united because Gambia's culture is English, while Senegal's is French. The main products are groundnuts, fish, and phosphates. In the capital, Dakar, there are many factories, and film-making is important.

SIERRA LEONE

Freetown, the capital of Sierra Leone, was founded as a home for freed slaves. The British first took ex-slaves to the town in 1787, and later the country became a British territory. The present-day Creoles are the descendants of the slaves. There are about 42,000 of them. The original people of Sierra Leone fall into about 18 groups. Most people are farmers, producing coffee, cocoa, and palm kernels. Minerals, especially diamonds and iron ore, are the most valuable resources.

TOGO

There are 30 main groups of people in Togo. About 70 percent have traditional religions. The others are Christians or Muslims. The main products are phosphates, cocoa, and coffee, but Togo is a poor country. Most people can only grow enough food to feed their families.

Central Africa

Most of the people who live in central, eastern, and southern Africa are called the Bantu, which means "people." They speak languages that belong to the Bantu family.

Left: The map shows the nations of west central Africa. Zaire, the largest country (formerly Congo), is about two-thirds of the size of Western Europe.

ANGOLA
Area: 481,353 square miles
Population: 8,200,000 (1988 est)   **Capital:** Luanda
Government: Republic   **Independent:** 1975
Major Languages: Bantu languages   **Currency:** Kwanza

Until 1975 Angola was ruled by Portugal. Then it gained independence, and most of the Portuguese left. The interior of the country consists of savanna-covered tablelands. There is a narrow, fairly dry plain on the coast. Farming is the main source of income, and the chief crop is coffee. Cattle-rearing, fishing, and the mining of oil, diamonds, and iron ore are also important. In recent years there has been civil war between rival factions aided by Soviet, Cuban, South African and U.S. arms.

CAMEROON
Area: 183,569 square miles
Population: 10,400,000 (1988 est)   **Capital:** Yaoundé
Government: Federal Republic   **Independent:** 1960
Major Languages: French, English   **Currency:** Franc

There are over 200 groups of people in Cameroon. Each group has its own language and traditions, even if it consists of only a few families. The south of the country is wet and covered by forest. The uplands are covered by grassland and savanna. Mount Cameroon is the highest peak in West Africa. The people are poor and mostly farmers, producing coffee, cocoa, and cattle. There are also aluminum mines.

CENTRAL AFRICAN REPUBLIC
Area: 240,535 square miles
Population: 2,800,000 (1988 est)   **Capital:** Bangui
Government: Republic   **Independent:** 1960
Major Languages: French   **Currency:** Franc

The Central African Republic is landlocked. Most of it is flat tableland, rainy in the south and drier in the north. Coffee and cotton are the chief products and exports, but most of the people are poor. In 1976 the country was formally named an empire when its president declared himself emperor. But in 1979 it reverted to a republic.

CONGO
Area: 132,047 square miles
Population: 2,200,000 (1988 est)   **Capital:** Brazzaville
Government: Republic   **Independent:** 1960
Major Languages: French   **Currency:** Franc

The climate of Congo, which is on the Equator, is hot and wet. The coast is a grassy plain, and inland there are huge forests and swamps. Most people live in the south. The Kongo, the largest group, live around the capital, Brazzaville. The chief product is timber, and oil, diamonds, cocoa, coffee, and sugar are important. Congo was once ruled by France, with which it still has links.

EQUATORIAL GUINEA
Area: 10,831 square miles
Population: 310,000 (1988 est)   **Capital:** Malabo
Government: Republic   **Independent:** 1968
Major Languages: Spanish   **Currency:** Ekuele

Equatorial Guinea consists of an island, Macias Nguema (called Fernando Póo before it was named after the country's first president), and an area of mainland called Rio Muni, which is covered in thick rain forest. Fertile Macias Nguema produces cocoa and coffee.

GABON
Area: 103,347 square miles
Population: 1,300,000 (1988 est)   **Capital:** Libreville
Government: Republic   **Independent:** 1960
Major Languages: French   **Currency:** Franc

Much of west central Africa is covered by thick rain forest. There are many crocodile-infested rivers. The people live on the savanna around the forest edge or in forest clearings.

Luanda is the capital of Angola, which became an independent republic in 1975. It is a major seaport.

Gabon is on the Equator, a hot wet country covered by forests. By African standards it is quite prosperous, and produces oil, manganese, uranium, and timber.

SÃO TOMÉ AND PRINCIPE
Area: 372 square miles
Population: 100,000 (1988 est)   **Capital:** São Tomé
Government: Republic   **Independent:** 1975
Major Languages: Portuguese   **Currency:** Dobra

São Tomé and Principe is a group of volcanic islands in the Gulf of Guinea. The largest island is São Tomé. Cocoa is the chief product.

ZAIRE
Area: 905,567 square miles
Population: 31,900,000 (1988 est)   **Capital:** Kinshasa
Government: Republic   **Independent:** 1960
Major Languages: French   **Currency:** Zaire

Zaire is the second-largest nation in Africa, about two-thirds the size of Western Europe. It used to be called the Congo (like one of its neighbors). Among the 200 groups of people in Zaire are the pygmies who live in the forests in the center of the country. With so many groups of people, there have been problems and conflict. Much of the country is in the humid and hot Zaire River basin. In the north and south there are savanna lands. Mountains and lakes, including Lake Tanganyika, border the eastern part. Zaire's chief resources are copper and other minerals. But most of the people work on the land, producing palm products, coffee, and rubber for export.

East Africa

Right: The map shows the countries of eastern Africa.

Most of eastern Africa is tropical. The interior consists of high tablelands, which are comparatively cool. Around the coast there are hot and humid plains. The area is dominated by the East African Rift Valley, which was formed when the land sank between breaks in the Earth's crust. There are lakes in the valley and volcanoes along its edges.

Fishing is important in Mozambique, which has a larger coastal plain than other East African nations.

COUNTRY	CAPITAL	AREA (sq mi)	POPULATION (1988 est)	GOVERNMENT	MAJOR LANGUAGES	CURRENCY	INDEPEN-DENCE
Burundi	Bujumbura	10,747	5,000,000	Republic	Bantu languages	Franc	1962
Comoros	Dzaoudzi	838	400,000	Republic	Comoran, French	Franc	1975
Kenya	Nairobi	224,961	22,500,000	Republic	English, Swahili	Shilling	1963
Madagascar	Tananarive	226,658	10,700,000	Republic	French, Malagasy	Franc	1960
Malawi	Lilongwe	45,747	7,500,000	Republic	Chichewa, English	Kwacha	1964
Mauritius	Port Louis	790	1,200,000	Monarchy	English, French	Rupee	1968
Mozambique	Maputo	302,329	14,800,000	Republic	Portuguese	Metical	1975
Rwanda	Kigali	10,169	6,900,000	Republic	Kinyarwanda, French	Franc	1962
Seychelles	Victoria	171	100,000	Republic	English, Creole	Rupee	1976
Tanzania	Dodoma	364,900	23,600,000	Republic	Swahili, English	Shilling	1961
Uganda	Kampala	91,134	16,000,000	Republic	English, Swahili	Shilling	1962
Zambia	Lusaka	290,586	7,200,000	Republic	English, native languages	Kwacha	1964

BURUNDI
Burundi is a small, densely populated nation. It has three main groups of people: the Hutu farmers who speak Bantu; the Hamitic, cattle-rearing Tutsi; and a few pygmies. Most people are poor. The main product is coffee.

COMOROS
Comoros is a group of islands in the northern Mozambique Channel. It used to be a French territory, and the main activity is farming.

KENYA
Most of this beautiful country is a high tableland, but there are mountains and an arm of the East African Rift Valley, which contains a string of lakes. To the west, Lake Victoria fills a shallow depression in the plateau. With such magnificent scenery and national parks containing many wild animals, Kenya makes a great deal of money from tourism. Coffee and tea are also important, although nine-tenths of the land is too dry for cultivation. There are developing manufacturing industries. About 40 groups of African people and some Asians and Europeans live in Kenya. The largest groups are the Kikuyu and the Luo. However, one of the official languages of Kenya and Tanzania is Swahili, which is spoken by some Kenyans and is quite easy to learn.

MADAGASCAR
Madagascar is an island off the east coast of Africa. The people are a mixture of mainland Africans and Indonesians. In the east there are forests, in the center savanna, and in the southwest semidesert. Farming is important, and coffee, vanilla, and cloves are the chief crops.

MALAWI
Malawi is a very poor country; many of its people take jobs abroad. Part of the lake that Malawians call Lake Malawi is in neighboring Tanzania, where it is called Lake Nyasa. Malawi used to be called Nyasaland. Tobacco and tea are the most valuable products.

MAURITIUS
Mauritius is an island in the Indian Ocean. It has Africans, Chinese, Europeans, and people of mixed origin, but the largest group is Indian. The chief religions are Hinduism, Islam, and Christianity. Tea, tobacco, and vegetables are grown, but the main crop is sugarcane.

MOZAMBIQUE
Mozambique was a Portuguese territory, but it gained independence in 1975 and most of the Portuguese left the country. On the coast there are broad plains; inland lie tablelands and highlands. Most people are farmers. The chief exports are cashew nuts, copra (from coconuts), cotton, sugar, and tea. The ports Maputo (formerly Lourenço Marques), Beira, and Nacala handle the trade of inland African countries. Many people from Mozambique take jobs abroad, especially in South Africa.

RWANDA
Rwanda is a small and thickly populated country. About 90 percent of the people are Hutu, the rest are Tutsi or pygmy. The Tutsi used to rule Rwanda, but the Hutu rebelled against them in 1958. Since then, many Tutsi have been killed. Rwanda's main product is coffee, but it is a poor country.

SEYCHELLES
There are about 90 islands in the Seychelles, which is a nation in the Indian Ocean. The capital, Victoria, is on the largest island, Mahé. The people are African, Chinese, European, and of mixed origin. Copra and cinnamon are the chief products. Tourism is growing.

TANZANIA
Tanzania was formed in 1964 when mainland Tanganyika united with the island of Zanzibar. It is a large country, with some splendid national parks and Mount Kilimanjaro, Africa's highest mountain. There are about 125 groups of people and some Europeans and Asians. Most of the Tanzanians are farmers, and the most valuable products are sisal, cloves, coffee, and cotton.

UGANDA
Uganda, which surrounds Lake Victoria, has no coastline. Its main products are coffee, cotton, and tea. The largest group of people is the Baganda, but there are many others. In 1971 the army took over the government and General Idi Amin became president. His regime lasted for eight years, and during that time, many people were tortured and murdered and the economy collapsed. Amin was overthrown in 1979.

ZAMBIA
Zambia, once Northern Rhodesia, is a landlocked nation. Most of its people are farmers. The climate is pleasant in most of the country, which is tableland. However, some low-lying areas are very hot. There are six main languages and 66 dialects. Copper is the chief resource and accounts for more than 90 percent of the exports.

A Zambian dancer. About six out of every ten Zambians live in rural areas. They depend on farming for their living. But copper is the nation's most valuable resource.

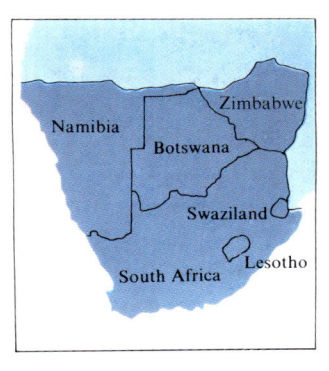

Above: The map shows the nations of southern Africa. Left: In the distance you can see Lake Kariba. It is on Zimbabwe's border with Zambia. It was formed by the building of the Kariba Dam.

Southern Africa

The pleasant climate and rich resources of southern Africa attract many European settlers. In South Africa about 17 percent of the people are of European origin, and in Zimbabwe about 5 percent. The other countries in this region all depend in some way on South Africa.

BOTSWANA
Area: 231,805 square miles
Population: 1,200,000 (1988 est)   **Capital:** Gaborone
Government: Republic   **Independent:** 1966
Major Languages: Bechuana, English   **Currency:** Pula

Botswana used to be called Bechuanaland. It is a vast country, and most of it is covered by a dry bush-covered plateau called the Kalahari Desert. Although Botswana has minerals, including diamonds, mining only began in the 1970s, and it is a poor country. Many people have to go to South Africa for work. The other major resource is cattle.

LESOTHO
Area: 11,720 square miles
Population: 1,560,000 (1988 est)   **Capital:** Maseru
Government: Monarchy   **Independent:** 1966
Major Languages: Sesotho, English   **Currency:** Maluti

Lesotho, formerly Basutoland, is one of Africa's poorest countries. Many of the people have to work in South Africa, which entirely surrounds Lesotho. It is a mountainous country, and the main products are cattle, mohair, and wool. Nearly all the people belong to the Basotho group.

NAMIBIA
Area: 318,261 square miles
Population: 1,300,000 (1988 est)   **Capital:** Windhoek
Government: Governed by South Africa
Major Languages: English, Afrikaans
Currency: South African rand

Namibia, formerly called South West Africa, is ruled by South Africa. The UN has condemned this rule and asked South Africa to grant Namibia independence. It is a large, dry country, containing the Namib Desert. About 12 percent of the people are Europeans. Minerals, especially diamonds, zinc, and lead, are the main resource.

SOUTH AFRICA
Area: 434,674 square miles
Population: 33,300,000 (1988 est)
Capitals: Cape Town, Pretoria
Government: Republic   **Independent:** 1910
Major Languages: English, Afrikaans   **Currency:** Rand

South Africa is the most powerful and industrialized nation in Africa. The center is mostly high, dry tableland, surrounded by mountains, plateaus, and coastal plains. There are four main groups of people in South Africa. About 70 percent are black Africans, of whom there are several groups, including the Zulu and the Xhosa. Some 17 percent are Europeans, or whites. Some of these are descended from early Dutch settlers and speak a language called Afrikaans. Others are descended from British, French, or German settlers. About 10 percent of the people are Coloreds (of mixed origin), and 3 percent are Asians.

Although the Europeans make up only 17 percent of the population, they control the government and business life of South Africa. They have a policy called *apartheid* (racial segregation), which tries to separate the people of South Africa. Marriages between people of different races are forbidden. Black African states called *homelands* have been set up. They cover only 13 percent of the country. Confrontation between blacks and the government increased during the late 1980s.

South Africa's manufacturing industries are the most important part of the economy. Minerals are also important; South Africa is the leading producer of gold, and asbestos, coal, diamonds, copper, iron, and uranium are also mined. Major farm products are cotton, dairy products, fruits, maize, meat, sugar, wheat, wine, and wool.

SWAZILAND
Area: 6,704 square miles
Population: 695,000 (1988 est)   **Capital:** Mbabane
Government: Monarchy   **Independent:** 1968
Major Languages: English, siSwati   **Currency:** Emalangeni

Swaziland has no coastline and is enclosed by South Africa and Mozambique. It is often called the Switzerland of Africa because of its beautiful mountain scenery. It is developing quickly, and sugar, timber, livestock, and minerals are its main products.

ZIMBABWE
Area: 150,804 square miles
Population: 9,000,000 (1988 est)   **Capital:** Harare
Government: Republic
Major Languages: English, native languages   **Currency:** Dollar

Zimbabwe is the former British colony of Southern Rhodesia. It became a self-governing British colony in 1923 and was ruled by the European settlers. But 95 percent of the population are black Africans (the largest groups are the Ndebele and the Shona), so this government was not representative of the majority of the people. It was for this reason that Britain refused to grant independence to Rhodesia in the early 1960s when the Rhodesian whites asked for it. In 1965 Rhodesia declared itself independent, but Britain and the UN said that this act was illegal. Finally, in 1979, the ruling government withdrew. In 1980, with a properly representative government, the country gained independence as the Republic of Zimbabwe. Zimbabwe is a relatively prosperous country. Its main exports are tobacco, asbestos, copper, chrome ore, clothing, and meat.

Above: A miner in a South African gold mine. South Africa is the world's top gold producer, and gold is the country's most valuable export.

Below: Zulu women in beaded headdresses at a festival. The Zulus are the largest single group of black African people in South Africa. There are more than 4 million of them.

OCEANIA

Wake Is (US)
Mariana Is
Guam (US)
Marshall Is (US)
Caroline Islands (US)

Equator

NAURU

Arafura Sea

Bismarck Archipelago
PAPUA NEW GUINEA
▲ Mt Wilhelm
■ Port Moresby

Solomon Is

Tuvalu Is

• Darwin

Coral Sea

Vanuatu

FIJI
Suva

INDIAN OCEAN

• Roebourne
• Townsville
• Cloncurry

New Caledonia (Fr)
■ Noumea

Gt Sandy Desert

Northern Territory

A U S T R A L I A

• Alice Springs

Queensland

Gibson Desert

Western Australia

• Kalgoorlie

Gt Victoria Desert

South Australia

Nullarbor Plain

L. Eyre

Toowoomba •   • Brisbane

Darling

New South Wales

• Newcastle
• Sydney
• Wollongong

G R E A T   D I V I D I N G   R A N G E

Tasman Sea

• Perth
• Albany

Great Australian Bight

• Adelaide

Murray

■ Canberra ▲
Victoria
• Ballarat
• Geelong • Melbourne
Mt Kosciusko

NEW ZEALAND
• Auckland
• Hamilton
• Rotorua

• Nelson
■ Welli...

Tasmania
• Launceston
• Hobart

South Is
▲ Mt Cook
• Christchurch

• Invercargill   • Dunedin

| 0 | 400 | 800 | 1200 miles |
| 0 | 400 | 800 | 1200 | 1600 kilometers |

■ Capital Cities

OCEANIA

The greater part of Oceania is Australia, much of which is empty desert. For this reason the continent has a low average population density. The next two countries in order of size are Papua New Guinea and New Zealand. Both have more people per square mile than Australia, though neither is densely populated. There are also about 30,000 Pacific Ocean islands. Some, like Fiji and Western Samoa, are fairly densely populated. Others are uninhabited.

FACTS AND FIGURES

Area: 3,290,000 square miles.
Population: 25,000,000
Population Density: 7.3 per square mile. On average, it is the most thinly populated continent, excepting Antarctica.
Countries: Oceania consists of Australia, New Zealand, Papua New Guinea, and more than 30,000 Pacific islands. Australia covers nine-tenths of the area of Oceania.
Highest Peaks: Mount Kosciusko, 7,310 feet above sea level, is Australia's highest peak; Mount Cook, 12,349 feet above sea level, is New Zealand's; and Mount Wilhelm, 14,793 feet above sea level, is Papua New Guinea's.
Lowest Point on Land: Lake Eyre, Australia, is 52 feet below sea level.
Longest Rivers: The longest river system is the Murray River and its tributaries in Australia. The Murray is 8,448 miles long. The Darling, one of its tributaries, is 8,104 miles long.

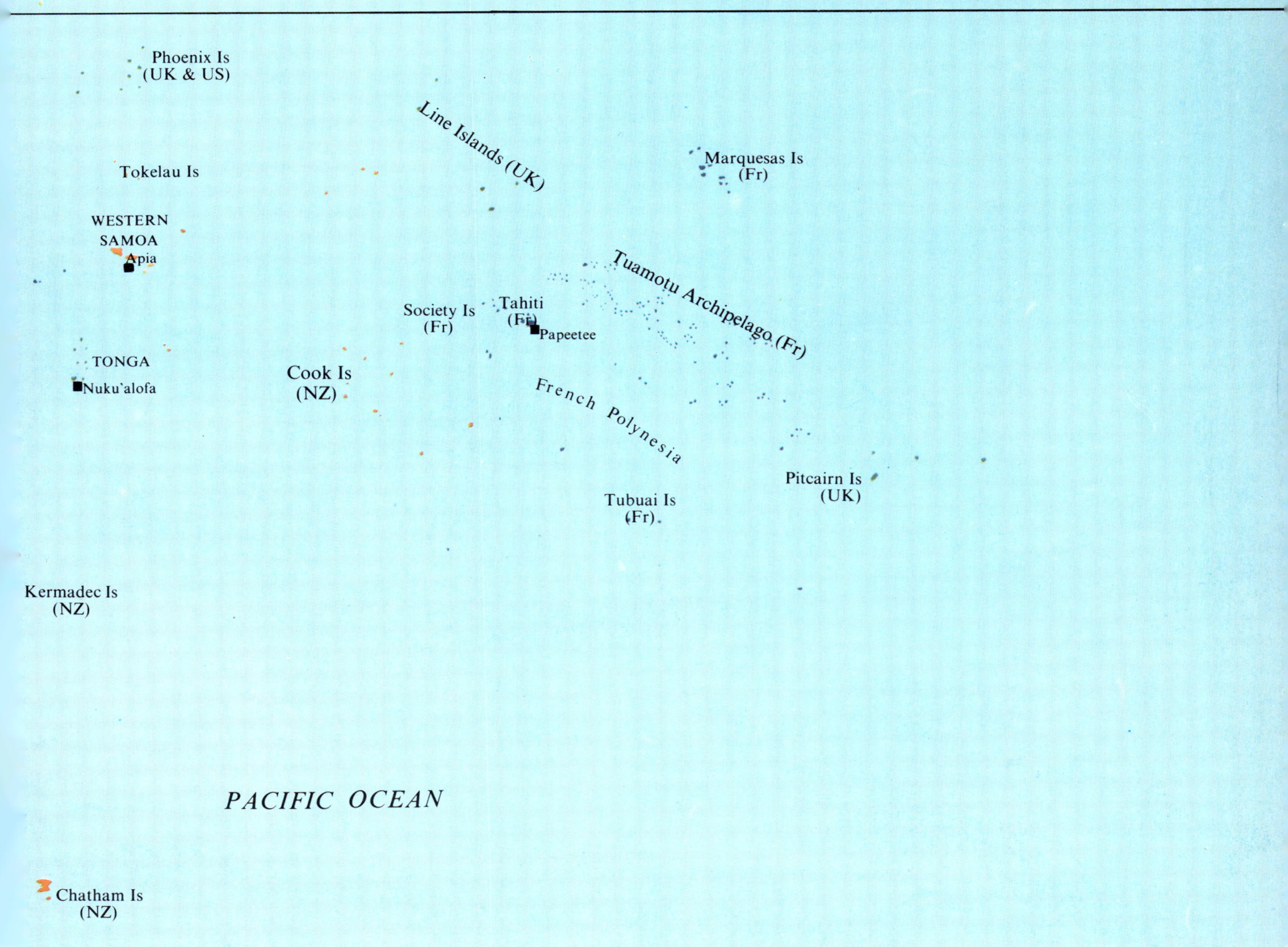

Phoenix Is (UK & US)
Tokelau Is
Line Islands (UK)
Marquesas Is (Fr)
WESTERN SAMOA — Apia
Tuamotu Archipelago (Fr)
Society Is (Fr) · Tahiti (Fr) Papeetee
TONGA — Nuku'alofa
Cook Is (NZ)
French Polynesia
Pitcairn Is (UK)
Tubuai Is (Fr)
Kermadec Is (NZ)

PACIFIC OCEAN

Chatham Is (NZ)

Australia

Left: Australia is the largest nation in Oceania.

Above left: A kangaroo carries its young in a pouch. Animals that do this are called *marsupials*.

Above: Ayers Rock is a massive sandstone inselberg (island mountain) in central Australia.

Area: 2,967,909 square miles
Population: 16,300,000 (1988 est) **Capital:** Wellington
Government: Monarchy
Major Languages: English   **Currency:** Dollar

Australia is the sixth-largest country in the world, but there are on average only about five people to every square mile. More than half of the people live in the four largest cities (Sydney, Melbourne, Brisbane, and Adelaide) and much of the island is empty desert.

Australia is a very flat country. To the west there are plateaus, most of which are desert. The vast, dry plains in the center provide pasture for huge herds of cattle. There are highlands in the east and southeast. Here there are sheep and dairy farming and mining. There is a fertile area around Perth in the southwest. The famous Great Barrier Reef, the largest coral reef in the world, runs along the northeastern coast.

The first people in Australia were probably the Tasmanian Aborigines. They were driven south to the island of Tasmania by the Australian Aborigines, who originated in Asia. There were about 2,000 in Tasmania in the late 1700s but by 1876 they had died out. The Australian Aborigines declined in number when they came into contact with European settlers. There were about 300,000

STATES AND TERRITORIES OF AUSTRALIA

STATE OR TERRITORY	AREA (sq mi)	POP. (1988 est)	CAPITAL
Australian Capital Terr.	939	247,000	Canberra
New South Wales	309,433	5,500,000	Sydney
Northern Terr.	520,280	139,000	Darwin
Queensland	667,000	2,510,000	Brisbane
South Australia	380,070	1,360,000	Adelaide
Tasmania	26,383	438,000	Hobart
Victoria	87,884	4,100,000	Melbourne
Western Australia	975,920	1,390,000	Perth

Beyond the eastern Pacific coast of Australia (far right), the land rises to form the Great Dividing Range, or eastern highlands. Rain that falls on the highlands seeps down through sloping rocks beneath the dry plains of central Australia. There, artesian wells bring it to the surface. To the west (far left), the land is desert.

Artesian Well

Above: The dry limestone Nullarbor Plain in southern Australia. Few people live there apart from some small settlements along the railway line.

Above: A beautiful Aborigine shield and boomerang. Once, all Aborigines lived a nomadic existence, hunting for food and water.

in the late 1700s. Now there are about 100,000 and many are of mixed blood. In 1788 Britain set up a convict settlement in Sydney. The first free settlers arrived in 1793, and the numbers of British immigrants soon increased, especially during gold rushes of the late 1860s and 1890s. After the Second World War, settlers began to arrive from other European countries.

The most valuable industries are manufacturing and mining. Australia is a leading producer of bauxite, iron ore, and lead, as well as mining other metals, coal, and oil. Australia's 150 million sheep mean that woolen goods are also important. There are 30 million cattle, and beef and dairy products are major exports. Only 2 percent of the land is used for crop-growing, but the yields are high. The many climates in Australia (from the tropical north to temperate Tasmania) enable a variety of crops to be produced.

Above: An aerial view of Sydney, the capital of New South Wales and the largest city in Australia.

Water-bearing Rock

New Zealand and the Pacific Islands

Right: Maori carvings.

The islands in the Pacific Ocean are named according to their original inhabitants. These names are Melanesia, Micronesia, and Polynesia. *Melanesia* means "black islands," and the people on these islands have dark skin and frizzy hair. This group includes Papua New Guinea, the Solomon Islands, and Fiji. *Micronesia* means "little islands." The Micronesian islands are north of Melanesia and include Nauru and Wake, the Caroline, Kiribati, Mariana, and Marshall islands. The people have straight hair and copper-colored skin. *Polynesia*, which means "many islands," spreads over a wide area. It is bounded by New Zealand in the southwest, Easter Island in the southeast, and Hawaii in the north. The Polynesians are taller than the other Pacific Islanders and have light-brown skin. They include the Maoris of New Zealand.

Oceania does not include Japan, Indonesia, or the Philippines, which are all parts of Asia; nor does it include islands near the Americas.

The city of Auckland is the largest in New Zealand and is a major port and manufacturing center. It is built on an isthmus in the northern part of North Island.

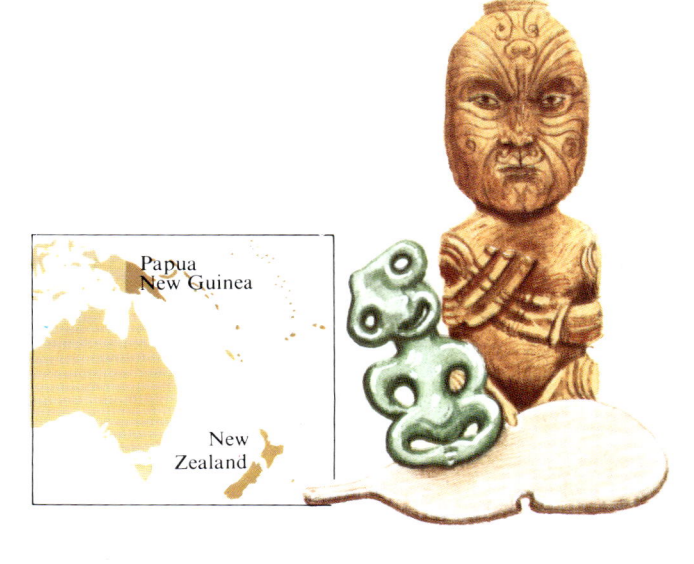

NEW ZEALAND
Area: 103,883 square miles
Population: 3,400,000 (1988 est)   **Capital:** Wellington
Government: Monarchy
Major Languages: English, Maori   **Currency:** Dollar

Two large islands, the North and South islands, and several smaller islands make up New Zealand. Probably the Maoris settled there about 600 years ago. In 1642, the Dutch sea captain Abel Tasman was attacked by them and driven away. Captain Cook arrived in 1769 and made friends with the Maoris. But when British people began to settle in New Zealand in the 1800s, the Maoris fought them, and there were wars between 1845 and 1879. Many Maoris died, and in 1869 only 42,000 were left. However, there are over 250,000 today.

SOME ISLAND TERRITORIES IN OCEANIA				
TERRITORY	CAPITAL	AREA (sq mi)	POPULATION (1988 est)	GOVERNMENT
Cook Islands	Avarua	91	18,000	Self-governing New Zealand territory
Fiji	Suva	7,055	700,000	Monarchy in British Commonwealth, independent 1970
Kiribati	Tarawá	291	63,000	Republic
Nauru	Nauru	8.2	8,200	Republic, independent 1968
New Caledonia	Noumea	7,358	148,000	French overseas territory
Papua New Guinea	Port Moresby	178,703	3,700,000	Monarchy, independent 1978
Solomon Islands	Honiara	11,506	300,000	British protectorate until independence in 1978
Tonga	Nuku'alofa	270	108,000	Monarchy, independent 1970
Tuvalu	Funafuti	10	8,100	British colony
Western Samoa	Apia	1,097	200,000	Monarchy, independent 1962

About 70 percent of New Zealanders live on the North Island, many of them on the fertile plains by the coast. Wellington, the capital, is on North Island, as is the largest city, Auckland. There are some mountains and several active volcanoes. There are many more mountains on the South Island (including the highest peak, Mount Cook), as well as numerous glaciers and ice fields. On the eastern coast there are fertile plains.

The climate is mild on the whole. Two-thirds of the people live in towns, but farming is the main activity. The farms are very efficient. There are about 56 million sheep, 10 million cattle, and 500,000 pigs, so leading exports are wool, beef, lamb, mutton, and dairy products. There is also some crop-farming, including cereals, fruits, tobacco, and vegetables. Many of the manufacturing industries process farm products and timber. There is some coal, iron ore, and oil, but most of New Zealand's electricity comes from hydro-electric power stations.

FIJI
Some 800 volcanic islands, most of them surrounded by coral reefs, make up Fiji. Viti Levu is the largest one. There are large Fijian and Indian communities, and some Europeans, Chinese, and other Pacific Islanders. Sugar, gold, and coconut oil are the main products.

NAURU
Nauru is a small coral island in Micronesia. It exports phosphates to Australia, New Zealand, and Japan. It imports food.

PAPUA NEW GUINEA
Papua New Guinea is made up of the eastern part of New Guinea (once ruled by Australia), islands of the Bismarck Archipelago, and Bougainville in the Solomon Islands. The climate is tropical. The interior mountains are heavily forested, and the plains are humid and hot. The main group of people are Melanesian, but there are some Negritos. Most of them live in the grassy valleys between the mountain ranges. Coconut and copra products, coffee beans, cocoa beans, and timber are the chief exports. Some manufacturing industries process farm products.

TONGA
Tonga is also known as the Friendly Islands. It is a Polynesian island group – the islands are made either of volcanic rock or of coral. Copra and bananas are the chief products.

WESTERN SAMOA
This is a Polynesian nation, which from 1920 to 1962 was ruled by New Zealand. The islands are volcanic and mountainous, and coral reefs border their coasts. Western Samoa's chief products are cocoa, bananas, and copra.

A market at Rabaul, which is a seaport of New Britain. It is in the Bismarck Archipelago, part of Papua New Guinea.

INDEX

A
Aborigine 50, 134, 135
Abu Dhabi 115
Acacia 29
Accra 124
Aconcagua, Mount 93, 99
Addis Ababa 122
Adelaide 134
Aegean Sea 38
Afghanistan 100, 114
Africa 9, 14, 27, 29, 30, 31, 34, 49, 50, 52, 53, 54, 55, 60, 61, 118–131
Air 12, 13, 20, 21
Air pressure 13, 20
Alaska 41, 83, 86, 87
Albania 62, 78
Algeria 42, 49, 52, 118, 120
Algiers 120
Alps 30, 31, 61, 70, 72, 74, 76
Alsace 73
Aluminum ore *see* Bauxite
Amazon, river 14, 44, 93, 96, 97
Amman 117
Amphibian 11, 27, 33
Amsterdam 69
Amur, river 101
Andes Mountains 14, 30, 31, 60, 92, 93, 94, 96, 97, 99
Andorra 62, 72, 73
Angola 118, 126
Animal life 10, 11, 13, 15, 18, 22, 23, 27, 28, 29, 32–33, 46, 49
Ankara 117
Antarctica 23, 24, 31, 44, 45, 60, 98
Anteater 32
Antelope 32
Anticyclone 20
Antwerp 68
Apennine Mountains 76
Appalachian Mountains 86
Aquitaine 73
Archipelago 108, 109, 137
Arctic 16, 22, 34, 61, 62, 63, 65
Arctic fox 22
Arctic hare 22
Ardennes 68, 69
Argentina 49, 92, 93, 98–99
Arizona 60, 86
Asbestos 84, 102, 131
Asia 9, 22, 27, 29, 30, 34, 51, 52, 54, 55, 60, 61, 63, 84, 86, 100–117
Aso, Mount 14
Assal, Lake 119
Asteroid 8
Asunción 98, 99
Atacama Desert 99
Athens 75
Atlantic Ocean 34, 35, 57, 61, 64, 65, 72, 75
Atlas Mountains 120, 121
Atmosphere 10, 12, 13
Atomic power 59
Auckland 136, 137
Australasia 32, 33, 34, 49, 52
Australia 29, 31, 34, 50, 52, 53, 54, 55, 58, 60, 132, 133, 134–135
Austria 31, 74
Automobile industry 72, 76, 77, 81, 86, 104
Avalanche 40
Ayers Rock 134

B
Baghdad 114
Bahamas 82, 90
Bahrain 100, 115
Baikal, Lake 14
Baltic Sea 16, 79, 80
Bananas 55, 91, 94, 95, 97, 109, 123, 124, 137
Bangkok 106
Bangladesh 49, 100, 110, 112
Baobab 29
Barbados 82, 90
Barcelona 77
Barley 54, 55, 73, 77, 78, 79, 85, 99, 102, 104, 120, 121
Basel 74
Bat 46
Bauxite 18, 58, 59, 91, 95, 108, 124, 126, 135
Beaufort scale 21
Beech tree 26
Beirut 117
Belfast 66
Belgium 62, 68, 69
Belgrade 74
Belize 90
Belo Horizonte 97
Benelux 69
Benin 118, 124
Ben Nevis 66
Bering Sea 57, 80, 84
Berlin 70
Bern 74
Bhutan 100, 110
Birch tree 26
Bird life 10, 11, 22, 23, 27, 32
Birmingham 66
Bison 29
Black Sea 63
Blanc, Mont 72
Bogota 94
Bohemia 78
Bolivia 58, 92, 97
Bombay 112
Bonn 70
Bordeaux 72
Borneo 108
Botswana 118, 130
Brahmaputra, river 110, 112
Brasilia 96, 97
Brazil 49, 92, 93, 96–97
Bremen 70
Brisbane 134
British Columbia 85
British Isles 66–67
Bruges 68
Brunei 100, 108
Brussels 68
Bucharest 79
Budapest 79
Buenos Aires 98
Bulgaria 78, 79, 80
Burma 100, 106
Burundi 118, 128
Bushmen 49, 50
Butterfly 27

C
Cactus 18
Cairo 120
Calcutta 112
California 41, 83, 86
Cambodia 100, 106
Camel 49, 123
Campine 68
Canada 14, 44, 49, 52, 58, 60, 82, 84–85
Canton 102, 103
Cape Town 130
Caracas 95
Carbon dioxide 13, 46
Caribbean Sea 82, 83
Carlsbad Caverns 46
Caspian Sea 14, 63, 80, 101
Cassava 55, 94, 124
Cattle 54, 61, 86, 94, 97, 98, 99, 102, 104, 112, 123, 126, 128, 130, 134, 137
Caucasoid race 50, 104
Caucasus Mountains 63
Caves 46–47
Central African Republic 118, 126
Central America 32, 54, 55, 60, 83, 90–91
Cereal crops 53, 54–55, 68, 69, 70, 73, 74, 75, 76, 77, 78, 79, 85, 86, 87, 91, 94, 95, 97, 98, 99, 102, 104, 105, 106, 108, 109, 110, 112, 113, 114, 116, 117, 120, 121, 123, 124, 131, 137
Chad 118, 122
Chemical industry 64, 70, 72, 74, 76, 120
Chicago 52, 87
Chile 58, 92, 93, 99
Chimpanzee 27
China 30, 41, 49, 51, 53, 60, 69, 78, 79, 80, 86, 100, 101, 102, 110
Climate 12, 16–17, 18, 19, 20
Cloud 9, 12, 21
Coal mining 58, 65, 66, 70, 72, 78, 79, 80, 86, 102, 104, 106, 108, 112, 135, 137
Cocoa 54, 94, 95, 97, 124, 125, 126, 127, 137
Coconut 54, 55, 108, 109, 112, 113, 129, 137
Coffee 54, 90, 91, 94, 95, 97, 108, 115, 124, 125, 126, 127, 128, 137
Cologne 70
Colombia 92, 94
Colombo 113
Colorado, river 60
Columbus, Christopher 90, 94
Comoros 118, 128
Congo 118, 127
Coniferous forests 18, 19, 26, 27, 64, 65, 85
Continental shelf 10, 34, 35, 56, 57
Continents 10, 15, 16, 24, 42, 60–61
    Africa 118–131
    Antarctica 22–23
    Asia 100–117
    Europe 62–81
    North America 83–91
    Oceania 132–137
    South America 92–99
Cook, Mount 133
Copenhagen 64
Copper 58, 59, 78, 84, 86, 97, 99, 104, 109, 129, 131
Coral 34, 84, 86, 134, 137

Corinth Canal 75
Costa Rica 90
Cotopaxi 30
Cotton 54, 86, 90, 91, 94, 97, 99, 102, 106, 112, 113, 114, 115, 117, 120, 122, 123, 126, 129, 131
Cracow 79
Crete 75
Crocodile 33, 127
Crust, Earth's 10, 35, 38, 39, 40
Cuba 90
Currents, ocean 16, 35, 36–37
Cyprus 100, 114, 116
Czechoslovakia 78, 80

D
Dacca 110
Damascus 117
Danube, river 63, 74, 78, 79
Darling, river 133
Dates 114, 121
Dead Sea 101
Death Valley 83, 86
Deccan plateau 112
Deciduous forests 19, 26, 32
Delhi 112
Delta 45, 106, 110
Denmark 61, 64
Desalination plant 57
Desert 15, 16, 18, 19, 24–25, 28, 29, 42, 55, 86, 99, 102, 103, 114, 115, 116, 118, 119, 120, 121, 122, 123, 130, 134
Developing countries 48, 52–53, 54, 60
Diamonds 95, 125, 126, 127, 130, 131
Dinosaur 11
Djakarta 108
Djibouti 118, 119, 122
Dodoma 118
Dolomite Mountains 31
Dominican Republic 90
Dortmund 70
Dresden 70
Dubai 115
Dublin 67
Duck 22
Duisberg 70
Dusseldorf 70
Dyke 69

E
Earth 8, 9, 10, 11, 12, 13, 14, 15, 30, 31
Earthquake 40–41, 65, 104
Echidna 32
Ecuador 30, 92, 94
Edinburgh 66
Egypt 55, 118, 120
Elba 76
Elbe, river 78
Elbruz, Mount 63
Electrical industries 69, 104
Electricity 44, 59, 65, 72, 137
Elephant 27
Elephant grass 29
Elm tree 26
El Salvador 90
Engineering 64, 65, 72, 74
England 66
Equator 9, 12, 16, 36, 94
Equatorial Guinea 118, 127
Erosion 24, 42–43
Eskimo 22, 51, 84
Essen 70
Estuary 44
Ethiopia 118, 122
Etna, Mount 76
Euphrates, river 114
Europe 9, 22, 30, 31, 34, 35, 45, 49, 50, 52, 54, 55, 60, 61, 62–81, 101

European Economic Community 68, 70
Everest, Mount 10, 14, 30, 101, 102, 113
Exosphere 12, 13
Eyre, Lake 133

F
Farming 18, 19, 24, 28, 48, 49, 52, 53, 54–55, 60, 63–137
Fault 31, 38, 40, 41
Fiber crops 54, 73, 87, 90, 91, 94, 97, 99, 102, 106, 110, 112, 113, 114, 115, 117, 120, 122, 123, 126, 129, 131
Fiji 34, 132, 137
Finland 61, 64, 65
Fish, fishing 11, 22, 32, 33, 56–57, 64, 65, 73, 75, 77, 85, 91, 97, 102, 104, 105, 109, 112, 113, 115, 121, 125, 126
Fjords 64, 65
Flax 54, 73
Florence 77
Food processing 64, 65, 75, 99, 137
Forecasting, weather 9, 20, 21
Forestry 65, 73, 77, 85, 102, 103, 108, 110, 113
Forests 18, 19, 26–27, 29, 32, 64, 65, 74, 85, 95, 96, 97, 99, 101, 104, 105, 109, 119, 124, 125, 126, 137
Fossils 10, 31
France 62, 72–73
Frankfurt 70
French Guiana 92, 93, 94
Frog 33
Frost 42
Fruit growing 48, 54, 55, 70, 72, 74, 75, 76, 77, 78, 79, 85, 91, 94, 95, 97, 98, 99, 104, 114, 116, 117, 120, 121, 131, 137
Fuji, Mount 104
Fulmar 23

G
Gabon 118, 127
Galaxy 8, 9
Gambia 118, 124
Ganges, river 110, 112
Gas 8, 9, 10, 12, 13, 38, 39
  production 52, 56, 58, 59, 66, 72, 79, 80, 86, 97, 114, 120
Geneva 74
Germany 62, 63, 70, 71, 80
Geyser 14, 65
Ghana 118, 124
Ghent 68
Gibbon 27
Giraffe 29, 32
Glacier 14, 15, 44, 45, 46, 64, 65
Glasgow 66
Goats 102, 104, 123
Gold 58, 59, 84, 94, 95, 124, 131, 135, 137
Gorilla 27, 32
Gothenberg 65
Grand Canyon 60, 86
Grasslands 18, 19, 28–29, 95, 98, 119, 126, 127, 128
Gravity 8, 10, 13, 36, 37, 45
Great Barrier Reef 34, 134
Great Dividing Range 31, 134–135
Great Lakes 83, 84, 86
Great Wall (China) 103
Greece 62, 75
Greenland 22, 64
Groundnuts 55, 102, 122, 123, 124, 125
Guadalajara 91
Guatemala 90

Guinea 58, 118, 124
Guinea-Bissau 118, 124
Gulf Stream 35, 37, 65
Guyana 92, 95

H
Haiti 90
Hamburg 70
Hammada 24
Hanoi 106
Harare 118, 131
Hawaii 31, 39, 86
Hedgehog 33
Helium 13
Helsinki 64
Hemp 54
Himalayas 14, 30, 31, 101, 112, 113
Hippopotamus 32
Hokkaido 104
Holland see Netherlands
Honduras 91
Hong Kong 48, 101, 103
Honshu 104
Hops 70, 78
Humidity 20
Hungary 78, 79, 80
Hurricane 9
Husky dog 22
Hwang Ho, river 101, 102
Hydroelectric power 44, 59, 65, 72, 137
Hydrogen 13

I
Ice 15, 22, 23, 42, 44, 45, 64, 65
Iceberg 45
Icebreaker 16
Iceland 14, 22, 64, 65
India 29, 30, 49, 51, 60, 61, 100, 110–112
Indian Ocean 34, 61
Indians, American 51, 84, 86, 90, 91, 93, 94, 96, 97
Indonesia 14, 38, 49, 58, 100, 108
Indus, river 112, 113
Industry 48, 52, 53, 60, 63–137
Ionosphere 13
Iran 14, 100, 114
Iraq 100, 114
Ireland 62, 67
Iron ore 16, 58, 59, 65, 66, 69, 72, 74, 78, 79, 80, 84, 86, 97, 99, 102, 104, 112, 125, 126, 131, 135, 137
Irrawaddy, river 106
Irrigation 55, 114, 116, 117, 123
Islamabad 113
Israel 52, 50, 100, 101, 114, 116
Italy 31, 62, 72, 75, 76
Ivory Coast 118, 125

J
Jaguar 27
Jamaica 58, 82, 91
Japan 14, 49, 52, 58, 60, 86, 101, 104
Java 38, 100, 108
Jerusalem 116
Jordan 100, 117
Jungle 26, 27
Jute 106, 110, 112
Jutland 64

K
Kabul 114
Kalahari Desert 130
Kampala 128, 129
Kangaroo 32, 134
Karachi 113
Karakoram Range 30
Karakuls 114
Kariba Dam 130
Karl-Marx-Stadt 70

139

Kashmir 112
Kathmandu 113
Kenya 118, 119, 128
Khartoum 123
Kilimanjaro, Mount 119
Koala 32
Korea 100, 104, 105
Krakatoa 14, 38
Kremlin 81
Kuala Lumpur 108
Kuwait 100, 115
Kyoto 104
Kyushu 104

L
Labrador Current 35
Lagos 125
Lahore 113
Landslide 40
Languages 50–51
Laos 100, 106
La Paz 97
Lapland, Lapps 22, 65
Lava 38, 39, 46
Lead 58, 59, 80, 84, 86, 97, 130, 135
Lebanon 100, 114, 117
Leipzig 70
Lemming 22
Lemur 32, 33
Lena, river 101
Leningrad 80
Lesotho 118, 130
Liberia 118, 125
Libya 118, 121
Lichen 19
Liechtenstein 74
Liège 68
Light-year 8
Lignite 70, 74, 78
Lille 72
Lima 97
Limestone 31, 43, 44, 46–47, 56, 135
Lion 32
Lisbon 77
Livestock farming 54, 61, 66, 67, 68, 73, 74, 85, 86, 94, 97, 98, 99, 102, 103, 104, 112, 114, 120, 122, 123, 126, 128, 130, 134, 135, 137
Llama 96, 97
Loire, river 73
Lombardy plain 76
Low Countries 68–69
Luanda 127
Luxembourg 62, 68, 69
Lyon 72

M
Macao 100, 101, 103
Macedonia 75
Machu Picchu 60
McKinley, Mount 83
Madagascar 118, 128
Madras 112
Madrid 77
Magnesium 56, 57
Mahogany 27
Maize 54, 55, 76, 79, 86, 91, 94, 95, 97, 99, 102, 106, 113, 124, 131
Malawi 118, 129
Malaysia 58, 100, 108
Maldive Islands 100, 112
Mali 118, 122
Malta 77
Mammals 10, 11, 27, 32, 33
Manchester 66
Manchuria 102
Manganese 80, 124, 127
Manila 109
Maori 136
Maracaibo, Lake 93, 95
Marseille 72

Mauna Loa 31
Mauritania 118, 123
Mauritius 118, 129
Mediterranean region 62, 63, 72, 73, 75–77, 120, 121
Mekong, river 101
Melanesia 136
Melbourne 134
Mesosphere 12
Mexico 60, 82, 83, 90, 91
Micronesia 136, 137
Mid-Atlantic Ridge 30, 35
Milan 77
Millet 98, 102, 112, 122, 123, 124
Minerals, mining 16, 56, 57, 58–59, 63–137
Mississippi, river 83
Missouri, river 83
Monaco 62, 72, 73
Mongolia 100, 103
Mongoloid race 50, 51, 104
Monkey 27, 32
Mons 68
Monte Carlo 73
Montevideo 99
Montreal 84
Moon 8, 36, 37
Moraine 64, 65
Morocco 118, 121
Moscow 80, 81
Moss 19, 22
Mountain building 14, 15, 16, 30–31, 42
Mozambique 118, 128, 129
Munich 70
Murray, river 133

N
Nagoya 104
Nairobi 128, 129
Namibia 118, 130
Namur 68
Naples 77
Narvik 16
Nauru 132, 137
Neagh, Loch 66
Negroid race 50
Neon 13
Nepal 14, 100, 102, 113
Netherlands 62, 68, 69
New Delhi 110
Newfoundland 85
New Guinea 50, 108
New Mexico 46
Newt 46
New York 87, 89
New Zealand 14, 29, 39, 52, 54, 60, 61, 132, 133, 136
Niagara Falls 44
Nicaragua 91
Nicosia 116
Niger 118, 123
Nigeria 49, 118, 125
Nile, river 14, 44, 45, 55, 93, 119, 120, 123
Nitrogen 12, 13
Noctuid moth 46
Nomad 24, 29, 65, 103, 115, 122
North America 14, 22, 28, 29, 31, 32, 34, 35, 45, 52, 55, 60, 82–91
North Atlantic Drift 16
Northern Ireland 66
North Sea 56, 57, 65
Norway 16, 61, 64, 65

O
Oak tree 26
Oats 54, 55, 73, 85, 86
Ob, river 101
Oceania 52, 60, 61, 132–137
Oceans 10, 16, 22, 34–35, 36–37, 39, 40, 57, 60, 61, 64, 65, 72, 75, 86
Oil 56, 58–59, 65, 66, 69, 72, 78, 79, 80, 84, 86, 91, 94, 95, 97, 99, 102, 108, 109, 114, 115, 117, 120, 121, 125, 126, 127, 135, 137
Oil seed crops 54, 55, 75, 76, 77, 78, 79, 87, 97, 99, 102, 104, 108, 109, 121, 122, 124, 125
Olives 54, 55, 75, 76, 78, 120
Olympus, Mount 75
Oman 100, 115
Ontario, Lake 84
Orangutan 27
Orinoco, river 95
Osaka 104
Oslo 65
Ostrich 32
Ottawa 84
Oxbow lake 45
Oxygen 12, 13
Ozone layer 12, 13, 97

P
Pacific Ocean 34, 35, 39, 60, 61, 86
Pacific Ocean Islands 132, 133, 137
Pakistan 49, 100, 110, 112, 113
Palm oil 108, 109, 124, 125, 127
Pampas 29, 98
Panama 82, 83, 91
Paper industry 27, 65
Papua New Guinea 132, 133, 137
Paraguay 92, 99
Paris 72, 73
Patagonia 99
Peking 102
Penguin 23
Perth 134
Peru 58, 60, 92, 93, 97
Petroleum *see* Oil
Philippines 101, 108, 109
Phnom Penh 106
Phosphates 86, 117, 121, 125, 137
Pig farming 54, 102, 137
Pine tree 27
Plains 14, 16, 19, 42, 44
Planets 8, 9, 10, 11, 12, 13, 14, 15
Plant life 10, 11, 12, 13, 14, 15, 18–19, 22, 23, 24, 25, 26, 29
Plateau 14, 16, 68, 69, 102, 112
Plates, continental 35, 38, 39, 40, 41
Platypus 32, 33
Po, river 76
Poland 62, 70, 78, 79, 80
Polar bear 22
Polar regions 8, 9, 12, 16, 19, 22–23
Pollution 49
Polynesia 136, 137
Population, world 48, 49, 52, 53
Portugal 75, 77
Potatoes 55, 68, 69, 70, 77, 79
Prague 78
Prairie 28, 29, 86
Prairie dog 28
Pretoria 130
Ptarmigan 22
Puerto Rico 91
Pygmies 50, 127, 128
Pyramids 120
Pyrenees 72, 73, 77

Q
Qatar 100, 115
Quebec 84
Quezon City 109
Quito 94

R
Rabat 121
Races 50–51
Radiation 12, 13
Rain 10, 16, 20, 21

Rangoon 106
Recife 97
Reclamation, land 68, 69
Red Sea 114
Reindeer 22, 65
Reptiles 11, 33
Reykjavik 65
Rhine, river 70, 71
Rhône, river 73
Rice 55, 76, 94, 95, 99, 102, 104, 105, 106, 108, 109, 110, 111, 112, 113, 114
Richter scale 41
Rift Valley 31
Rio de Janeiro 96, 97
River formation 10, 14, 15, 19, 44, 45
Riyadh 114
Rock 10, 14, 15, 18, 24, 38, 42, 43
Rocky Mountains 31, 86
Romania 62, 78, 79, 80
Rome 76, 77
Rotterdam 69
Rubber 54, 106, 108, 109, 113, 125, 127
Ruhr 70
Russia *see* USSR
Rwanda 118, 129
Rye 54, 70, 78, 79, 85

S
Sabah 108
Sahara 42, 118, 119, 120, 121
St. Lawrence Seaway 84
Salt 13, 18, 34, 56, 57, 123
Salvador 97
San Andreas Fault 41
Sand 16, 24, 25, 43, 56
San Francisco 41, 87
San Marino 62, 77
Santiago 99
Sao Paulo 97
Sao Tome and Principe 118, 127
Sarawak 108
Sardinia 76
Satellite 12, 13, 20
Saudi Arabia 100, 114
Savanna 14, 19, 29, 119, 126, 127, 128
Scandinavia 64, 65
Scotland 66
Seal 22
Seasons 8
Seismograph 40
Senegal 118, 125
Seoul 105
Severn, river 66
Seychelles 118, 129
Shale 44
Shanghai 102
Sheep 29, 54, 61, 97, 98, 99, 102, 104, 123, 134, 135, 137
Sheffield 66
Shikoku 104
Shipbuilding 64, 65, 69, 104, 109
Shrew 33
Siberia 81
Sicily 76, 77
Sierra Leone 118, 125
Sierra Nevada (Spain) 77
Sierra Nevada (USA) 41, 86
Silk production 76, 78, 102
Silt 19, 44, 45
Silver 58, 59, 64, 84, 91, 97
Singapore 100, 109
Sittang, river 106
Skua 23
Sloth 32
Snake 33
Snow 12, 18, 21, 22, 23, 44, 45
Snowy owl 22
Sofia 78

Soil 18–19, 43
Solar system 8, 9
Somalia 118, 123
Sorghum 55, 98, 102
South Africa 19, 29, 52, 58, 118, 119, 130, 131
South America 14, 29, 31, 34, 52, 54, 55, 60, 92–99
South Yemen 100, 115
Soybeans 55, 86, 97, 99, 104
Space 8, 9, 12
Spacecraft 9, 13
Spain 62, 77
Sri Lanka 27, 55, 100, 113
Stalactite 46, 47
Stalagmite 46, 47
Steel industry 58, 65, 68, 72, 74, 77, 78, 86, 91, 102, 120
Steppe 14, 16, 19, 29, 80
Stockholm 65
Stratosphere 12
Stuttgart 70
Sudan 49, 118, 123
Sugar beet 68, 69, 70, 73, 74, 78, 79, 86
Sugarcane 90, 91, 94, 97, 109, 112, 113, 116, 120, 127, 129, 131, 137
Sumatra 38, 108
Sun 8, 9, 12, 13, 21, 22, 42
Sunflower seeds 55, 79
Superior, Lake 14, 83
Surinam 92, 95
Swaziland 118, 131
Sweden 16, 61, 64, 65
Switzerland 61, 62, 74
Sydney 134, 135
Syria 100, 117
Szechwan 102

T
Tableland 14, 77, 112, 113, 122, 126, 128, 130
Taiwan 101, 102, 103
Taj Mahal 61
Tanganyika, Lake 119, 127
Tanzania 118, 119, 129
Tasmania 132, 134, 135
Tea 54, 55, 102, 108, 109, 112, 113, 128, 129
Teak 27, 106
Tehran 114
Temperature 10, 12, 13, 16, 17, 20, 42
Textile industry 53, 68, 69, 72, 74, 76, 77, 78, 91, 99, 112, 113, 114, 120
Thailand 100, 106, 107
Thames, river 66
Thermometer 20
Thessaly 75
Thrace 75
Tibet 14, 102
Tides 36, 37
Tientsin 102
Tigris, river 114
Timber industry 27, 65, 74, 85, 95, 97, 99, 102, 109, 125, 127, 131, 137
Timor 108
Tin 58, 59, 97, 106, 108, 109
Tirana 78
Titicaca, Lake 93
Tobacco 54, 70, 75, 78, 79, 86, 90, 97, 99, 102, 106, 108, 114, 117, 129, 131, 137
Togo 118, 125
Tokyo 87, 104
Tonga 133, 137
Tornado 21
Tributary 45
Trinidad and Tobago 91
Tripoli 121
Troposphere 12
Tundra 18, 19, 26, 80

Tunis 121
Tunisia 43, 118, 121
Turin 77
Turkey 40, 52, 54, 62, 63, 100, 101, 114, 117

U
Uganda 118, 129
Ulan Bator 103
United Arab Emirates 100, 115
United Kingdom 62, 66, 79
United Nations 52, 53, 102
Upper Volta 118, 123
Uranium 58, 59, 84, 86, 127, 131
Uruguay 99
USA 14, 23, 44, 46, 48, 49, 52, 54, 55, 58, 60, 70, 79, 80, 82, 83, 86–87, 88–89, 104, 105
USSR 14, 49, 51, 53, 54, 55, 58, 60, 62, 63, 70, 78, 79, 80–81, 83, 84, 100, 101, 104, 105

V
Valencia 77
Valleys 15, 30, 31, 42, 44, 45
Valparaiso 99
Vanuatu 132
Vatican City 63, 76, 77
Vegetables 54, 55, 68, 69, 70, 73, 74, 76, 77, 78, 79, 87, 94, 114, 116, 117, 120, 121, 129, 137
Vegetation 18–19
Veld 29
Venezuela 92, 93, 95
Vesuvius 76
Victoria, Lake 118, 119, 129
Vienna 74
Vientiane 106
Vietnam 100, 106
Volcano 10, 14, 30, 31, 38–39, 40, 42, 65, 76, 86, 104, 105, 108, 109, 137
Volga, river 63
Vosges Mountains 72

W
Wales 66
Walrus 22
Warsaw 79
Washington, D.C. 86, 87
Waterfall 15, 44
Waves 36
Weather 9, 12, 20–21, 23
Wellington 137
Western Sahara 118, 121
Western Samoa 133, 137
West Indies 60, 83, 90–91
West Irian 108
Wheat 53, 54, 55, 69, 73, 75, 76, 77, 78, 79, 85, 86, 98, 99, 102, 104, 112, 113, 114, 120, 121, 131
Wind 12, 20, 21, 42, 43
Wine 70, 72, 73, 75, 76, 77, 78, 79, 99, 120, 121, 131
Wool 97, 98, 99, 114, 130, 131, 135

Y
Yangtze, river 101, 102
Yemen 100, 115
Yenisey, river 101
Yokohama 104
Yugoslavia 74

Z
Zagreb 74
Zaire 118, 119, 127
Zambezi, river 118, 119
Zambia 61, 118, 129, 130
Zimbabwe 118, 130, 131
Zinc 58, 59, 84, 97, 130
Zurich 74

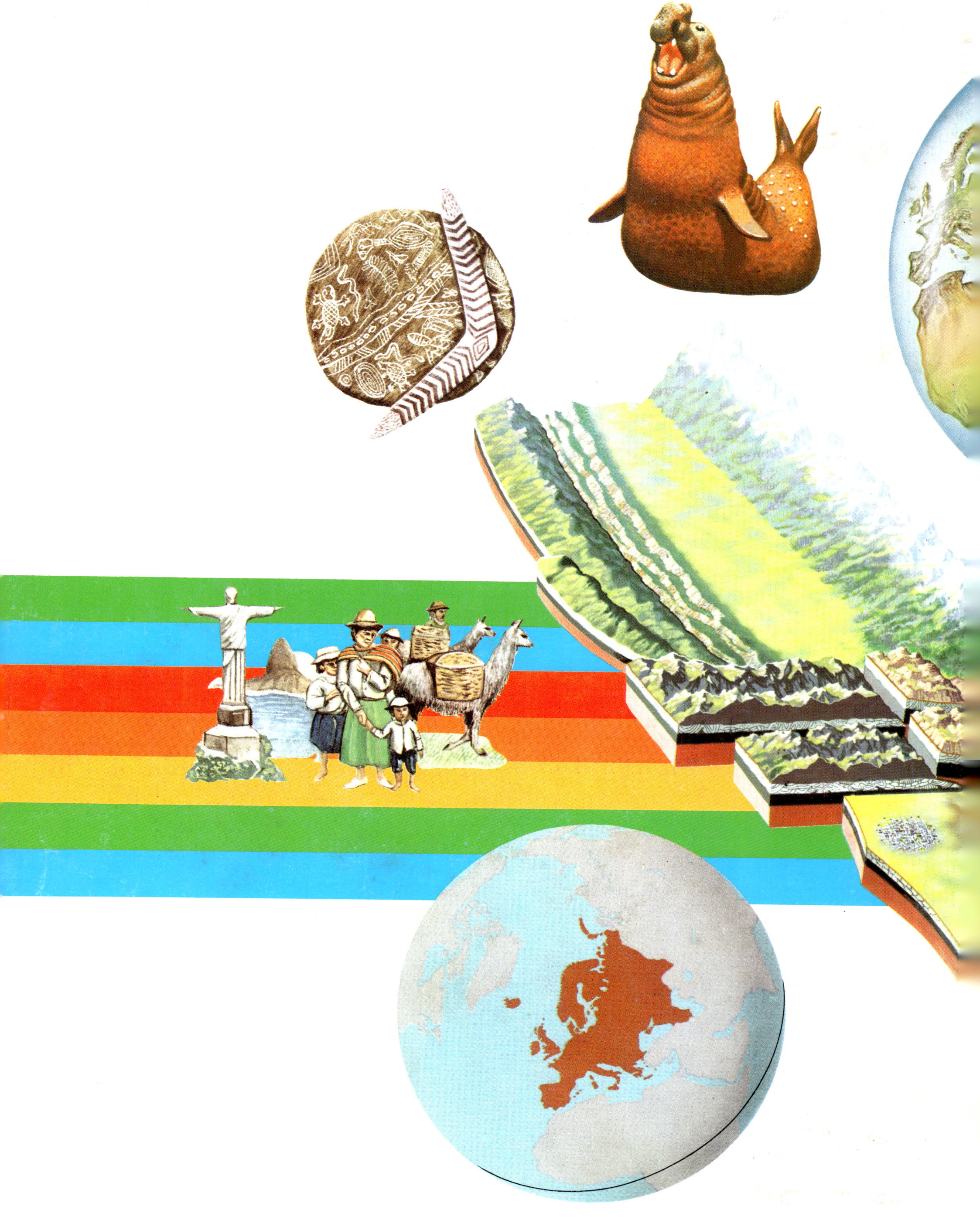